LOLA

A GHOST STORY

WRITTEN BY
J. TORRES

ILLUSTRATED BY
ELBERT OR

LETTERED BY
JILL BEATON

ART ASSIST BY
JONAS DIEGO

BOOK DESIGN BY
KEITH WOOD

EDITED BY
JAMES LUCAS JONES
& JILL BEATON

ONI PRESS

PUBLISHED BY ONI PRESS, INC.

JOE NOZEMACK
PUBLISHER

JAMES LUCAS JONES
EDITOR IN CHIEF

RANDAL C. JARRELL
MANAGING EDITOR

KEITH WOOD
ART DIRECTOR

CORY CASONI
MARKETING DIRECTOR

JILL BEATON
ASSISTANT EDITOR

DOUGLAS E. SHERWOOD
PRODUCTION ASSISTANT

ONI PRESS, INC.
1305 SE MARTIN LUTHER KING JR. BLVD.
SUITE A
PORTLAND, OR 97214
USA

WWW.ONIPRESS.COM

FIRST EDITION: OCTOBER 2009
ISBN 978-1-934964-33-0

3 5 7 9 10 8 6 4 2

PRINTED IN CHINA.

For my beloved Lola Gloria, whose
stories inspired this story.

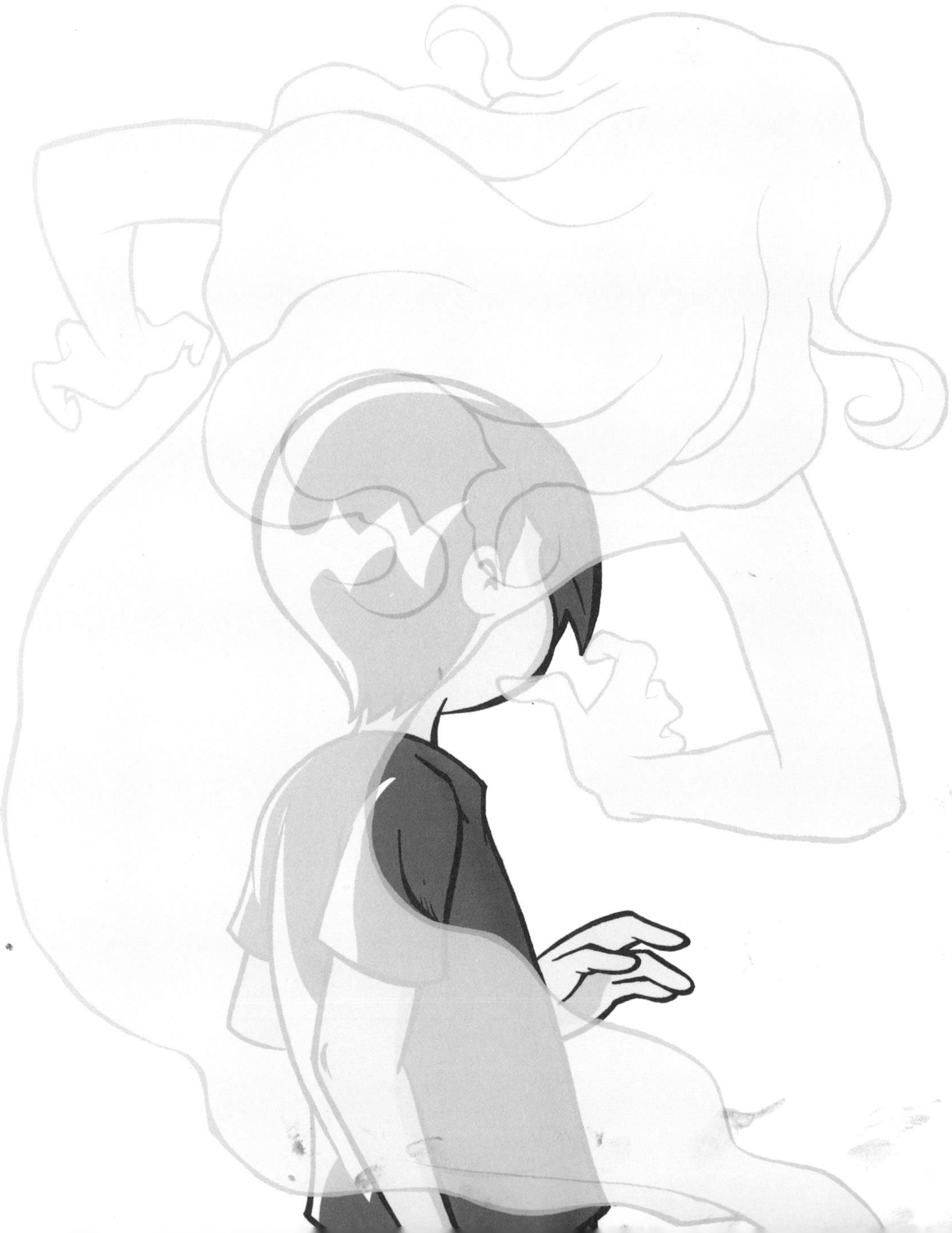

ACT

I

LOLA

A GHOST STORY

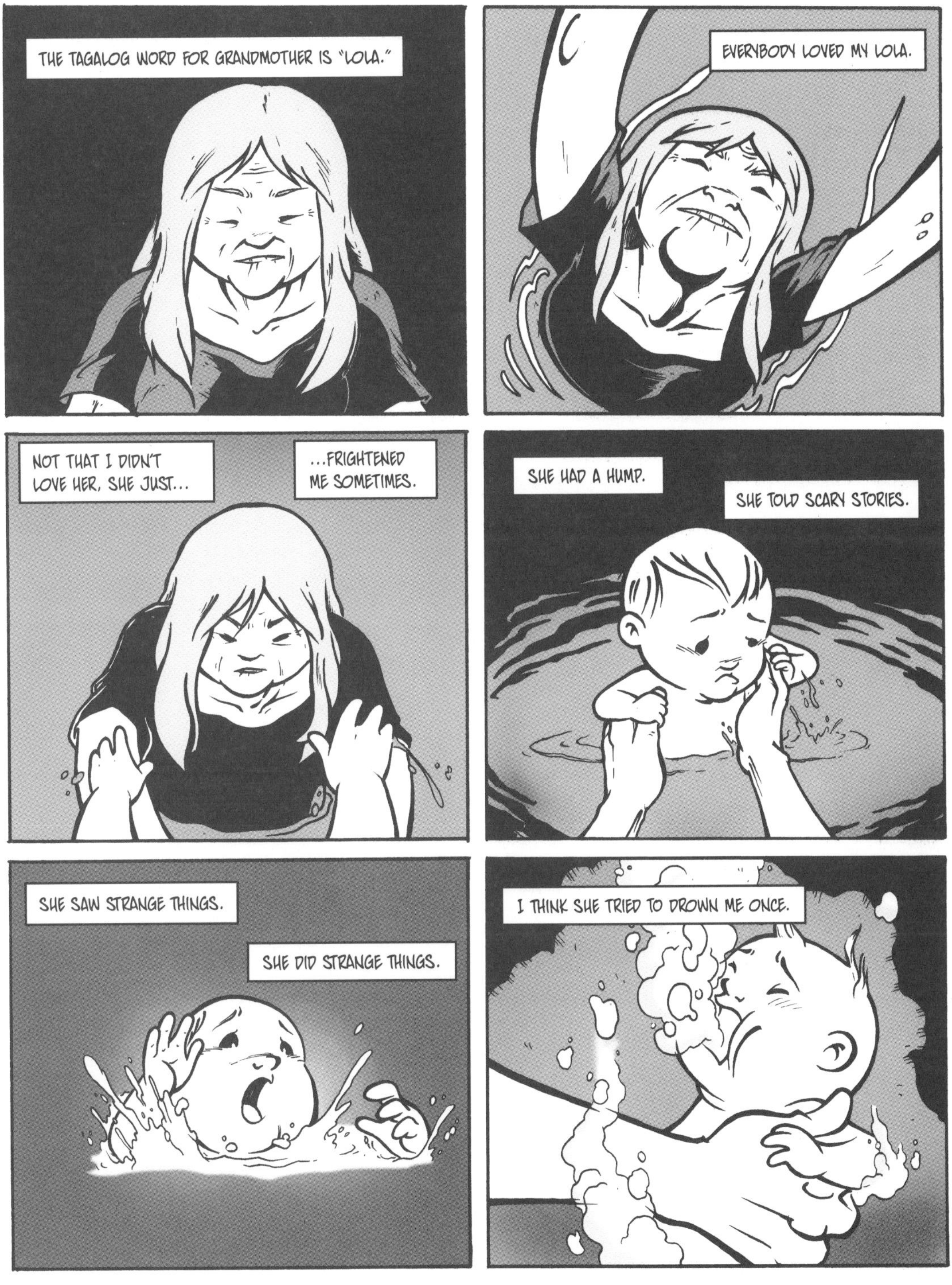
THE TAGALOG WORD FOR GRANDMOTHER IS "LOLA."
EVERYBODY LOVED MY LOLA.
NOT THAT I DIDN'T LOVE HER, SHE JUST...
...FRIGHTENED ME SOMETIMES.
SHE HAD A HUMP.
SHE TOLD SCARY STORIES.
SHE SAW STRANGE THINGS.
SHE DID STRANGE THINGS.
I THINK SHE TRIED TO DROWN ME ONCE.

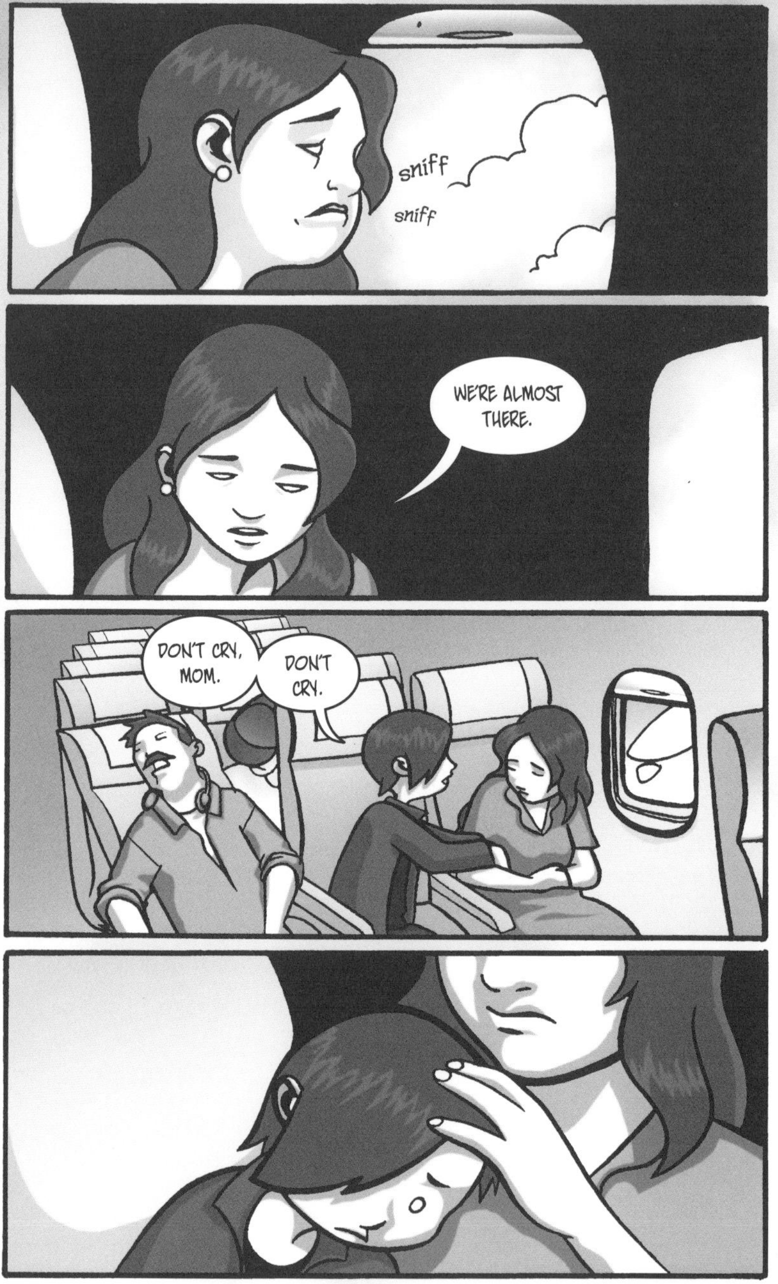
sniff
sniff
WE'RE ALMOST THERE.
DON'T CRY, MOM.
DON'T CRY.

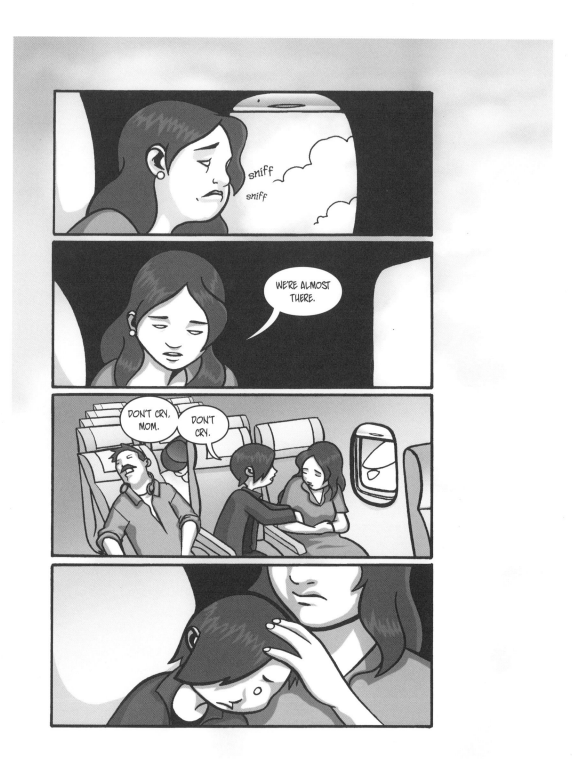

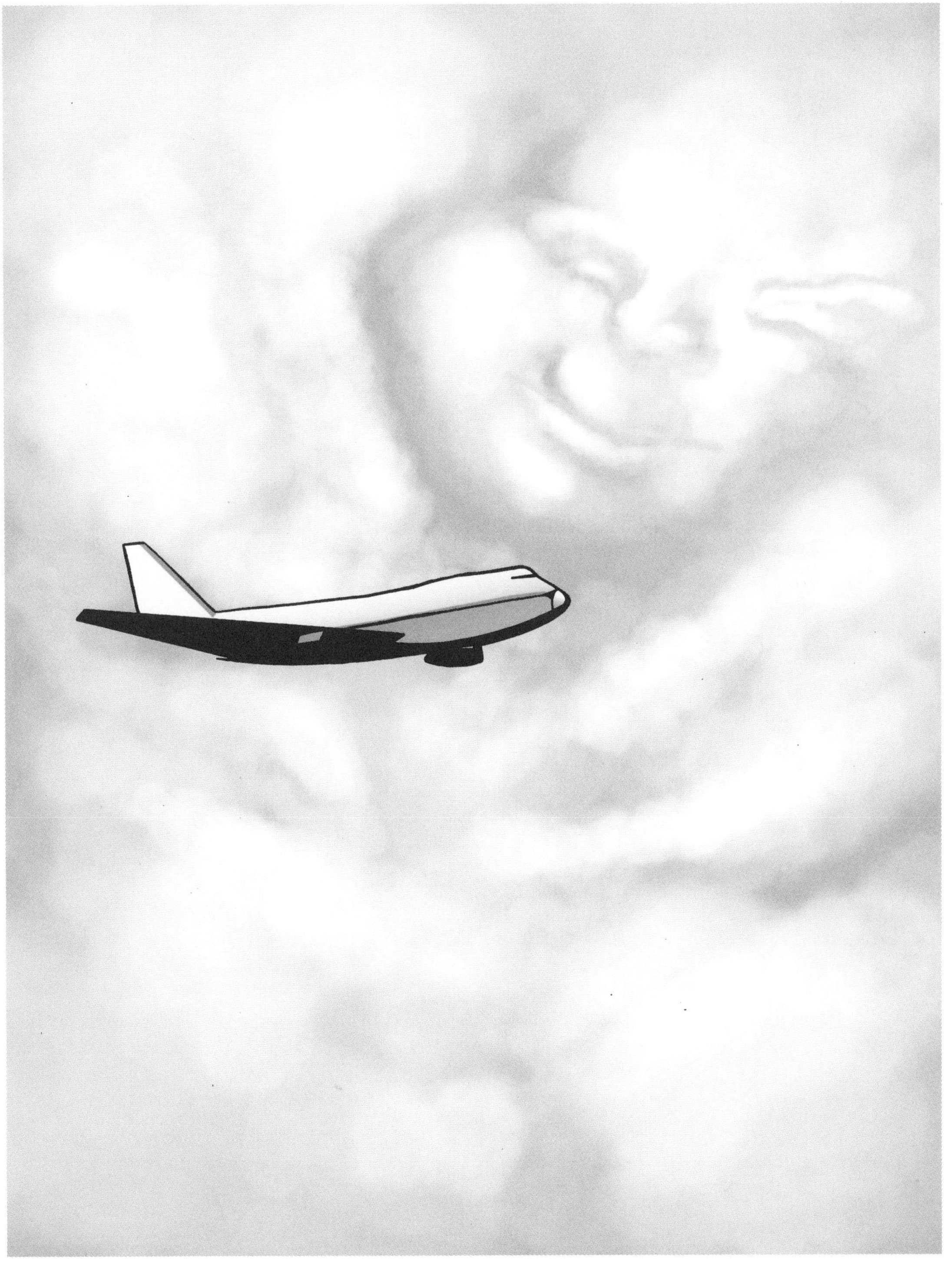

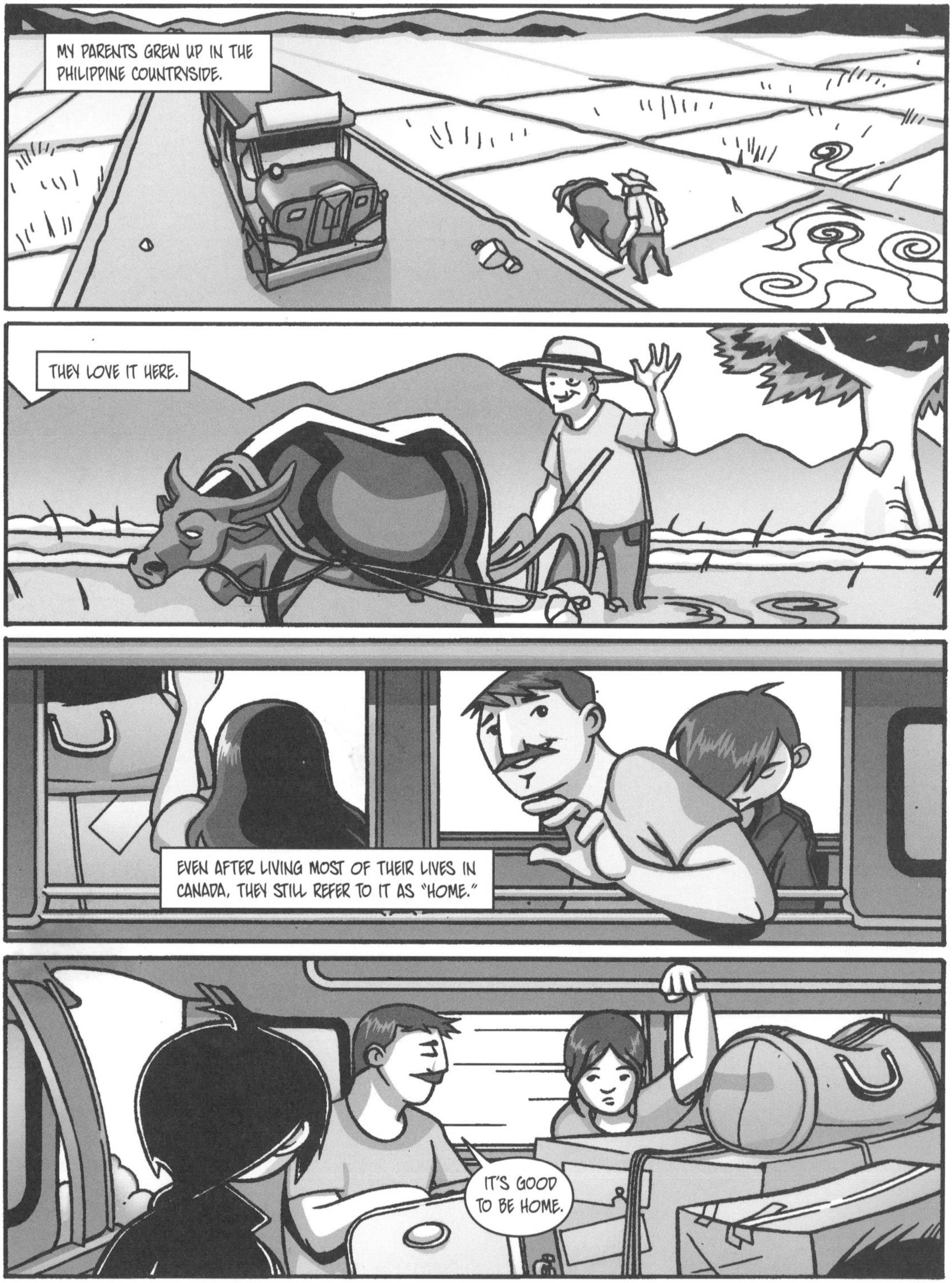
MY PARENTS GREW UP IN THE PHILIPPINE COUNTRYSIDE.
THEY LOVE IT HERE.
EVEN AFTER LIVING MOST OF THEIR LIVES IN CANADA, THEY STILL REFER TO IT AS "HOME."
IT'S GOOD TO BE HOME.

LOLA A GHOST STORY

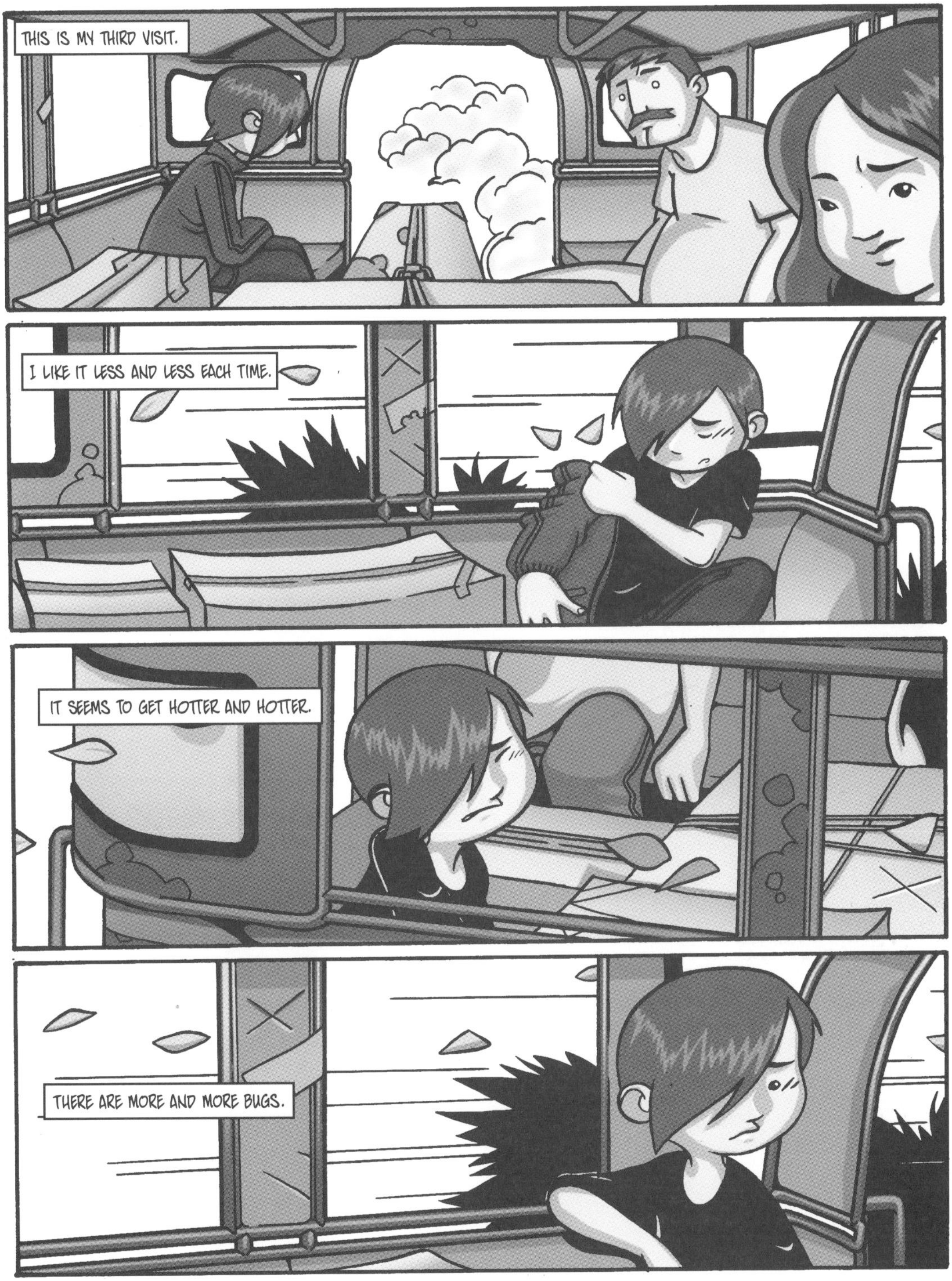
THIS IS MY THIRD VISIT.
I LIKE IT LESS AND LESS EACH TIME.
IT SEEMS TO GET HOTTER AND HOTTER.
THERE ARE MORE AND MORE BUGS.

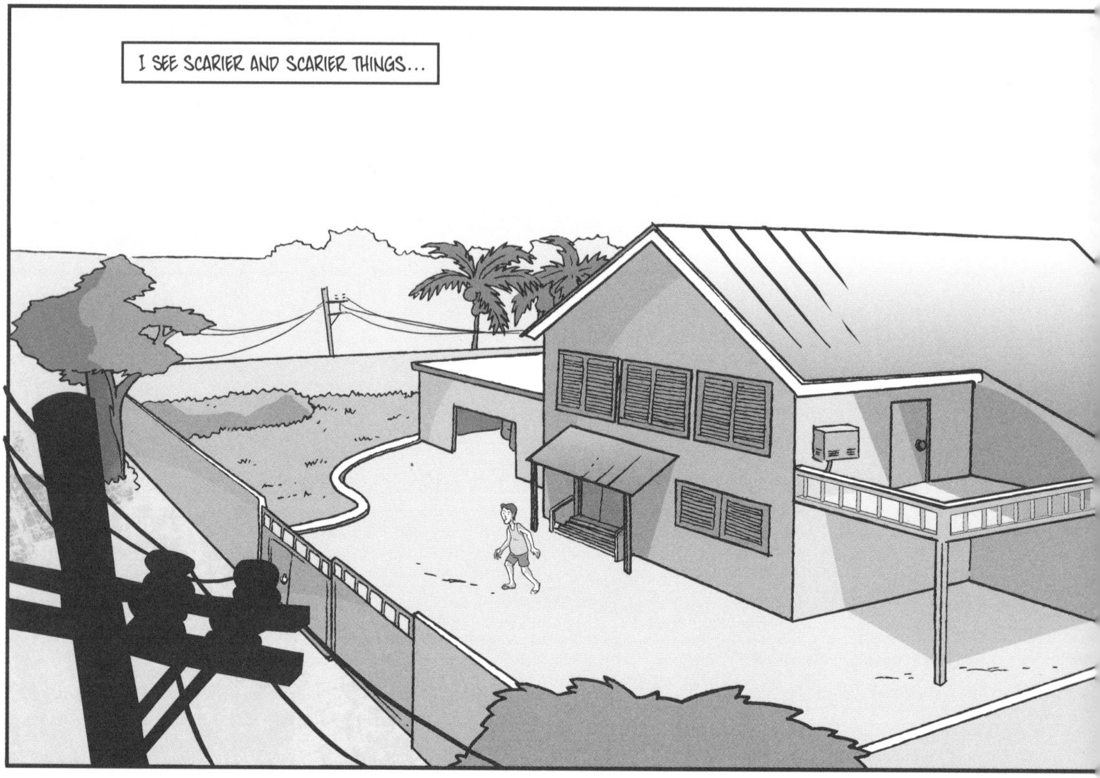
I SEE SCARIER AND SCARIER THINGS...

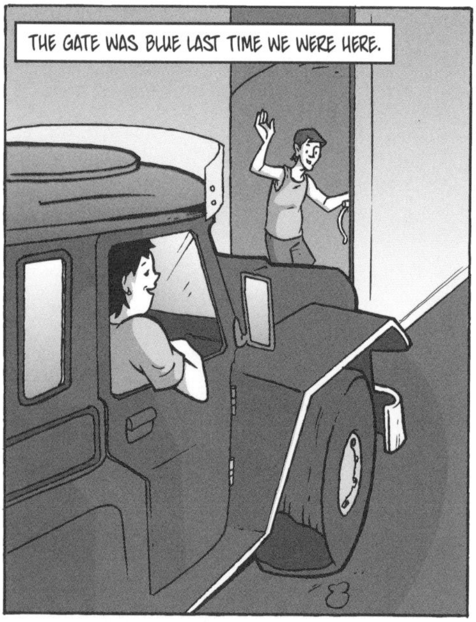
THE GATE WAS BLUE LAST TIME WE WERE HERE.

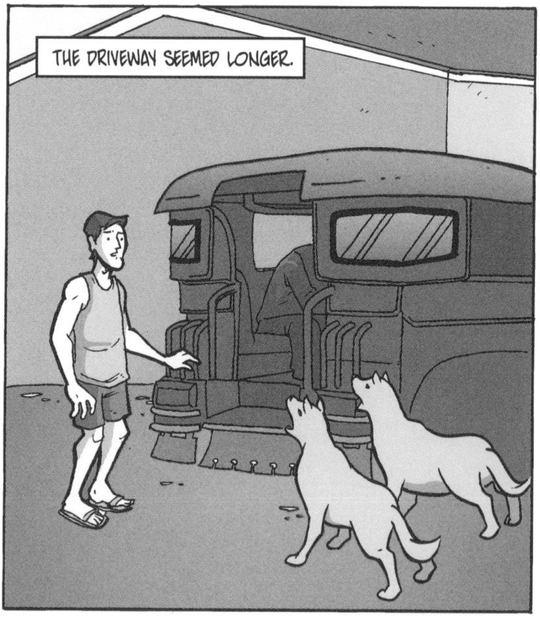
THE DRIVEWAY SEEMED LONGER.

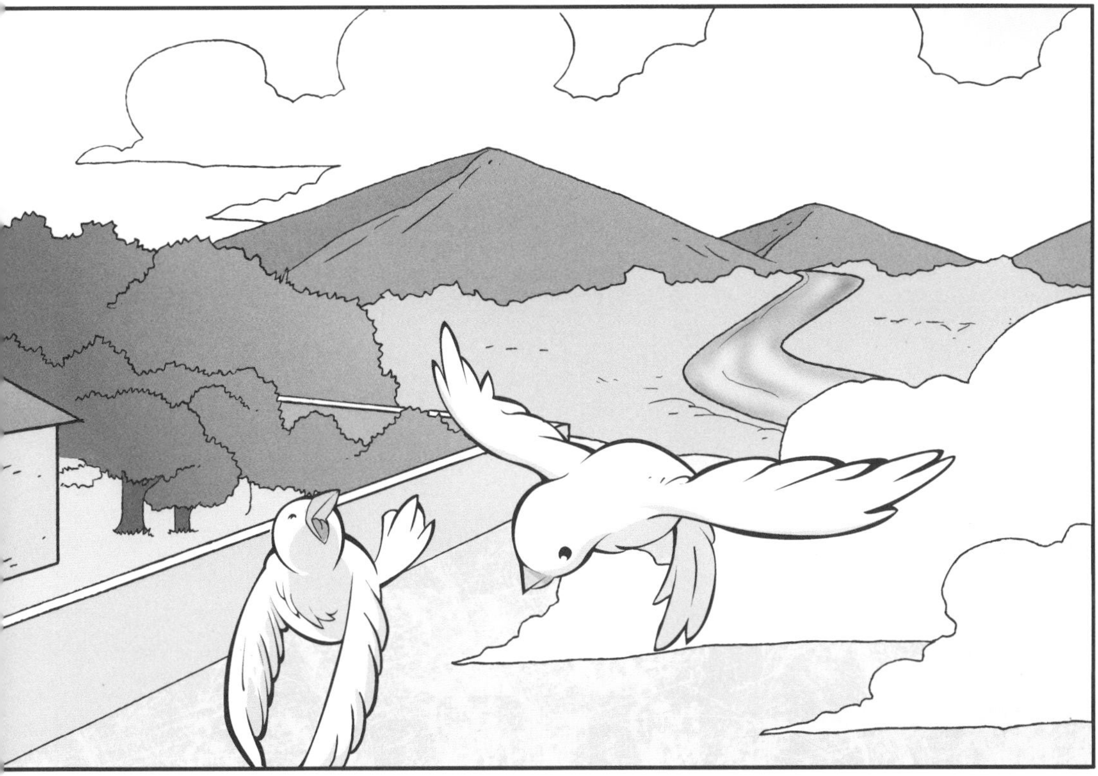

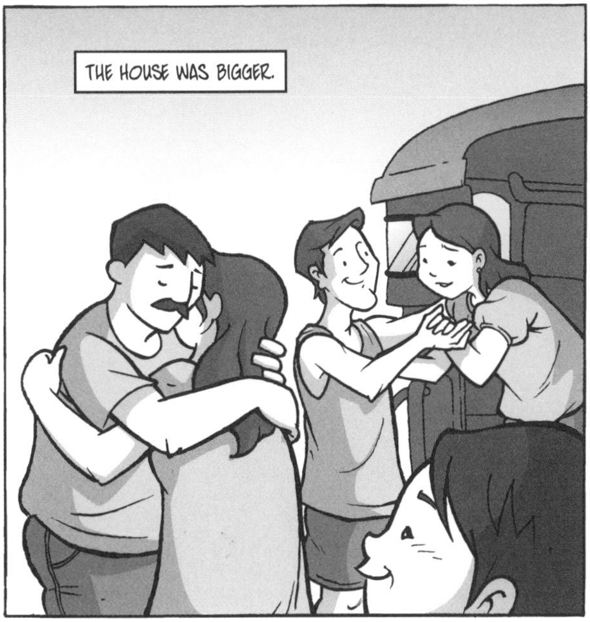
THE HOUSE WAS BIGGER.

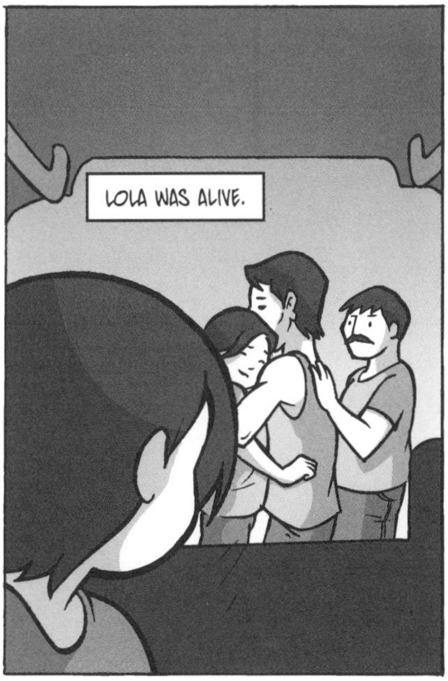
LOLA WAS ALIVE.

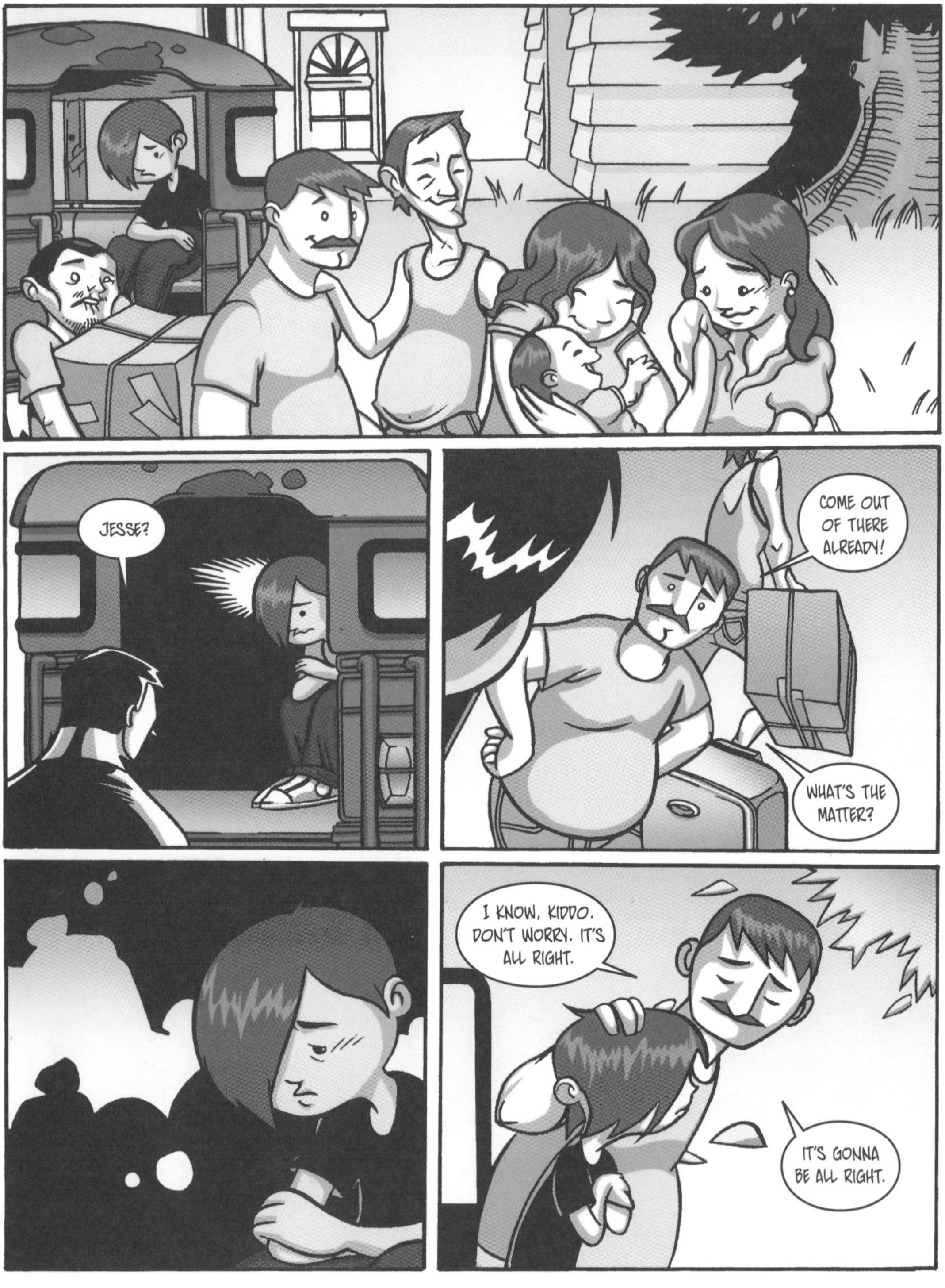
JESSE?
COME OUT OF THERE ALREADY!
WHAT'S THE MATTER?
I KNOW, KIDDO. DON'T WORRY. IT'S ALL RIGHT.
IT'S GONNA BE ALL RIGHT.

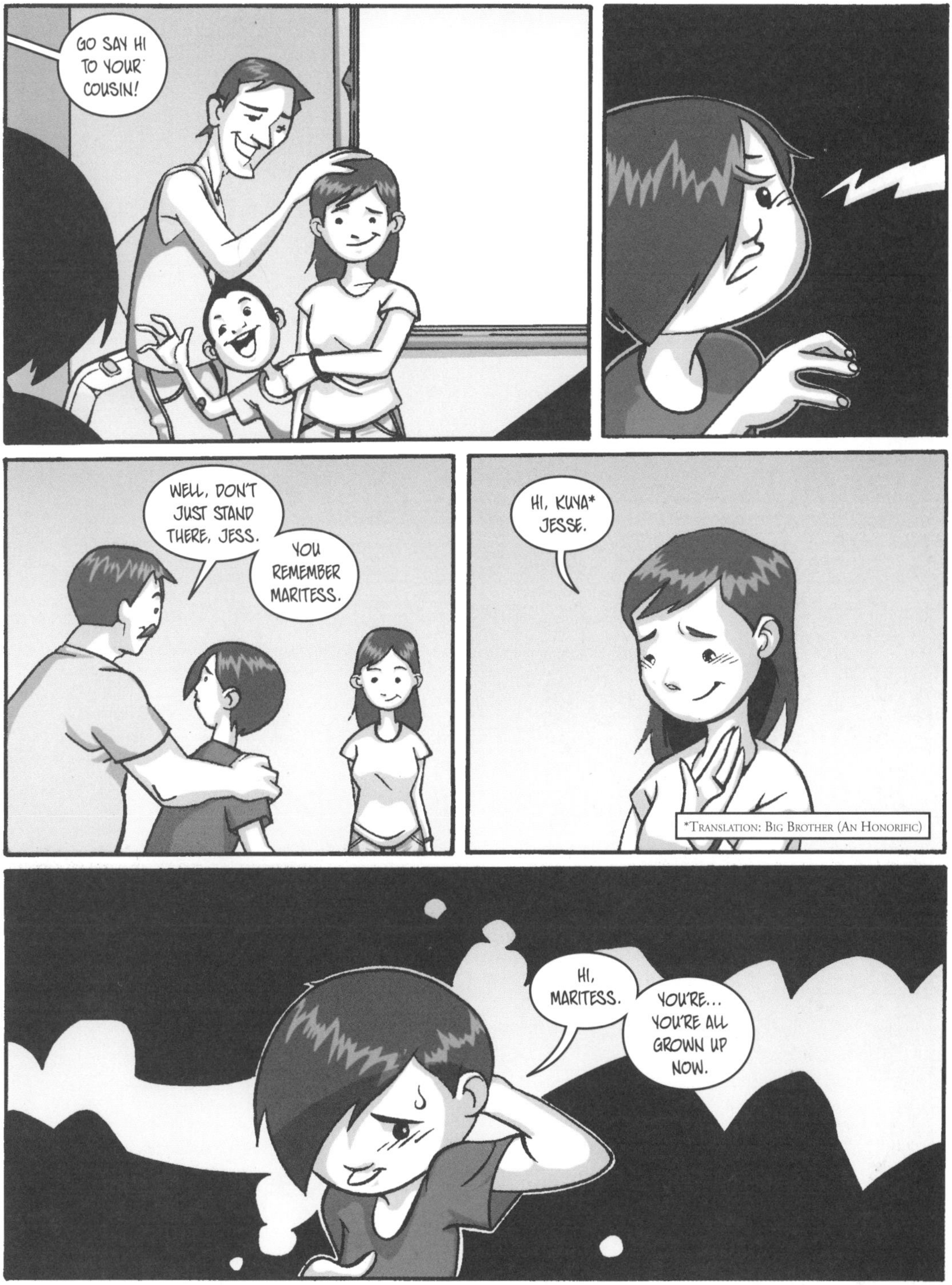
GO SAY HI TO YOUR COUSIN!
WELL, DON'T JUST STAND THERE, JESS.
YOU REMEMBER MARITESS.
HI, KUYA* JESSE.
*TRANSLATION: BIG BROTHER (AN HONORIFIC)
HI, MARITESS.
YOU'RE... YOU'RE ALL GROWN UP NOW.

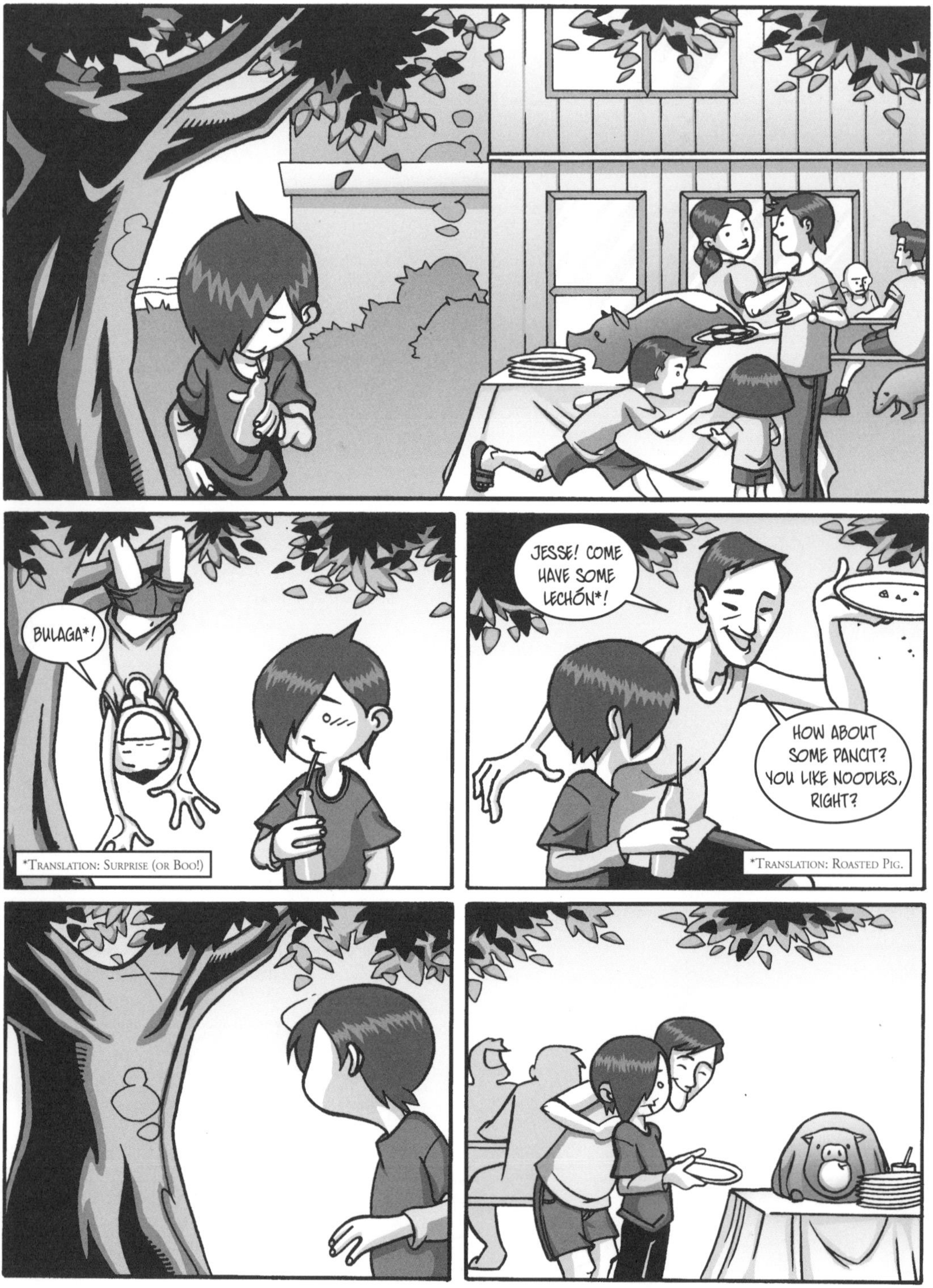
BULAGA*!
*Translation: Surprise (or Boo!)
JESSE! COME HAVE SOME LECHÓN*!
HOW ABOUT SOME PANCIT? YOU LIKE NOODLES, RIGHT?
*Translation: Roasted Pig.

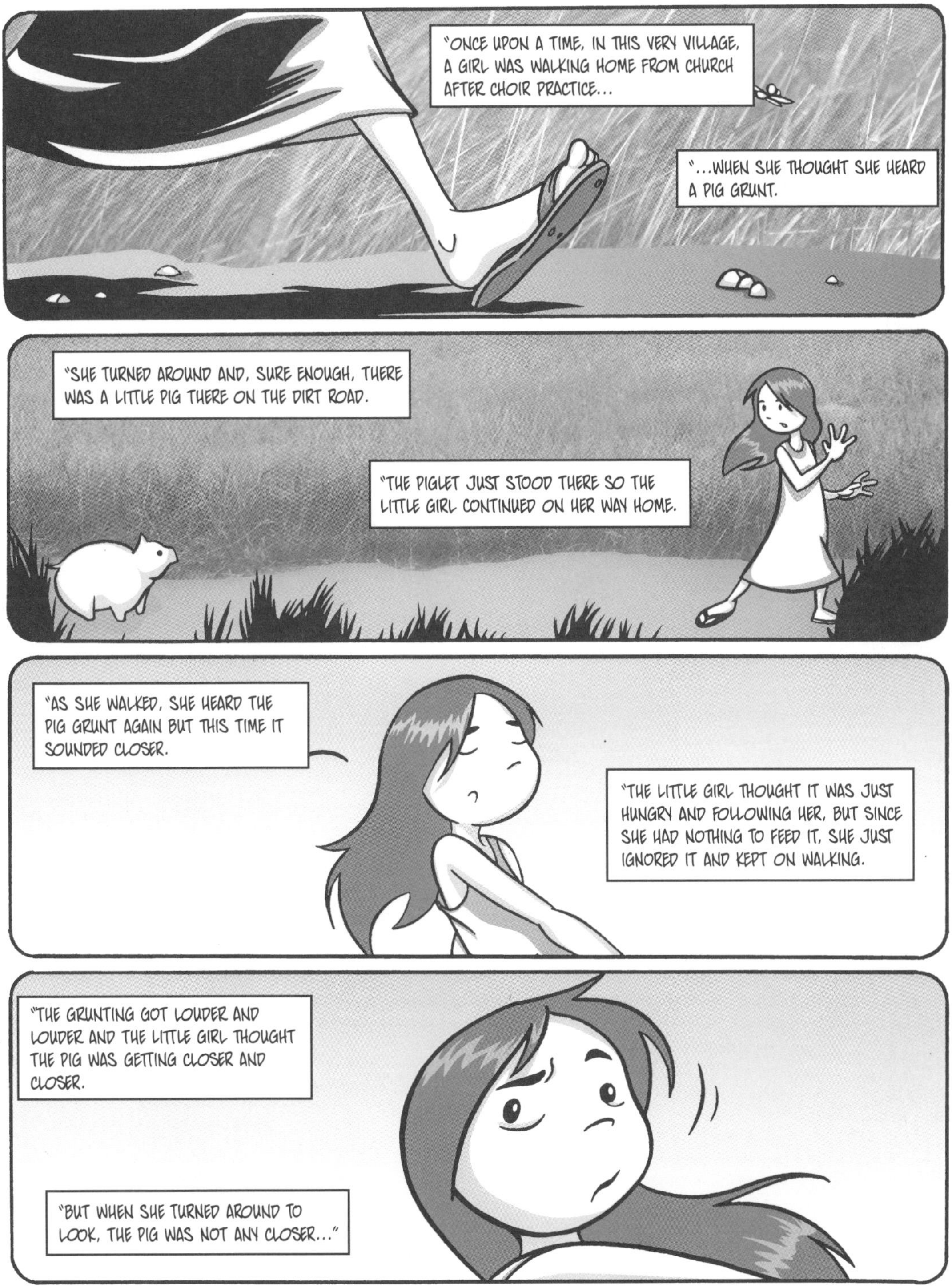
"ONCE UPON A TIME, IN THIS VERY VILLAGE, A GIRL WAS WALKING HOME FROM CHURCH AFTER CHOIR PRACTICE...
"...WHEN SHE THOUGHT SHE HEARD A PIG GRUNT.
"SHE TURNED AROUND AND, SURE ENOUGH, THERE WAS A LITTLE PIG THERE ON THE DIRT ROAD.
"THE PIGLET JUST STOOD THERE SO THE LITTLE GIRL CONTINUED ON HER WAY HOME.
"AS SHE WALKED, SHE HEARD THE PIG GRUNT AGAIN BUT THIS TIME IT SOUNDED CLOSER.
"THE LITTLE GIRL THOUGHT IT WAS JUST HUNGRY AND FOLLOWING HER, BUT SINCE SHE HAD NOTHING TO FEED IT, SHE JUST IGNORED IT AND KEPT ON WALKING.
"THE GRUNTING GOT LOUDER AND LOUDER AND THE LITTLE GIRL THOUGHT THE PIG WAS GETTING CLOSER AND CLOSER.
"BUT WHEN SHE TURNED AROUND TO LOOK, THE PIG WAS NOT ANY CLOSER..."

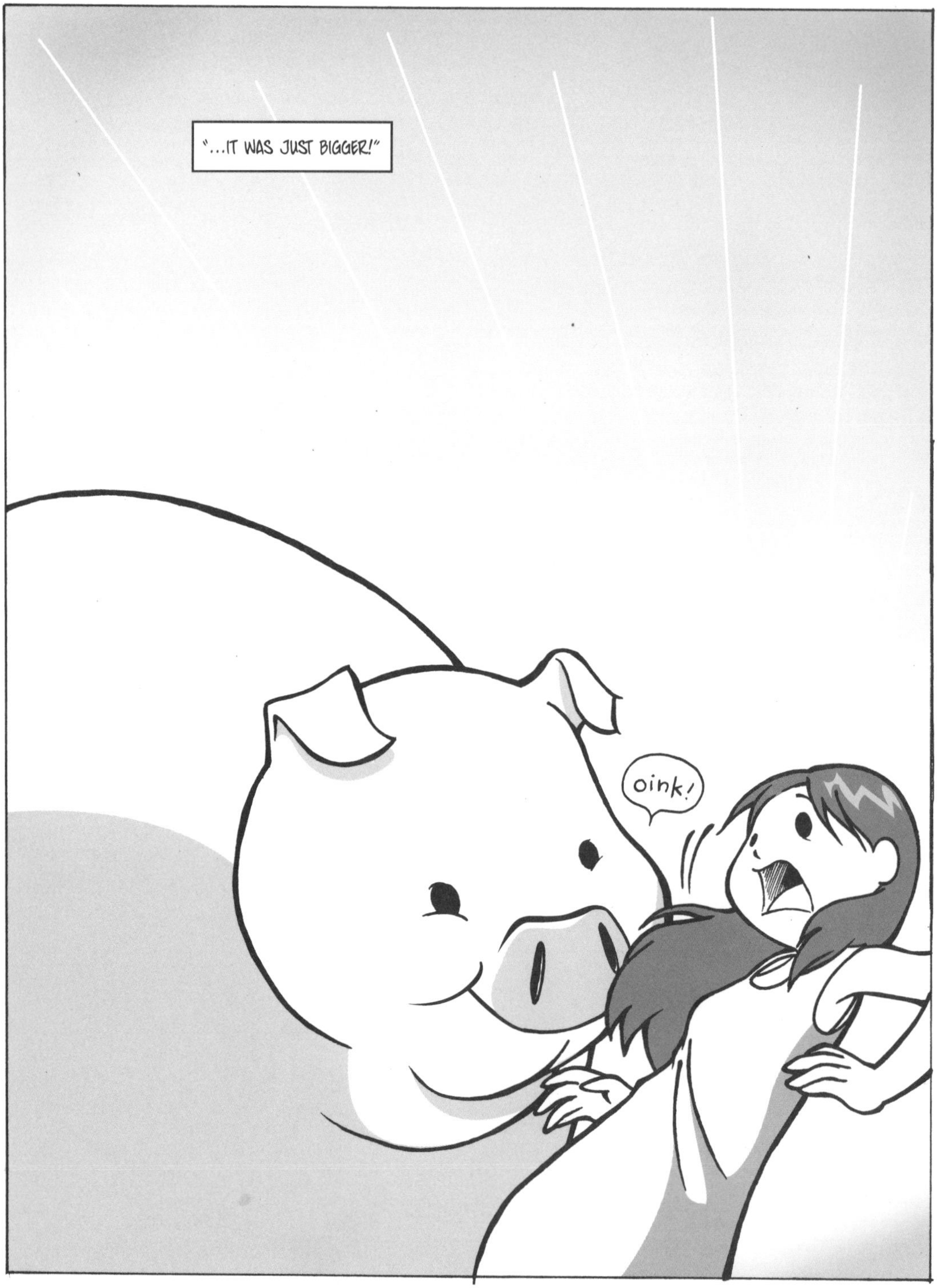
"...IT WAS JUST BIGGER!"
oink!

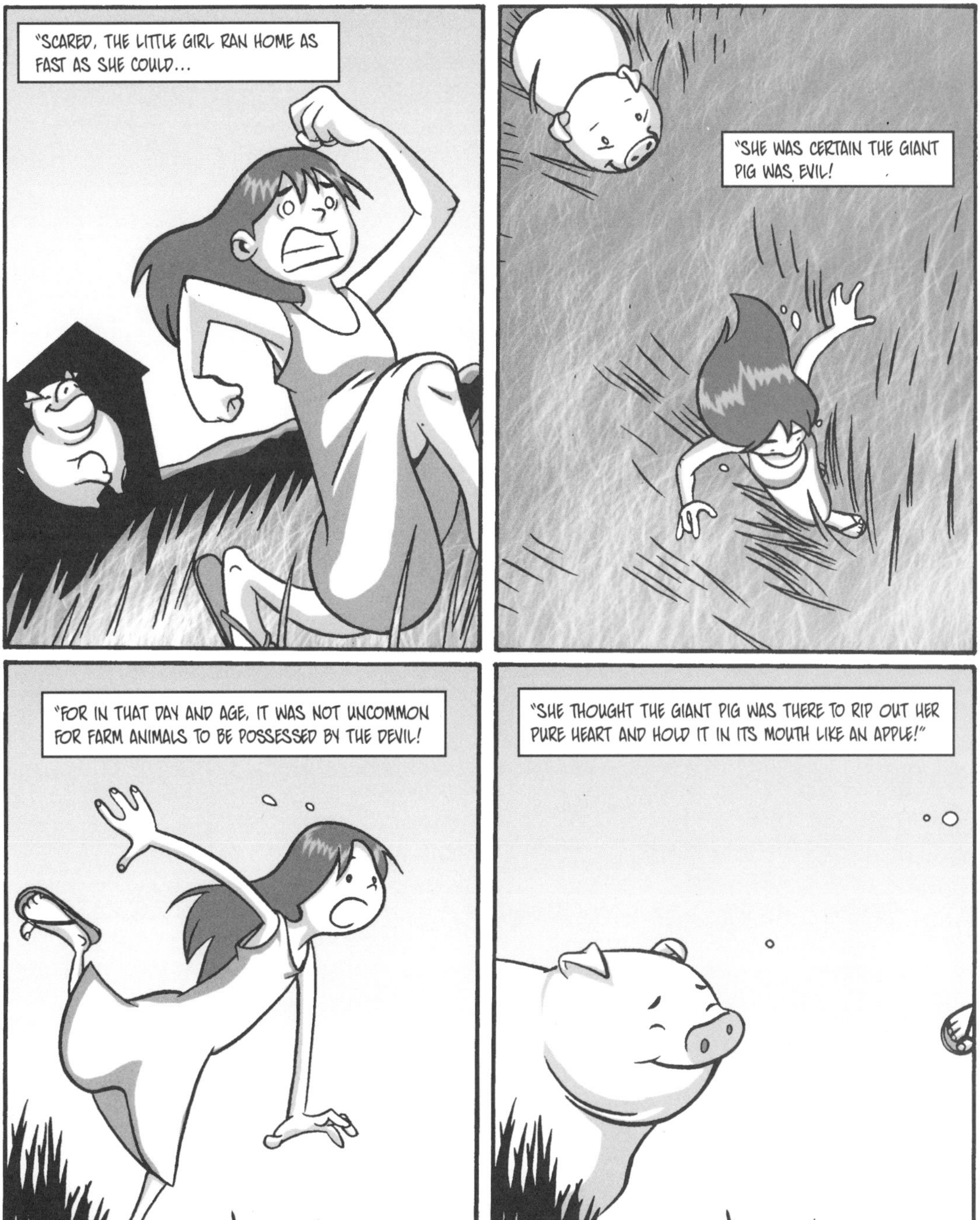
"SCARED, THE LITTLE GIRL RAN HOME AS FAST AS SHE COULD...
"SHE WAS CERTAIN THE GIANT PIG WAS EVIL!
"FOR IN THAT DAY AND AGE, IT WAS NOT UNCOMMON FOR FARM ANIMALS TO BE POSSESSED BY THE DEVIL!
"SHE THOUGHT THE GIANT PIG WAS THERE TO RIP OUT HER PURE HEART AND HOLD IT IN ITS MOUTH LIKE AN APPLE!"

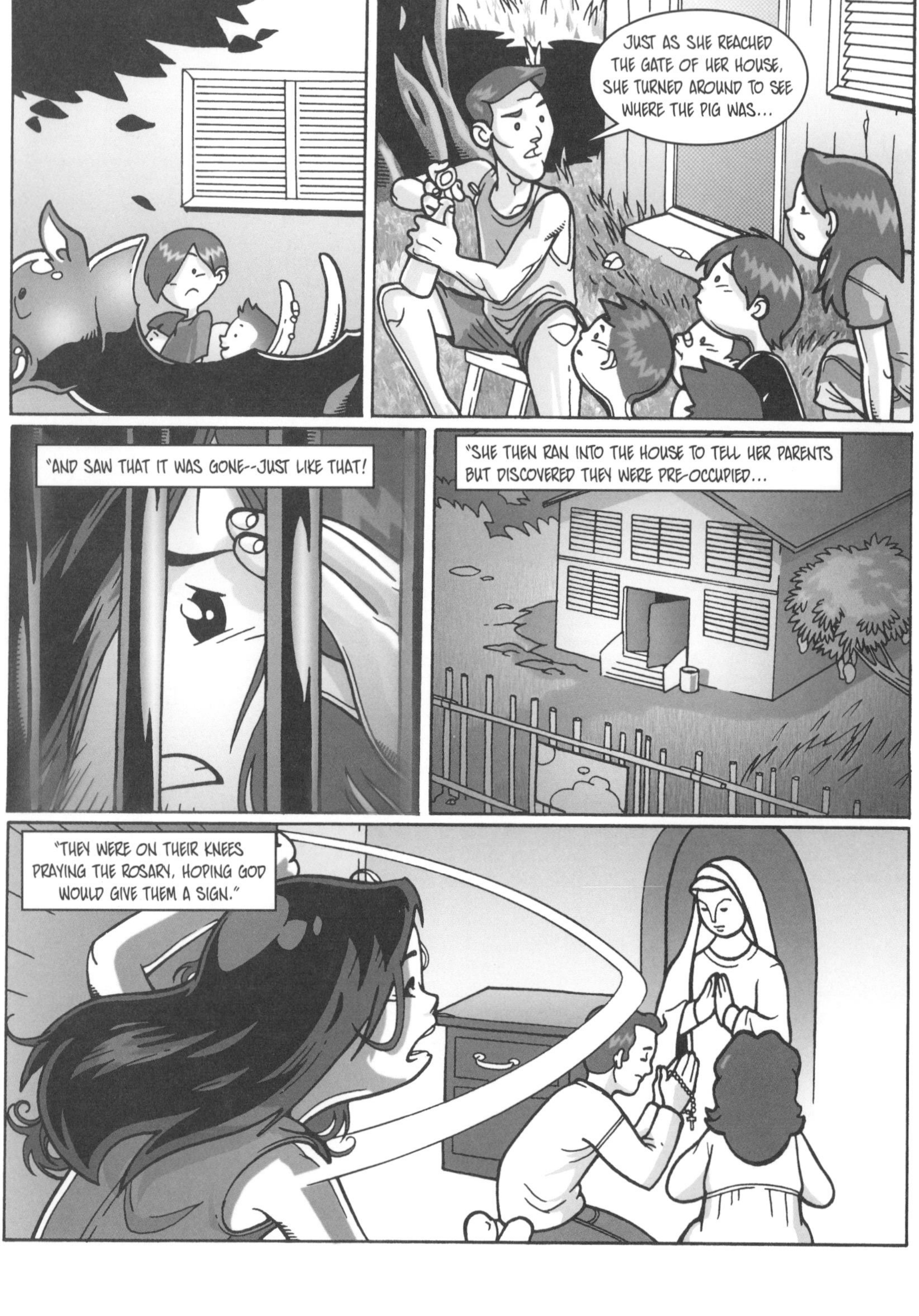
JUST AS SHE REACHED THE GATE OF HER HOUSE, SHE TURNED AROUND TO SEE WHERE THE PIG WAS...
"AND SAW THAT IT WAS GONE--JUST LIKE THAT!
"SHE THEN RAN INTO THE HOUSE TO TELL HER PARENTS BUT DISCOVERED THEY WERE PRE-OCCUPIED...
"THEY WERE ON THEIR KNEES PRAYING THE ROSARY, HOPING GOD WOULD GIVE THEM A SIGN."

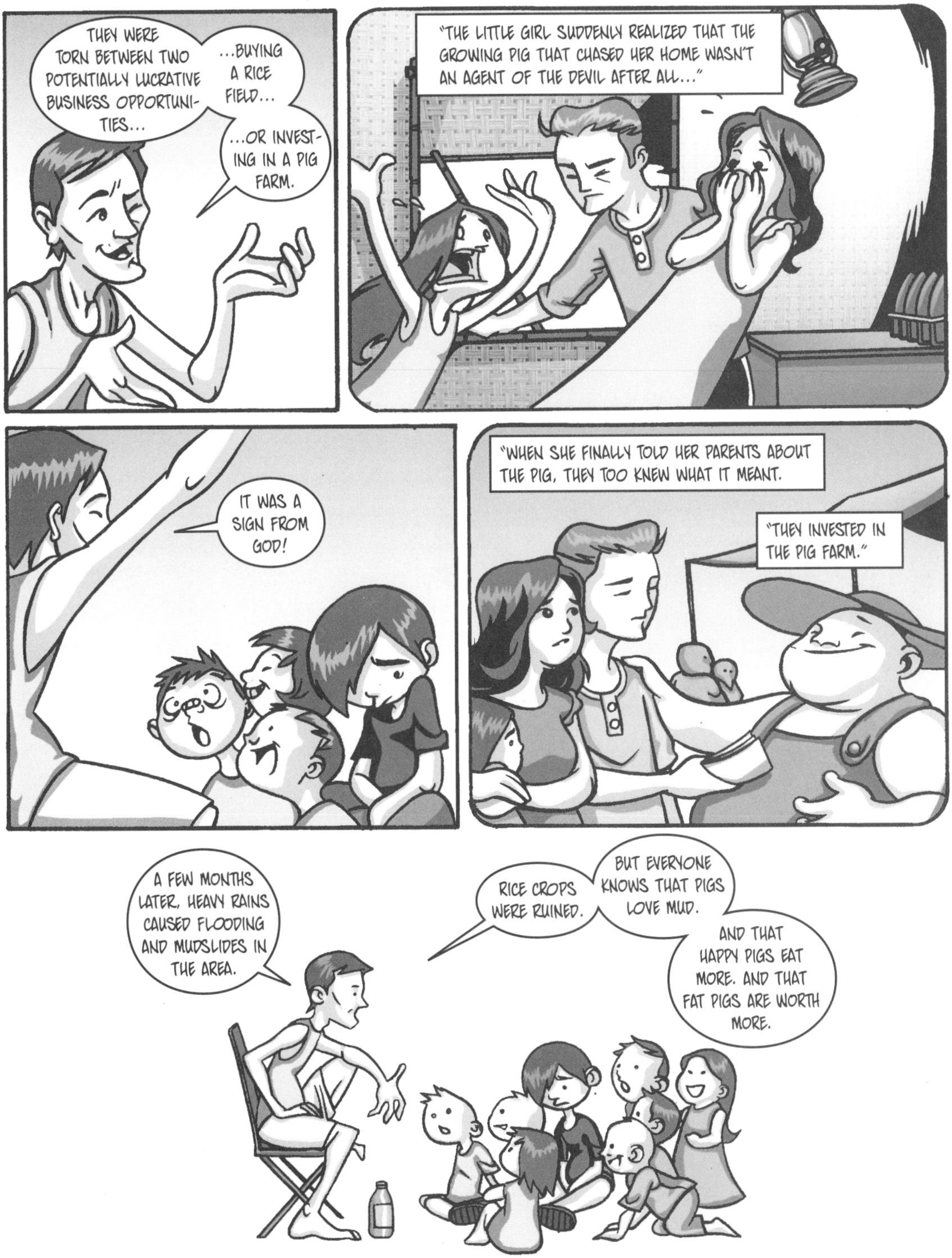
THEY WERE TORN BETWEEN TWO POTENTIALLY LUCRATIVE BUSINESS OPPORTUNI-TIES...
...BUYING A RICE FIELD...
...OR INVEST-ING IN A PIG FARM.
"THE LITTLE GIRL SUDDENLY REALIZED THAT THE GROWING PIG THAT CHASED HER HOME WASN'T AN AGENT OF THE DEVIL AFTER ALL..."
IT WAS A SIGN FROM GOD!
"WHEN SHE FINALLY TOLD HER PARENTS ABOUT THE PIG, THEY TOO KNEW WHAT IT MEANT.
"THEY INVESTED IN THE PIG FARM."
A FEW MONTHS LATER, HEAVY RAINS CAUSED FLOODING AND MUDSLIDES IN THE AREA.
RICE CROPS WERE RUINED.
BUT EVERYONE KNOWS THAT PIGS LOVE MUD.
AND THAT HAPPY PIGS EAT MORE. AND THAT FAT PIGS ARE WORTH MORE.

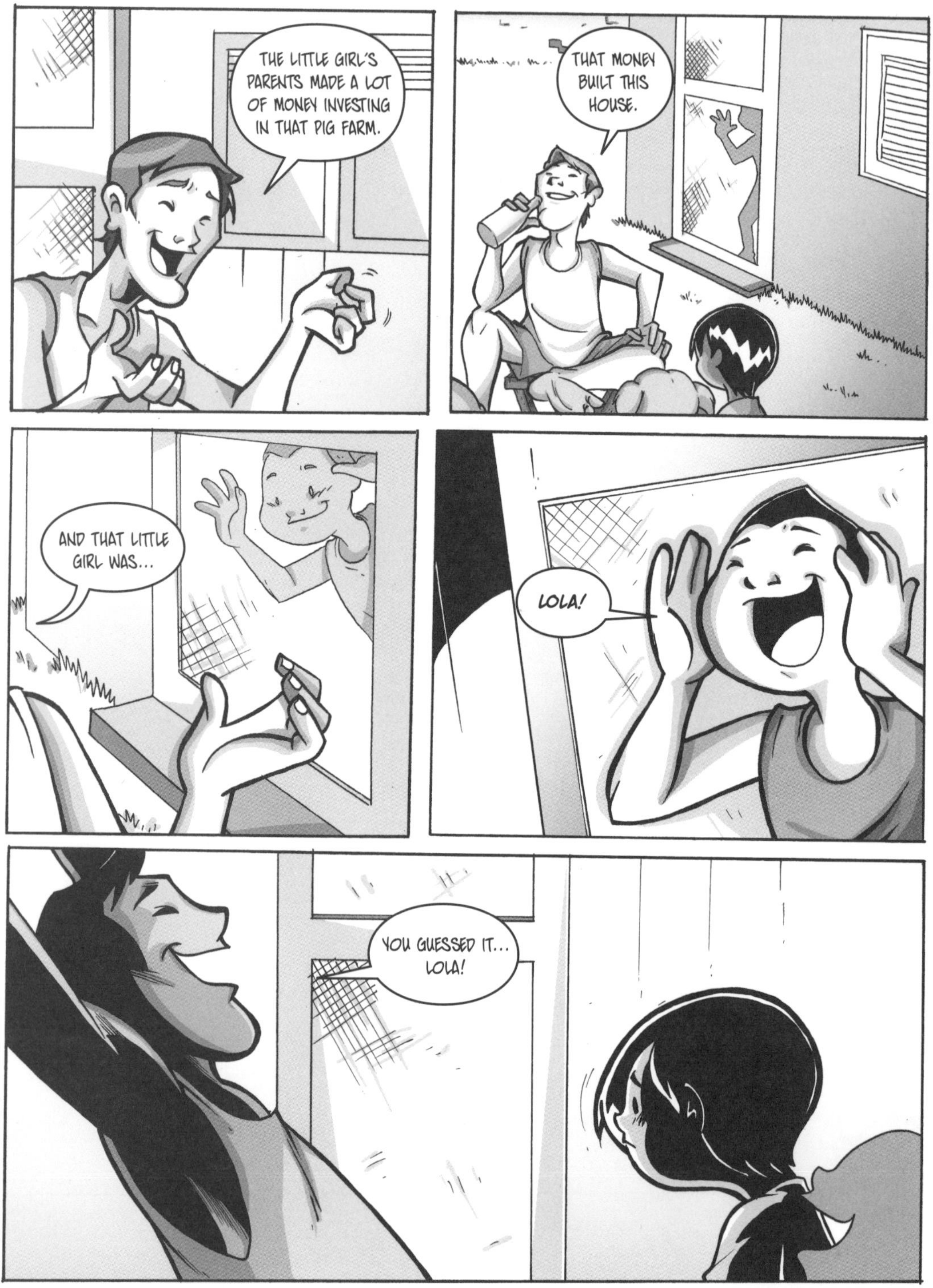
THE LITTLE GIRL'S PARENTS MADE A LOT OF MONEY INVESTING IN THAT PIG FARM.
THAT MONEY BUILT THIS HOUSE.
AND THAT LITTLE GIRL WAS...
LOLA!
YOU GUESSED IT... LOLA!

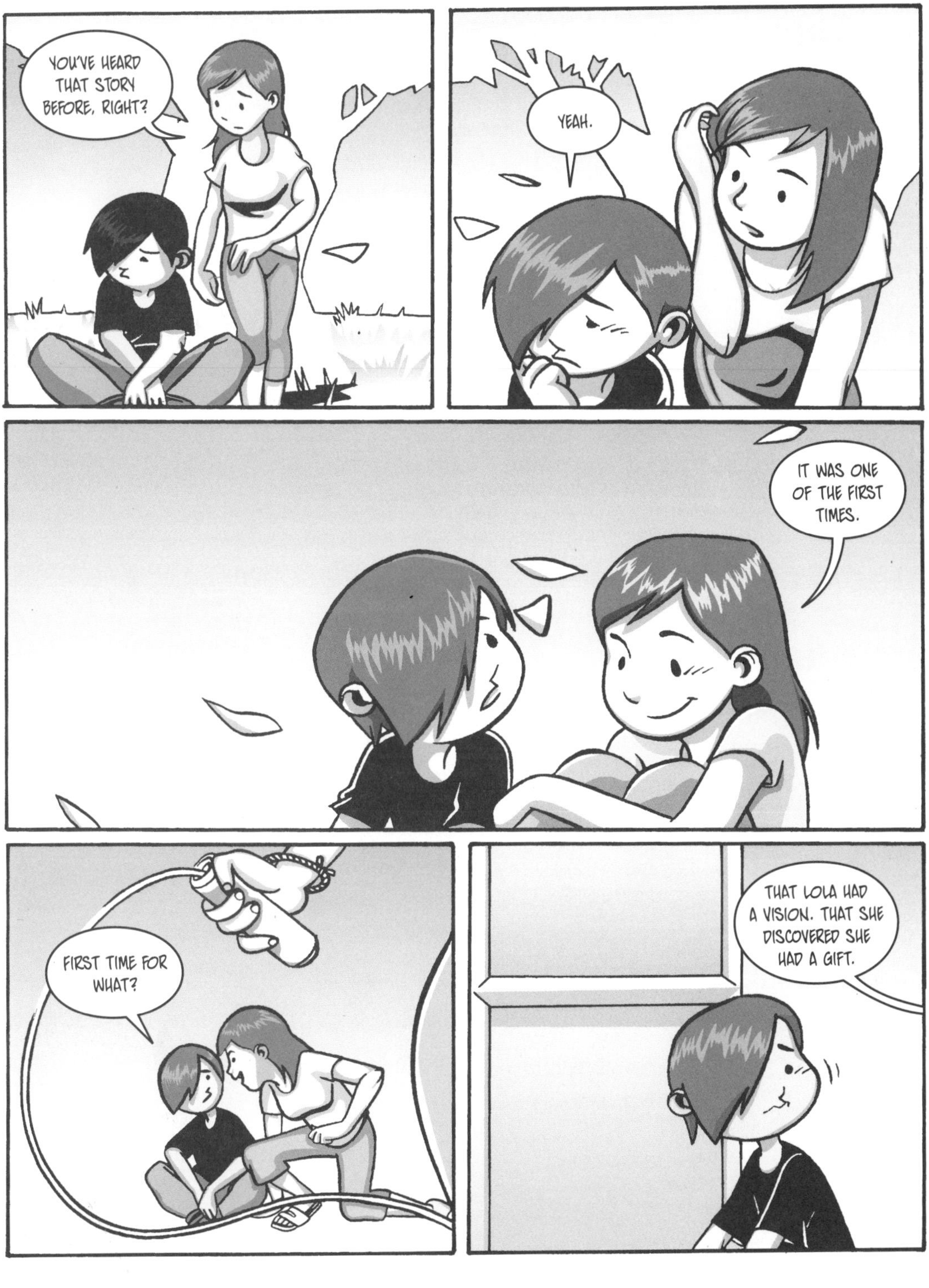
YOU'VE HEARD THAT STORY BEFORE, RIGHT?
YEAH.
IT WAS ONE OF THE FIRST TIMES.
FIRST TIME FOR WHAT?
THAT LOLA HAD A VISION. THAT SHE DISCOVERED SHE HAD A GIFT.

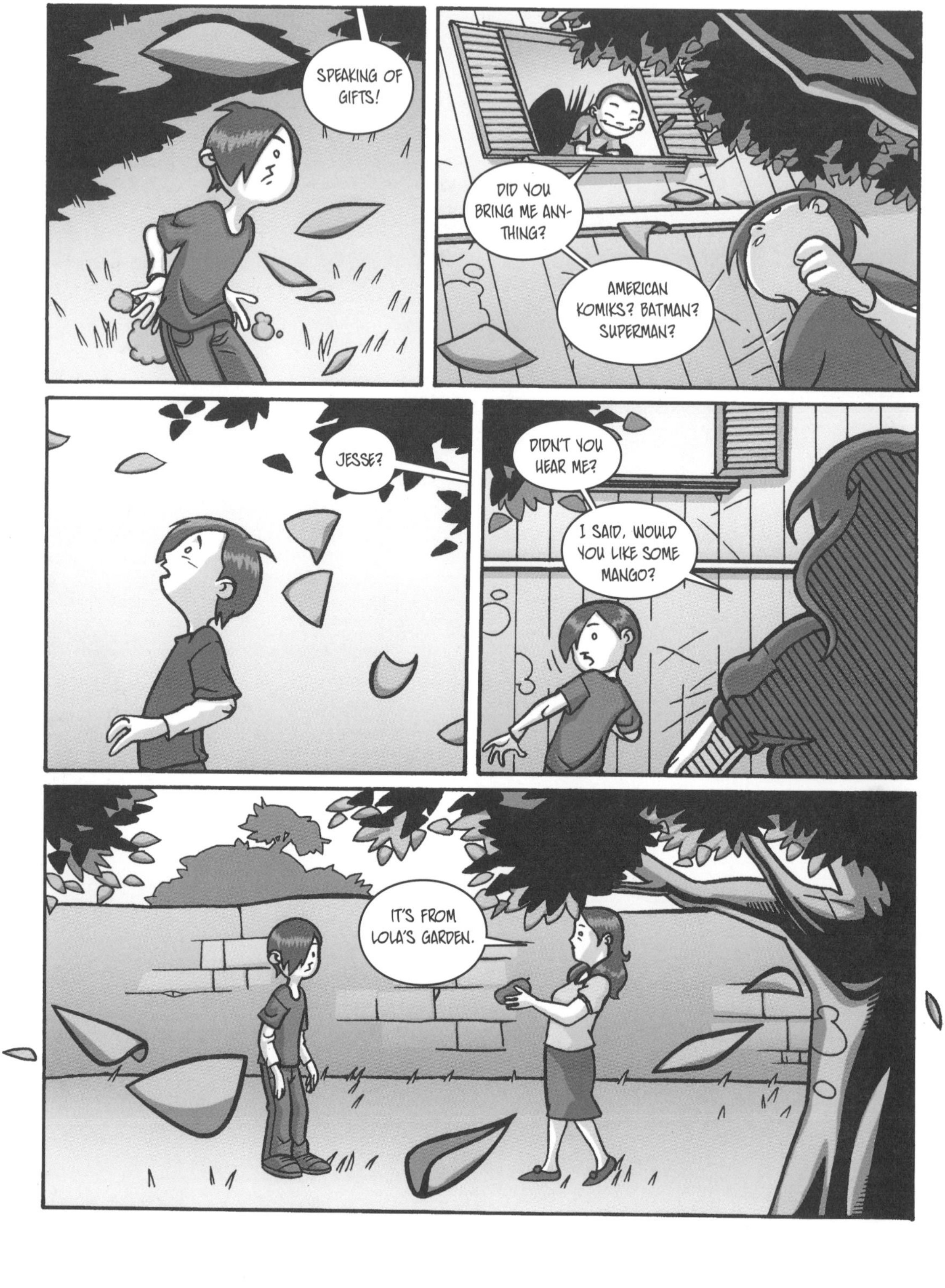
SPEAKING OF GIFTS!
DID YOU BRING ME ANY-THING?
AMERICAN KOMIKS? BATMAN? SUPERMAN?
JESSE?
DIDN'T YOU HEAR ME?
I SAID, WOULD YOU LIKE SOME MANGO?
IT'S FROM LOLA'S GARDEN.

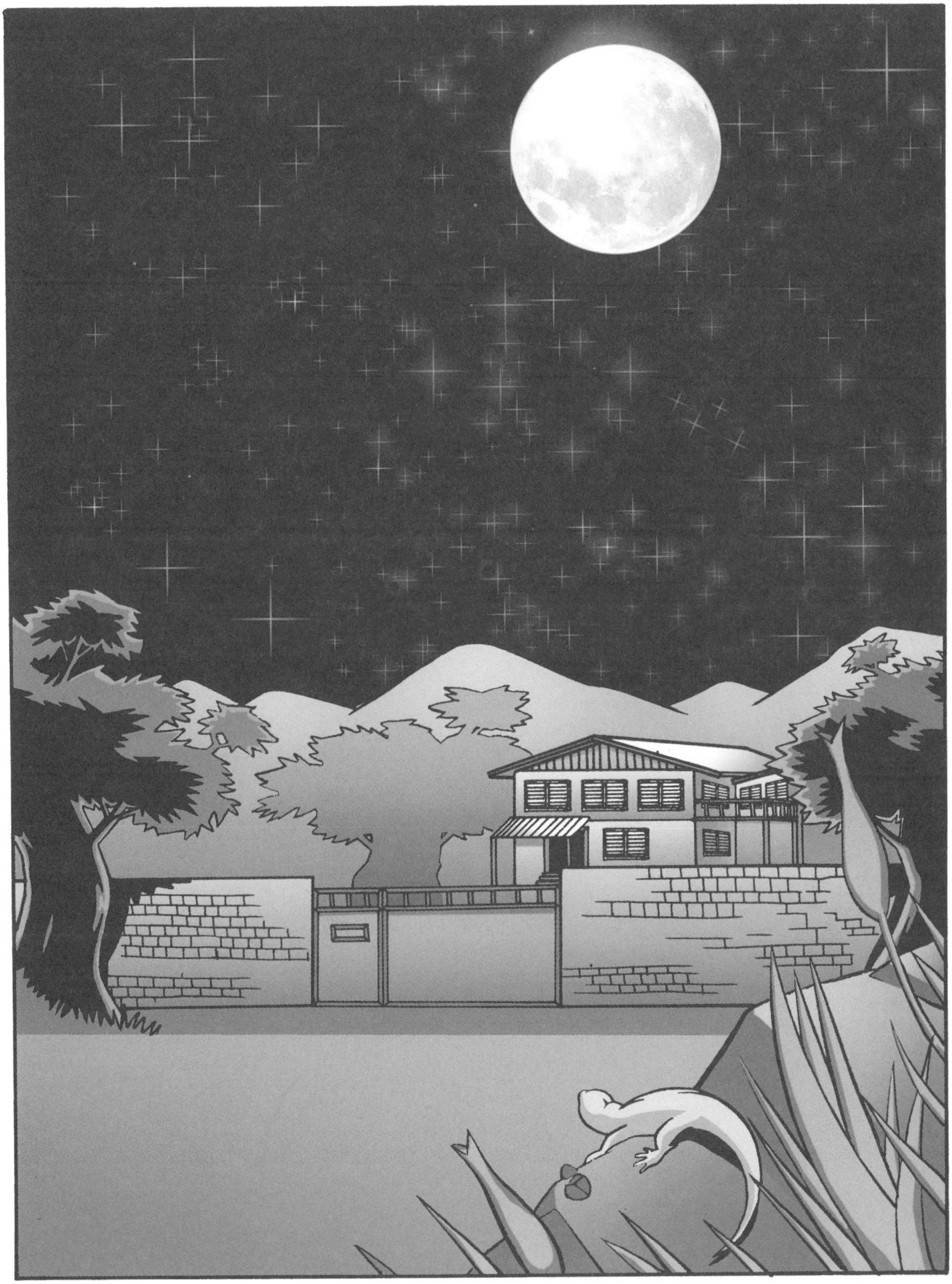

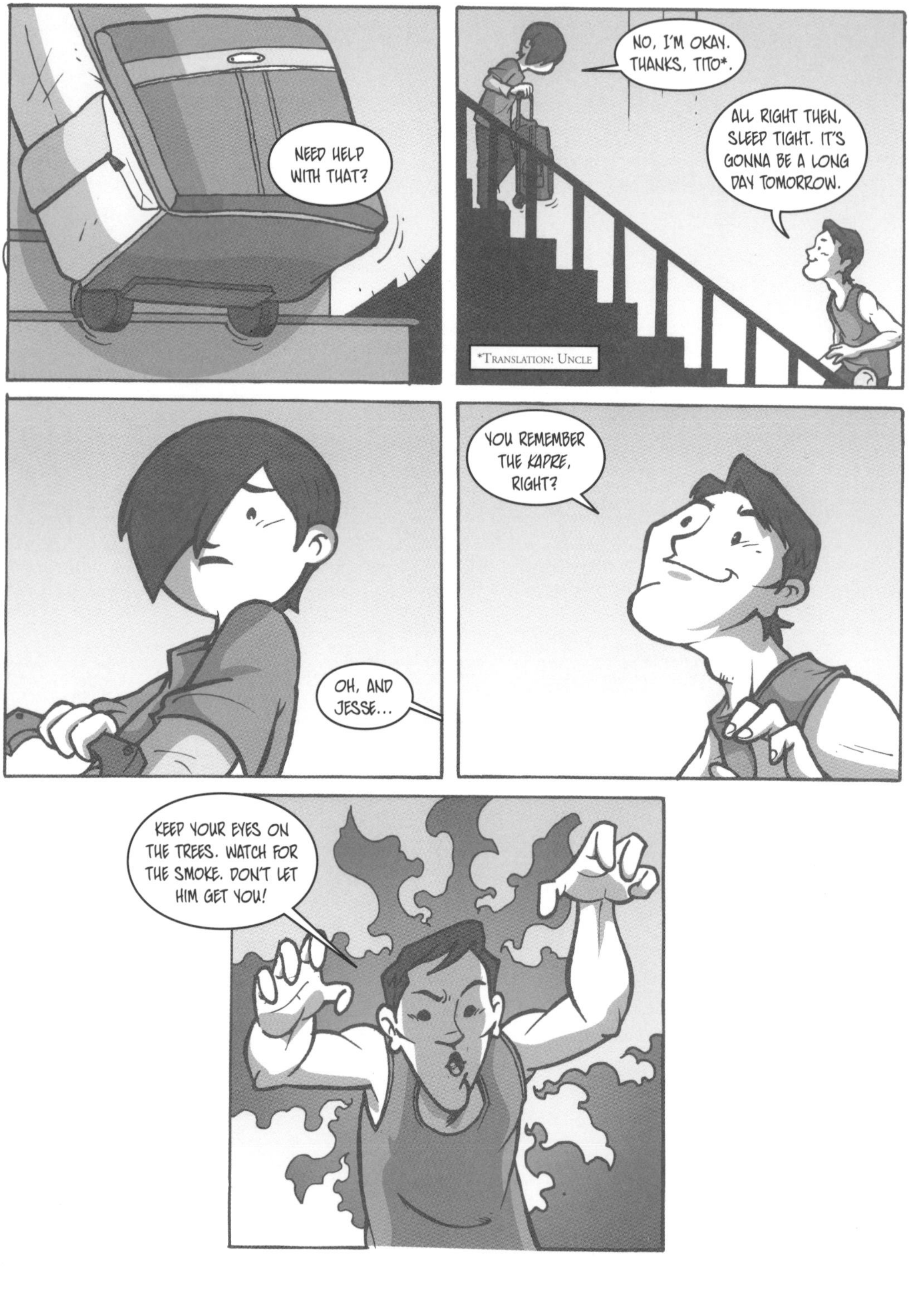
NEED HELP WITH THAT?
NO, I'M OKAY. THANKS, TITO*.
ALL RIGHT THEN, SLEEP TIGHT. IT'S GONNA BE A LONG DAY TOMORROW.
*Translation: Uncle
OH, AND JESSE...
YOU REMEMBER THE KAPRE, RIGHT?
KEEP YOUR EYES ON THE TREES. WATCH FOR THE SMOKE. DON'T LET HIM GET YOU!

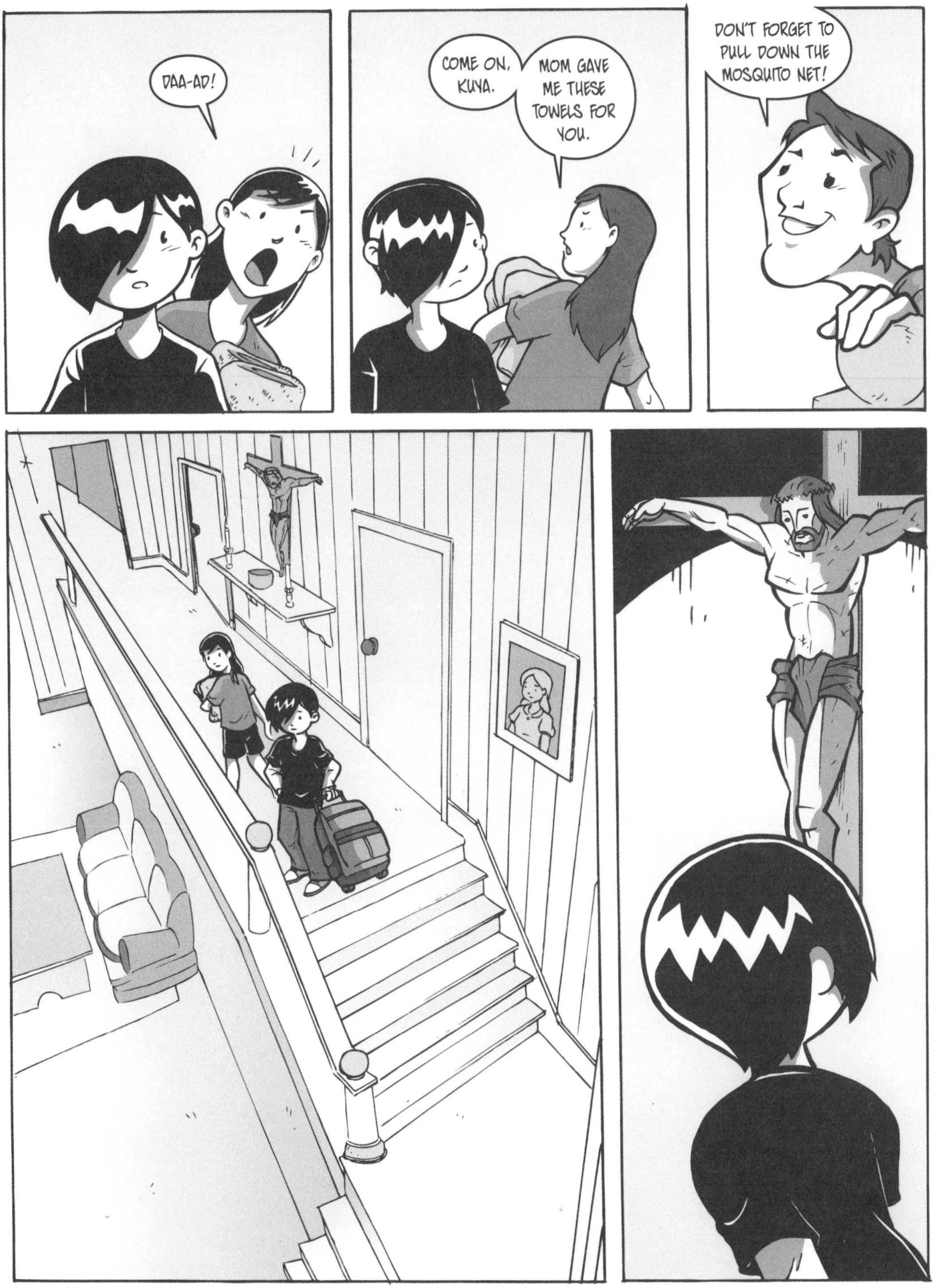
DAA-AD!
COME ON, KUYA.
MOM GAVE ME THESE TOWELS FOR YOU.
DON'T FORGET TO PULL DOWN THE MOSQUITO NET!

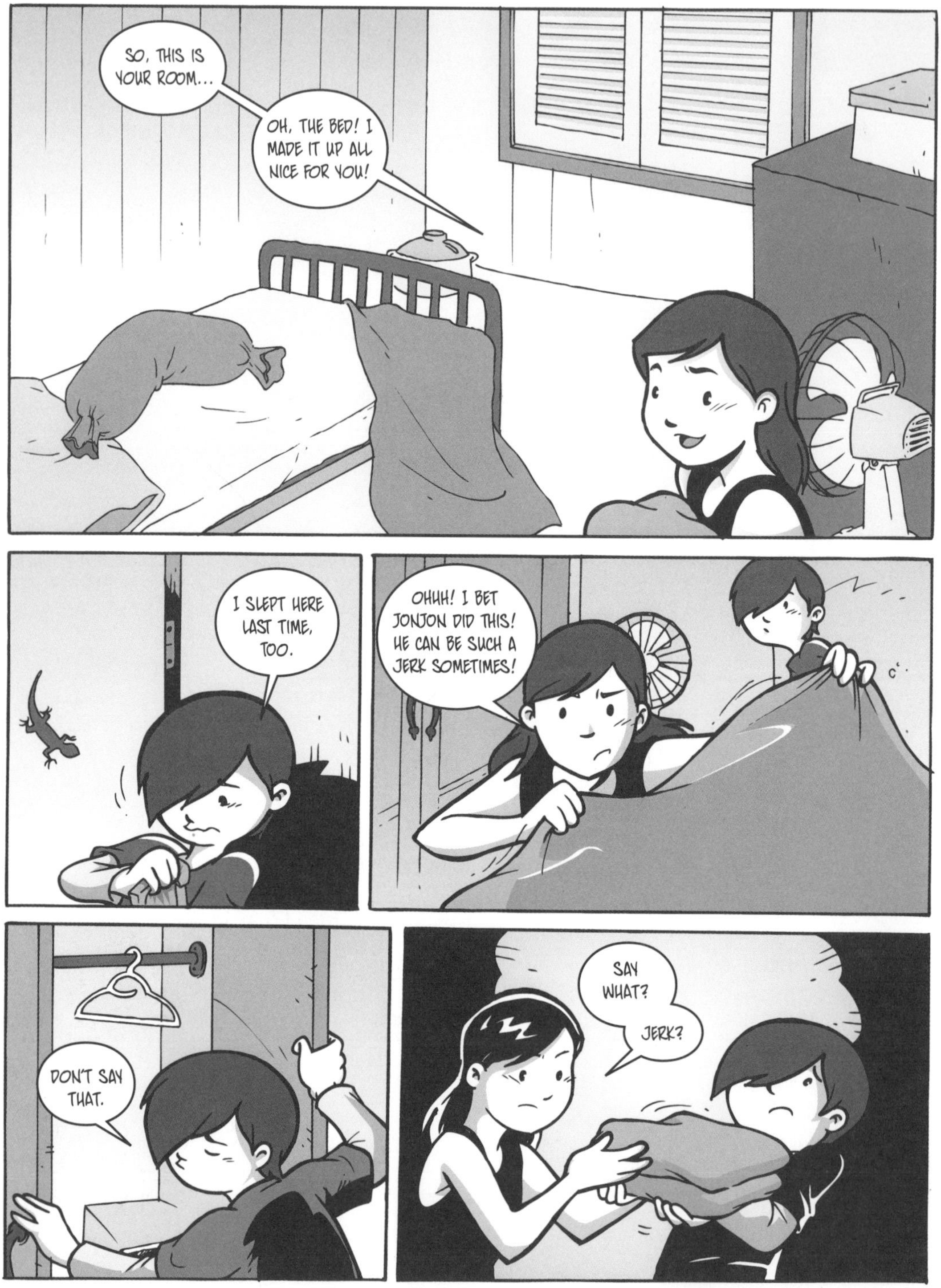
SO, THIS IS YOUR ROOM...
OH, THE BED! I MADE IT UP ALL NICE FOR YOU!
I SLEPT HERE LAST TIME, TOO.
OHHH! I BET JONJON DID THIS! HE CAN BE SUCH A JERK SOMETIMES!
DON'T SAY THAT.
SAY WHAT?
JERK?

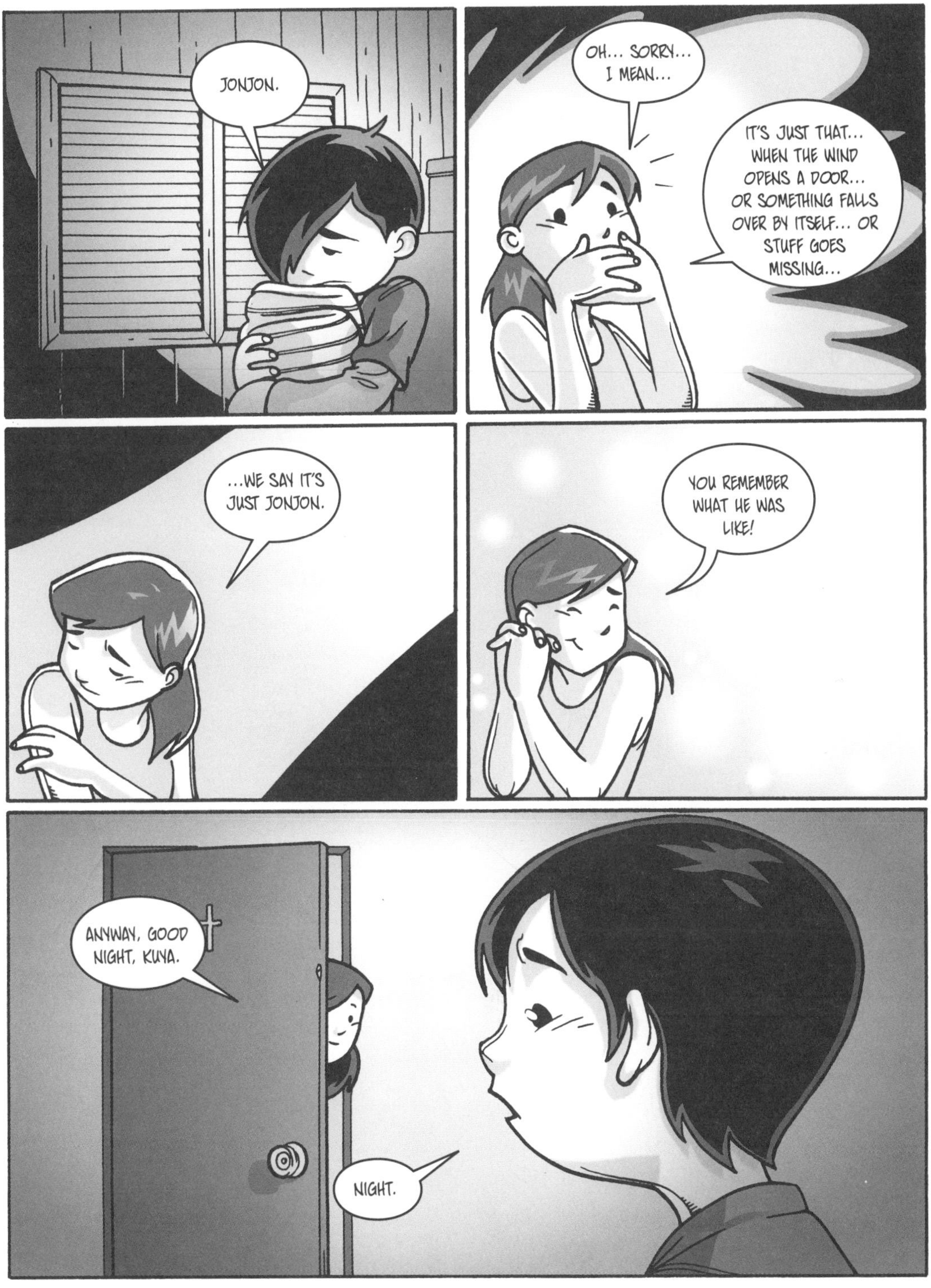
JONJON.
OH... SORRY... I MEAN...
IT'S JUST THAT... WHEN THE WIND OPENS A DOOR... OR SOMETHING FALLS OVER BY ITSELF... OR STUFF GOES MISSING...
...WE SAY IT'S JUST JONJON.
YOU REMEMBER WHAT HE WAS LIKE!
ANYWAY, GOOD NIGHT, KUYA.
NIGHT.

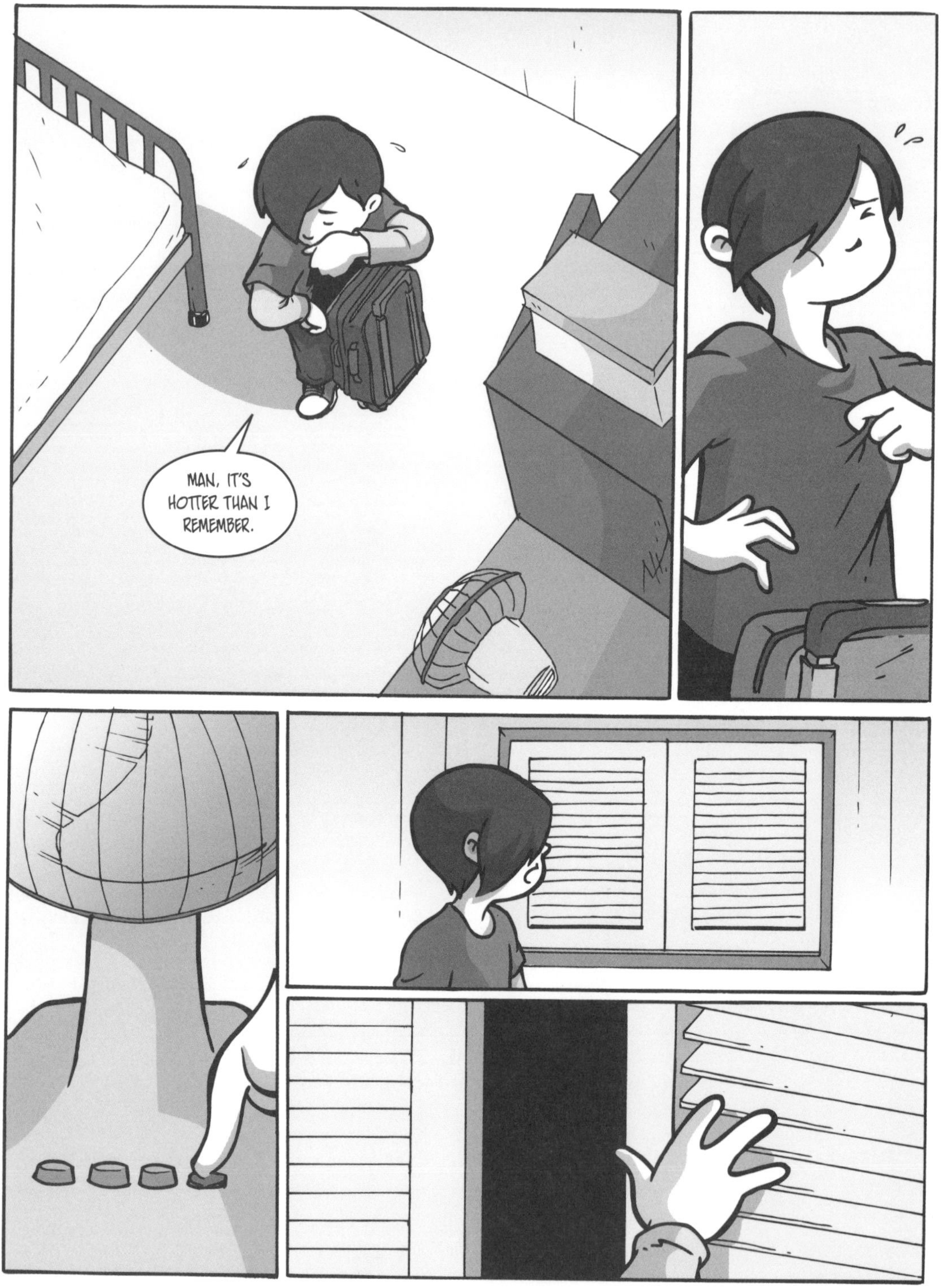
MAN, IT'S HOTTER THAN I REMEMBER.

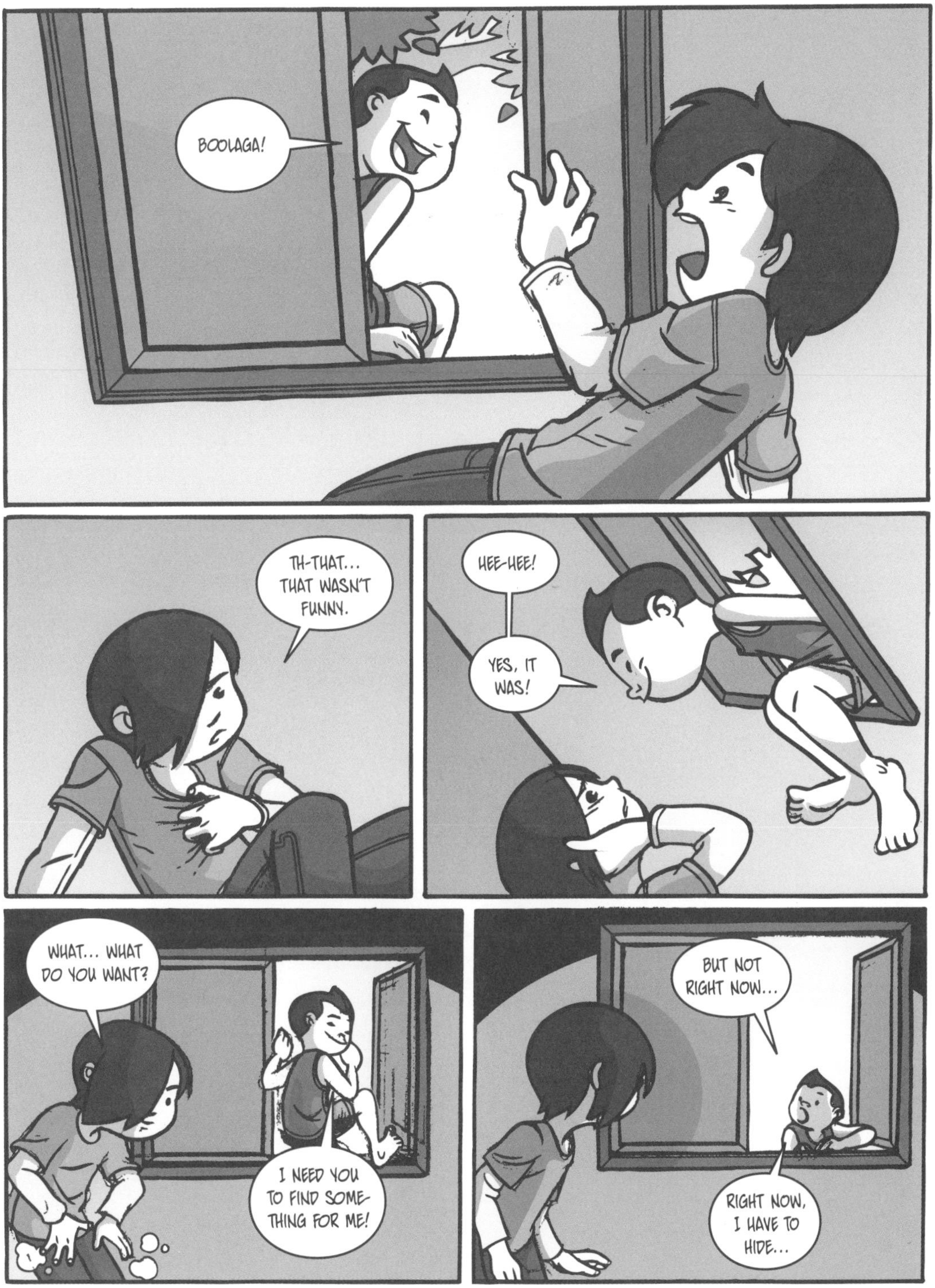
BOOLAGA!
TH-THAT... THAT WASN'T FUNNY.
HEE-HEE!
YES, IT WAS!
WHAT... WHAT DO YOU WANT?
I NEED YOU TO FIND SOME-THING FOR ME!
BUT NOT RIGHT NOW...
RIGHT NOW, I HAVE TO HIDE...

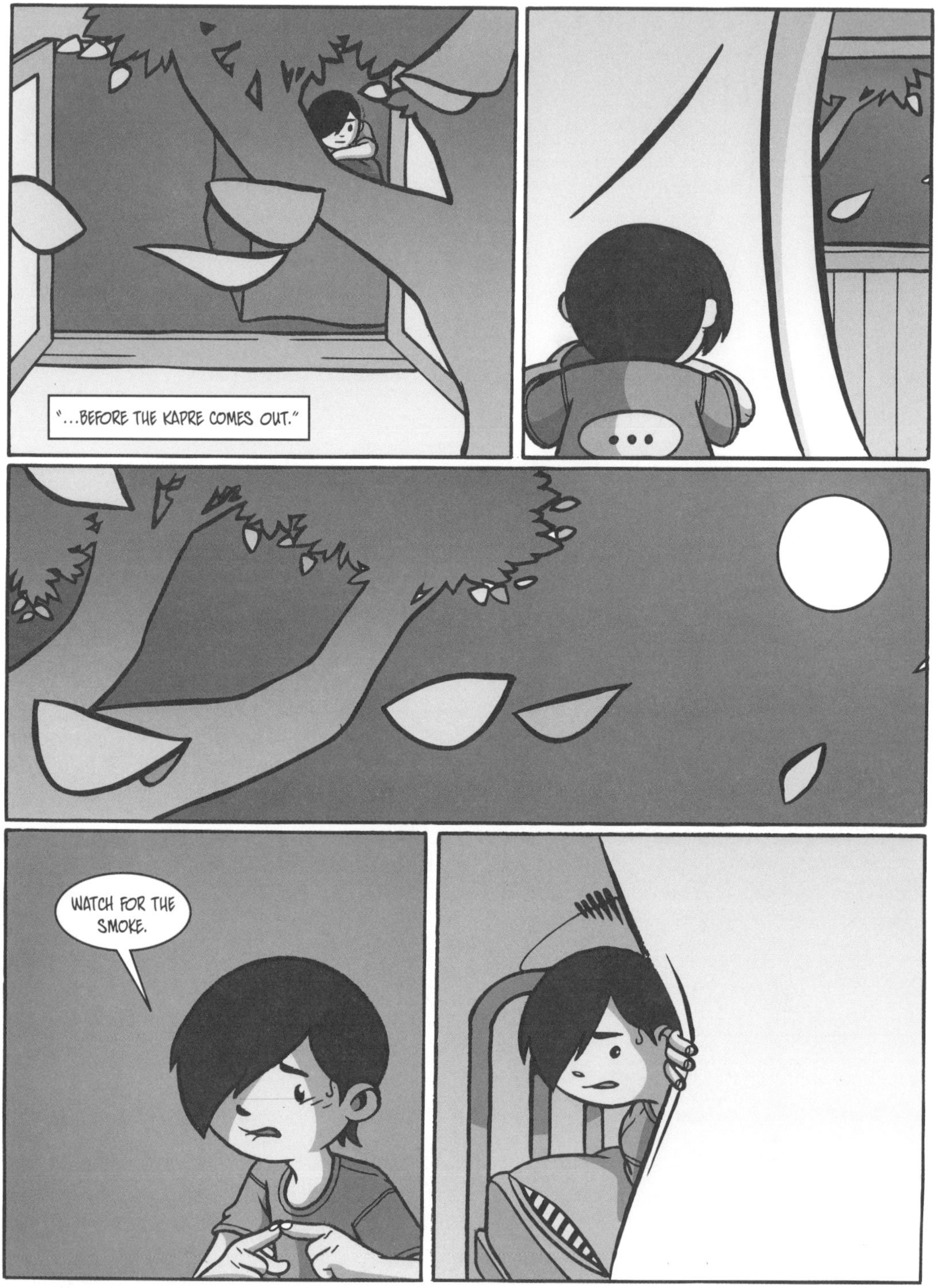
"...BEFORE THE KAPRE COMES OUT."
WATCH FOR THE SMOKE.

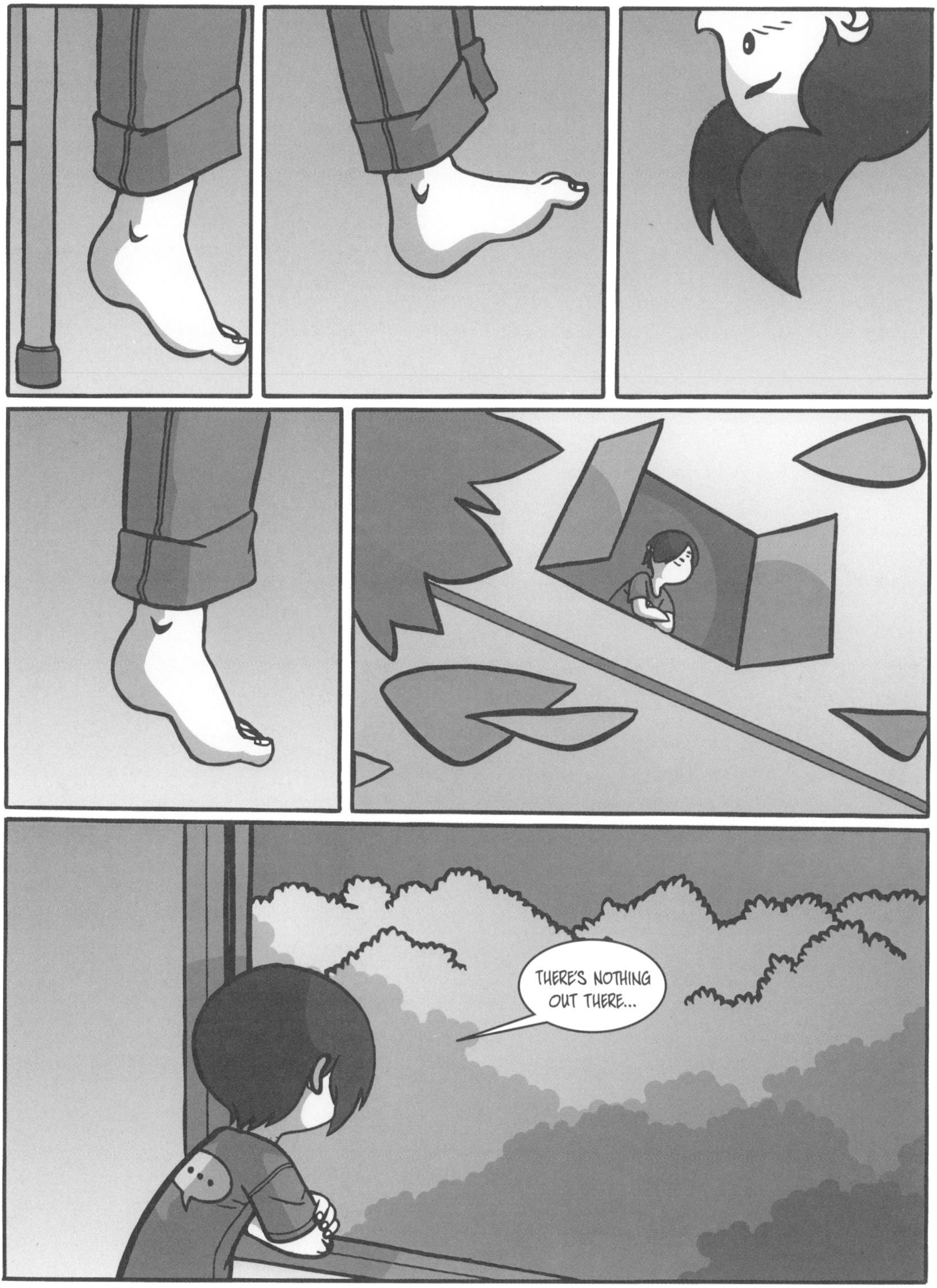
THERE'S NOTHING OUT THERE...

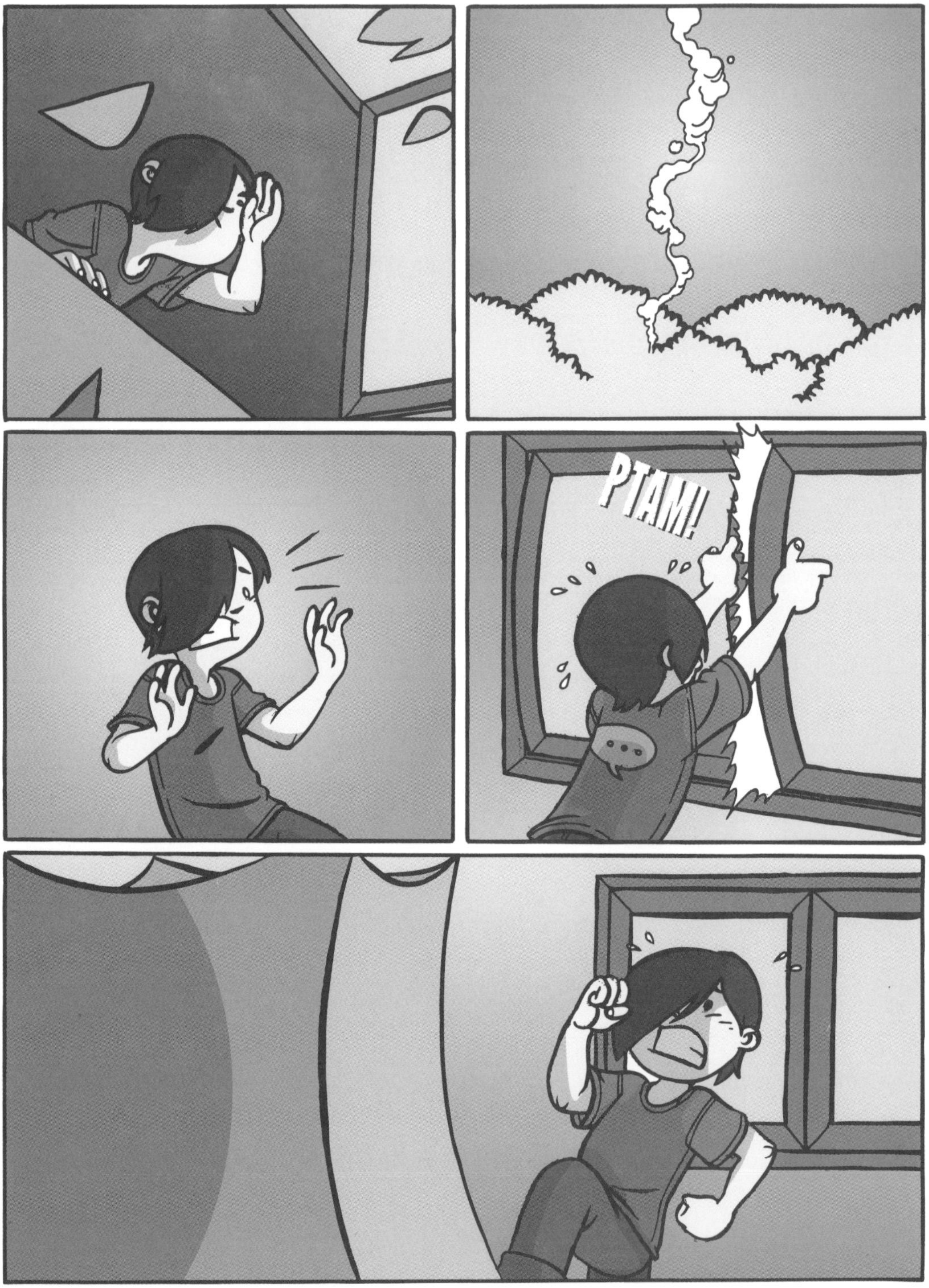
PTAM!

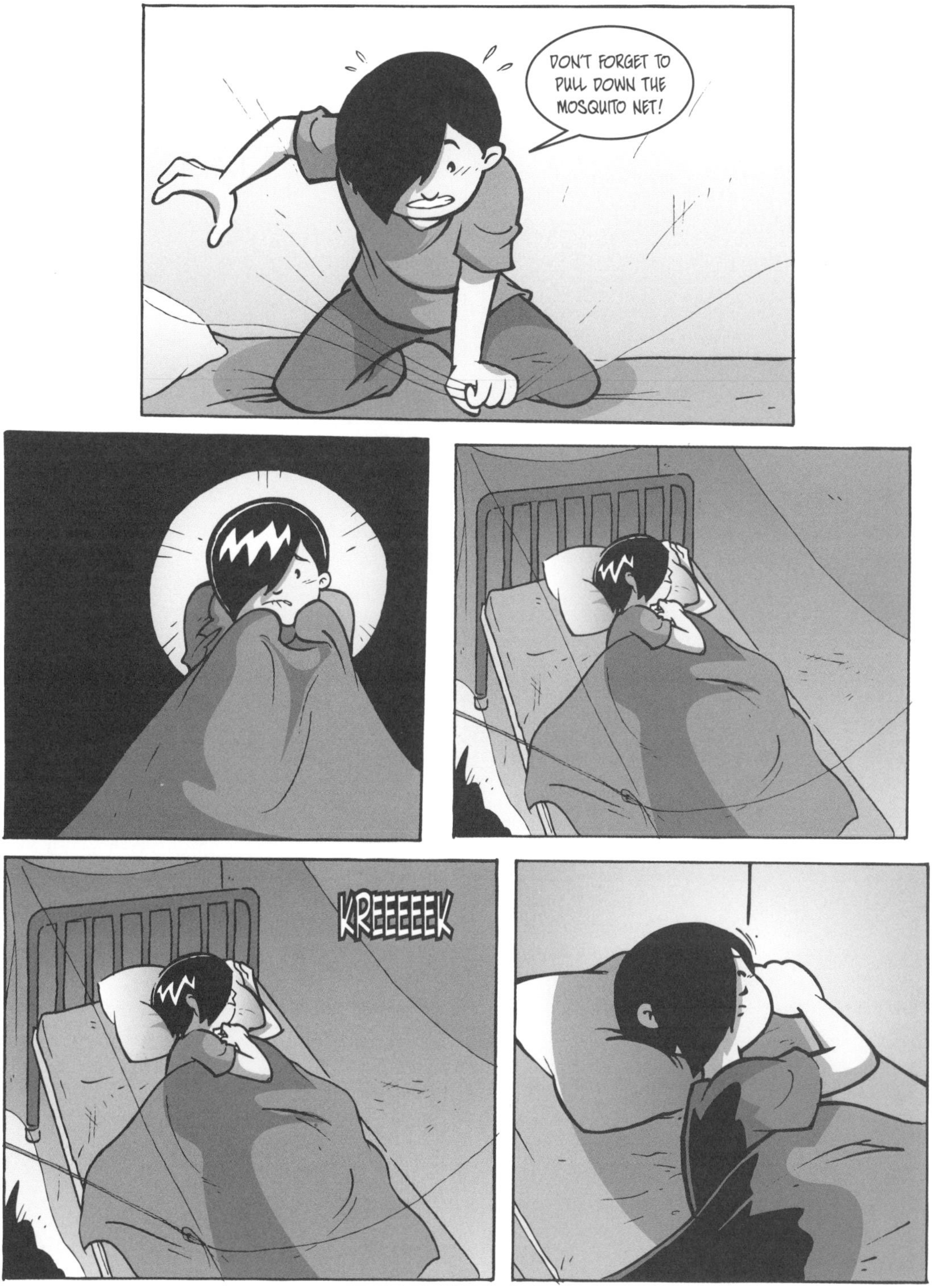
DON'T FORGET TO PULL DOWN THE MOSQUITO NET!
KREEEEEK

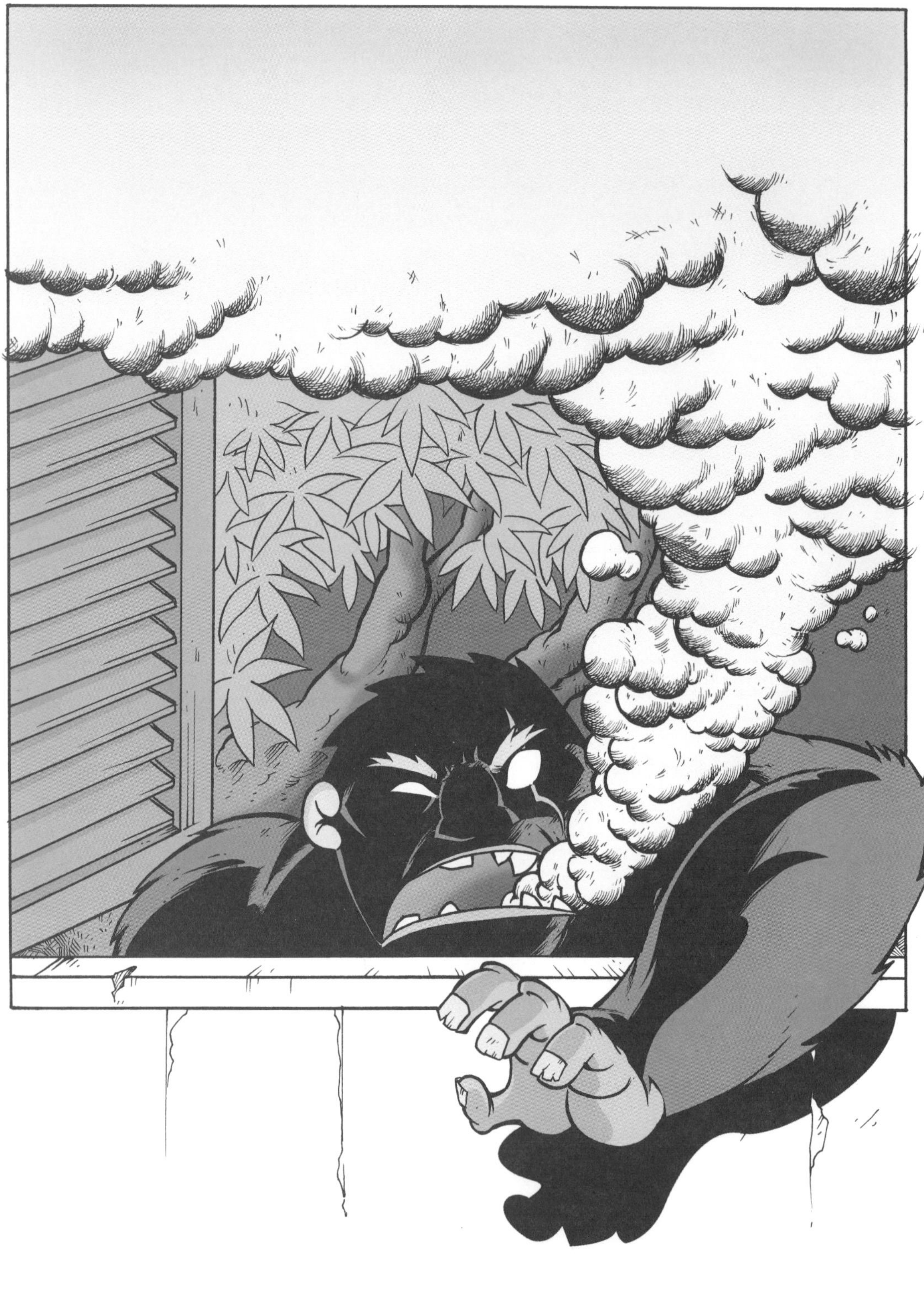

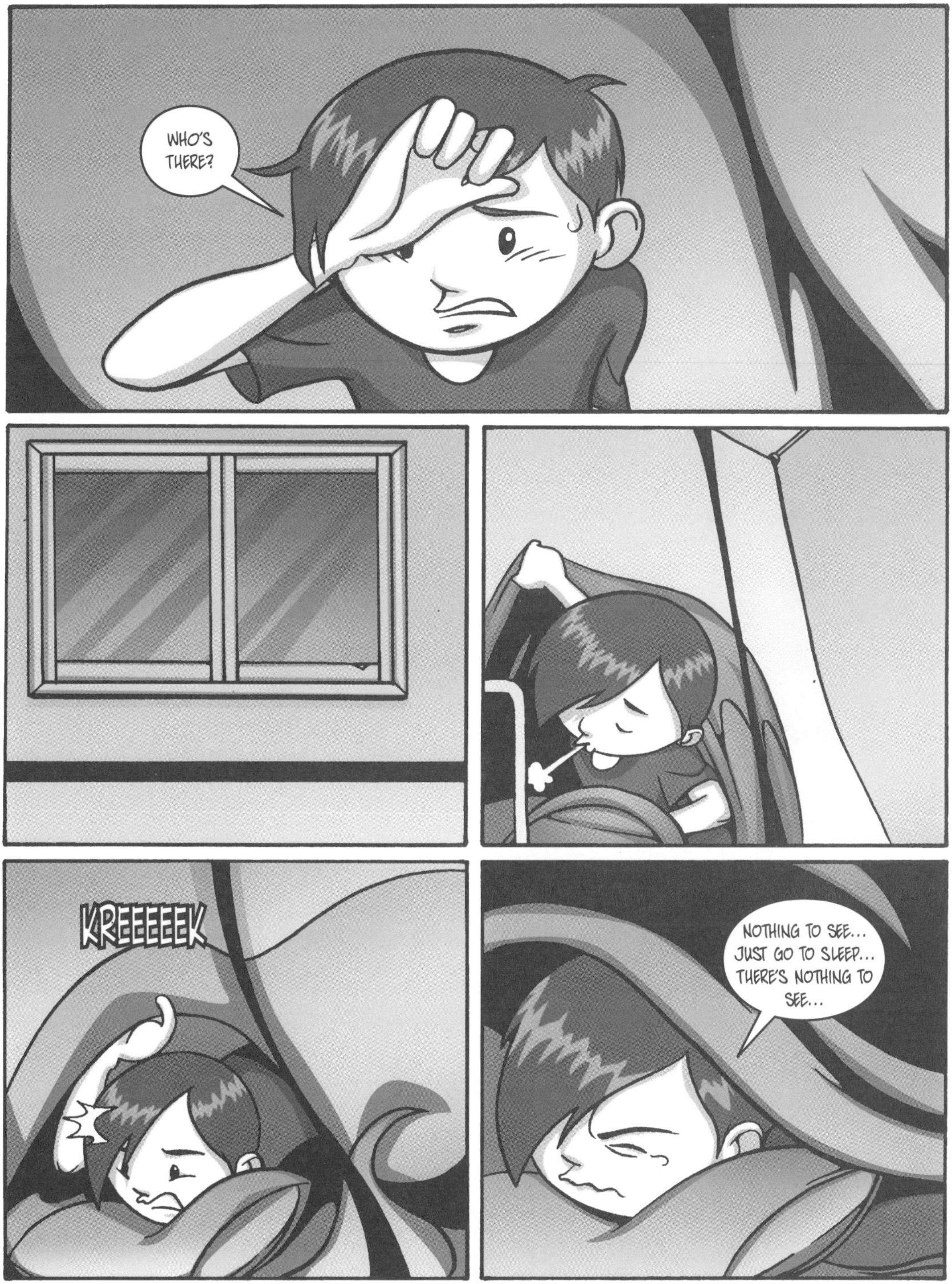
WHO'S THERE?
KREEEEEK
NOTHING TO SEE... JUST GO TO SLEEP... THERE'S NOTHING TO SEE...

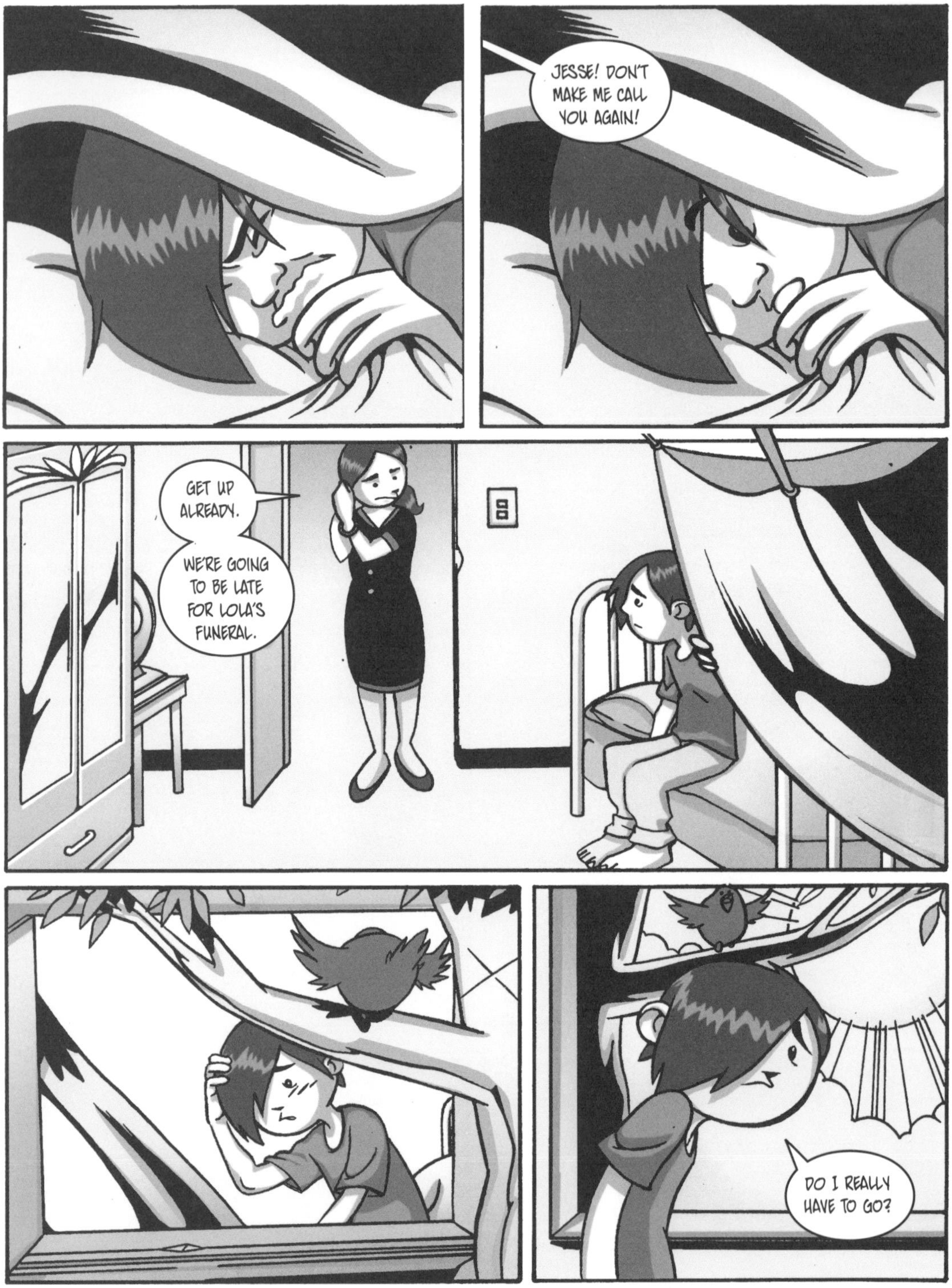
JESSE! DON'T MAKE ME CALL YOU AGAIN!
GET UP ALREADY.
WE'RE GOING TO BE LATE FOR LOLA'S FUNERAL.
DO I REALLY HAVE TO GO?

ACT

II

LOLA

A GHOST STORY

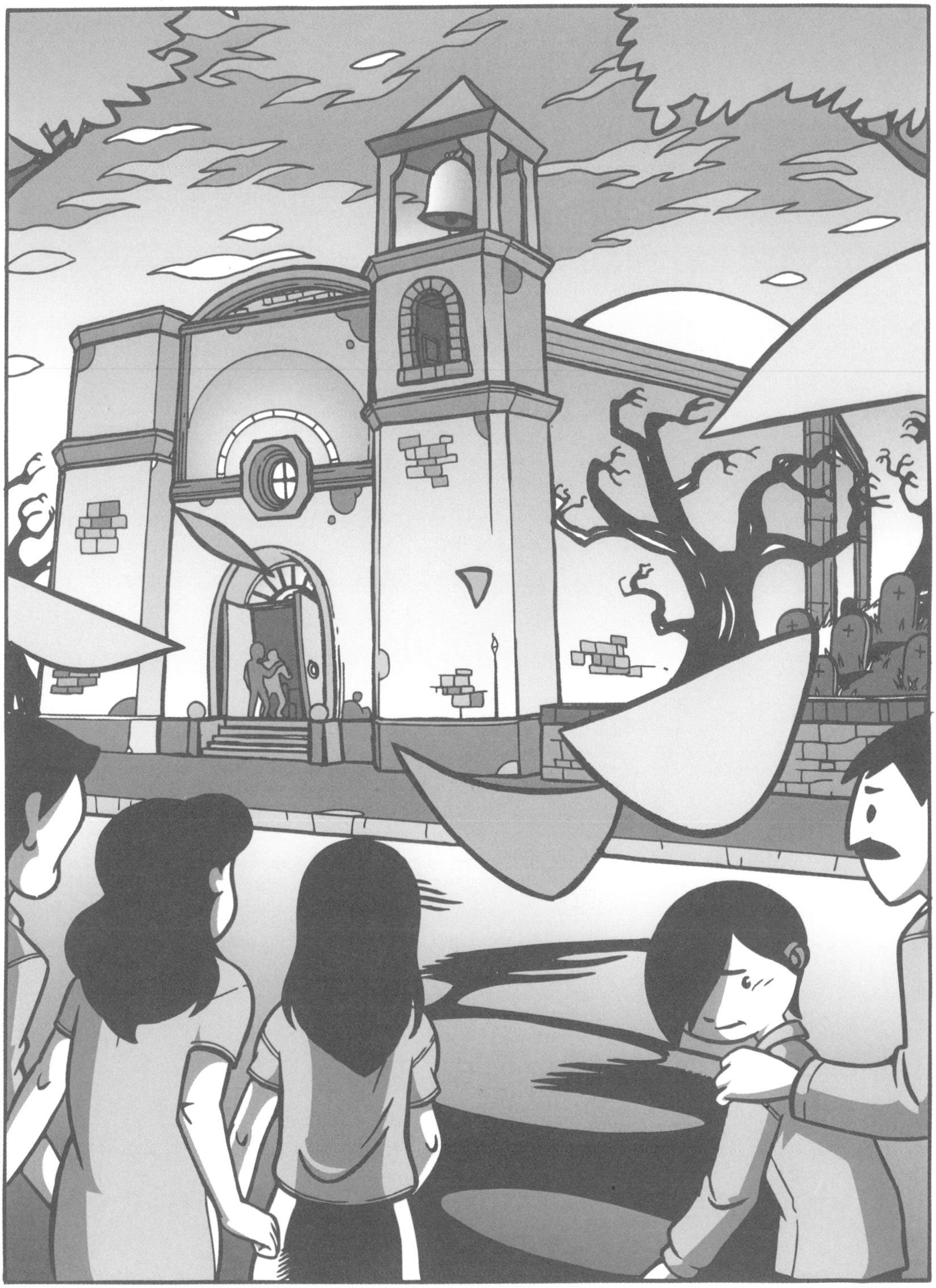

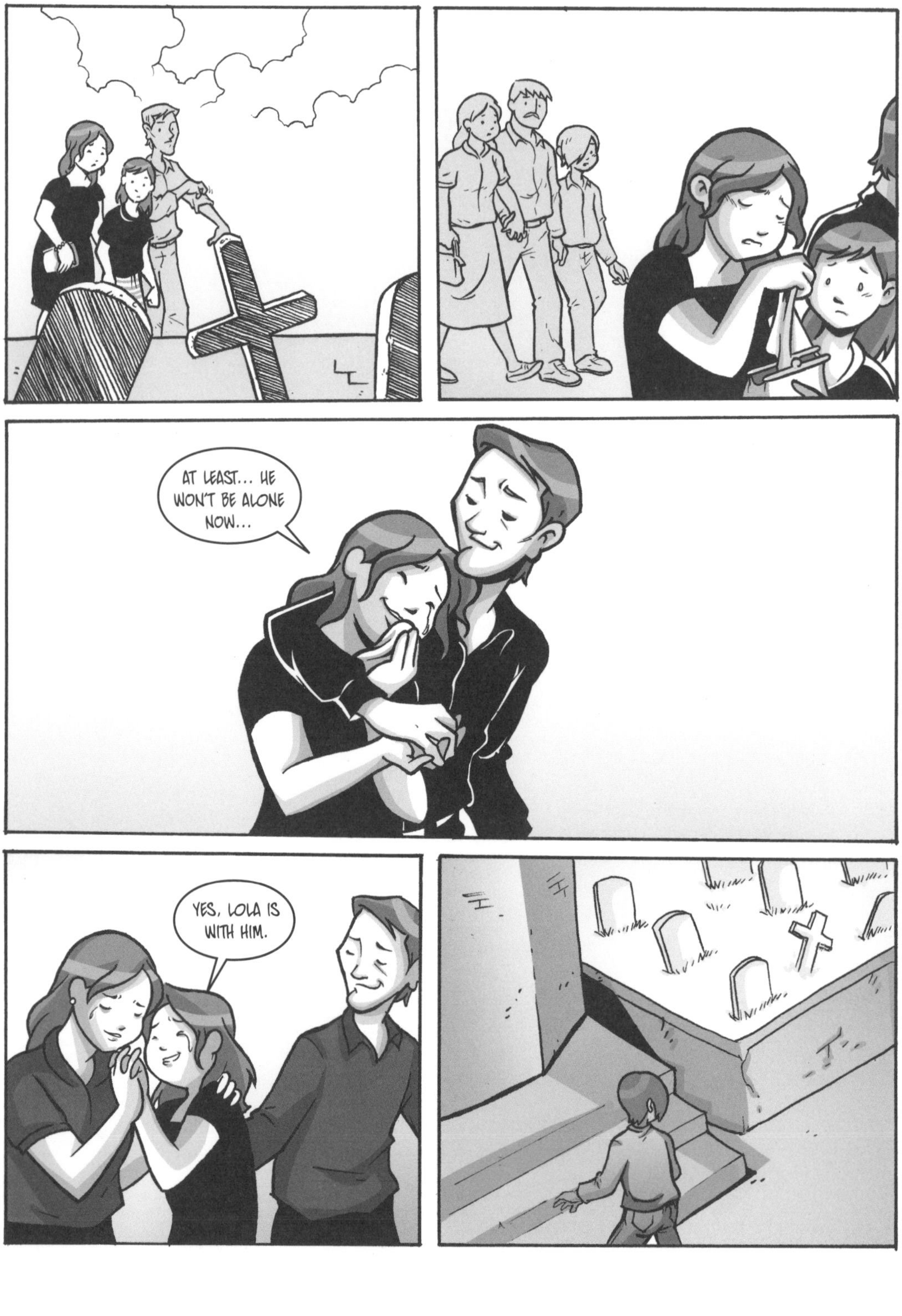
AT LEAST... HE WON'T BE ALONE NOW...
YES, LOLA IS WITH HIM.

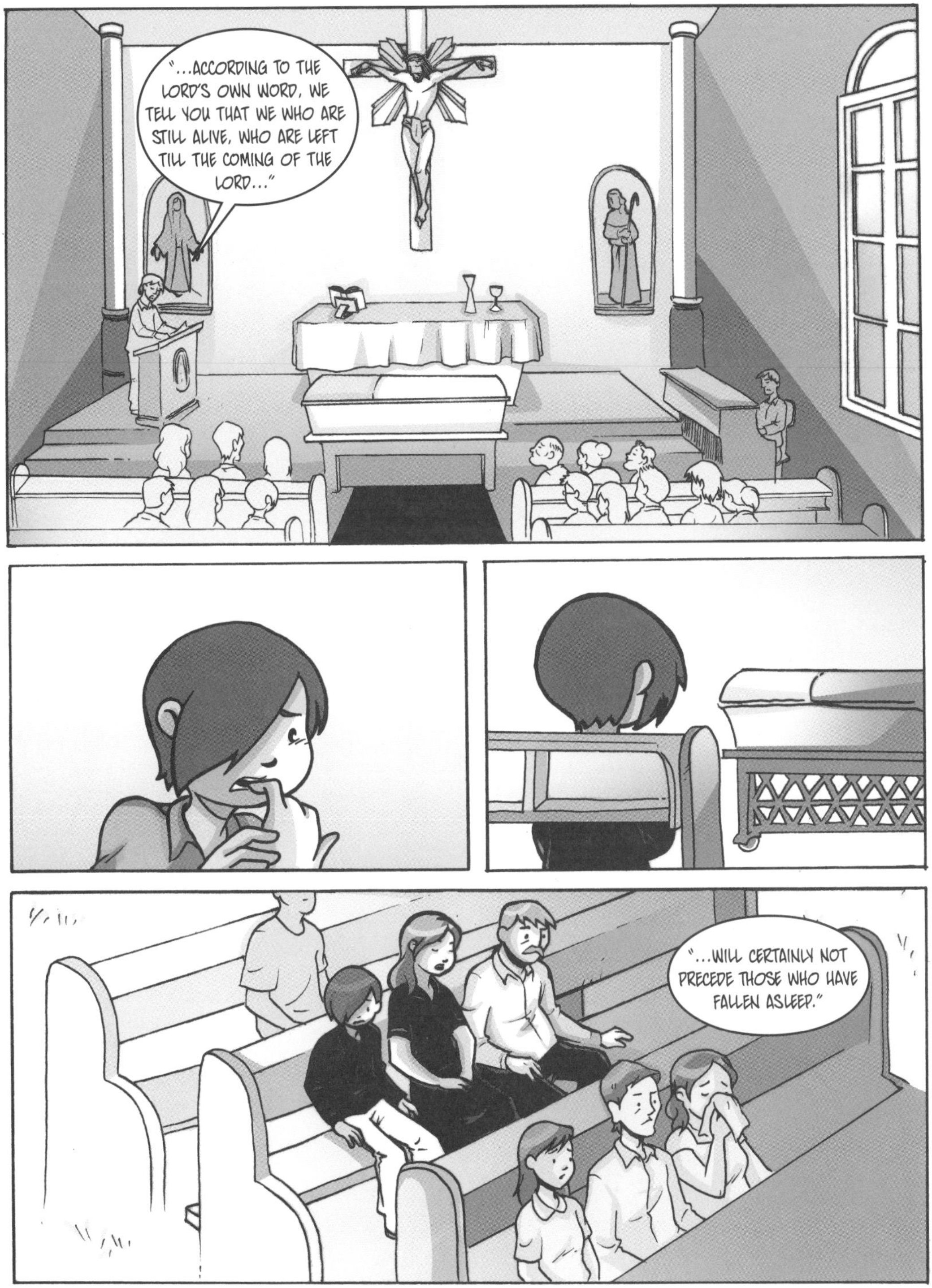
"...ACCORDING TO THE LORD'S OWN WORD, WE TELL YOU THAT WE WHO ARE STILL ALIVE, WHO ARE LEFT TILL THE COMING OF THE LORD..."
"...WILL CERTAINLY NOT PRECEDE THOSE WHO HAVE FALLEN ASLEEP."

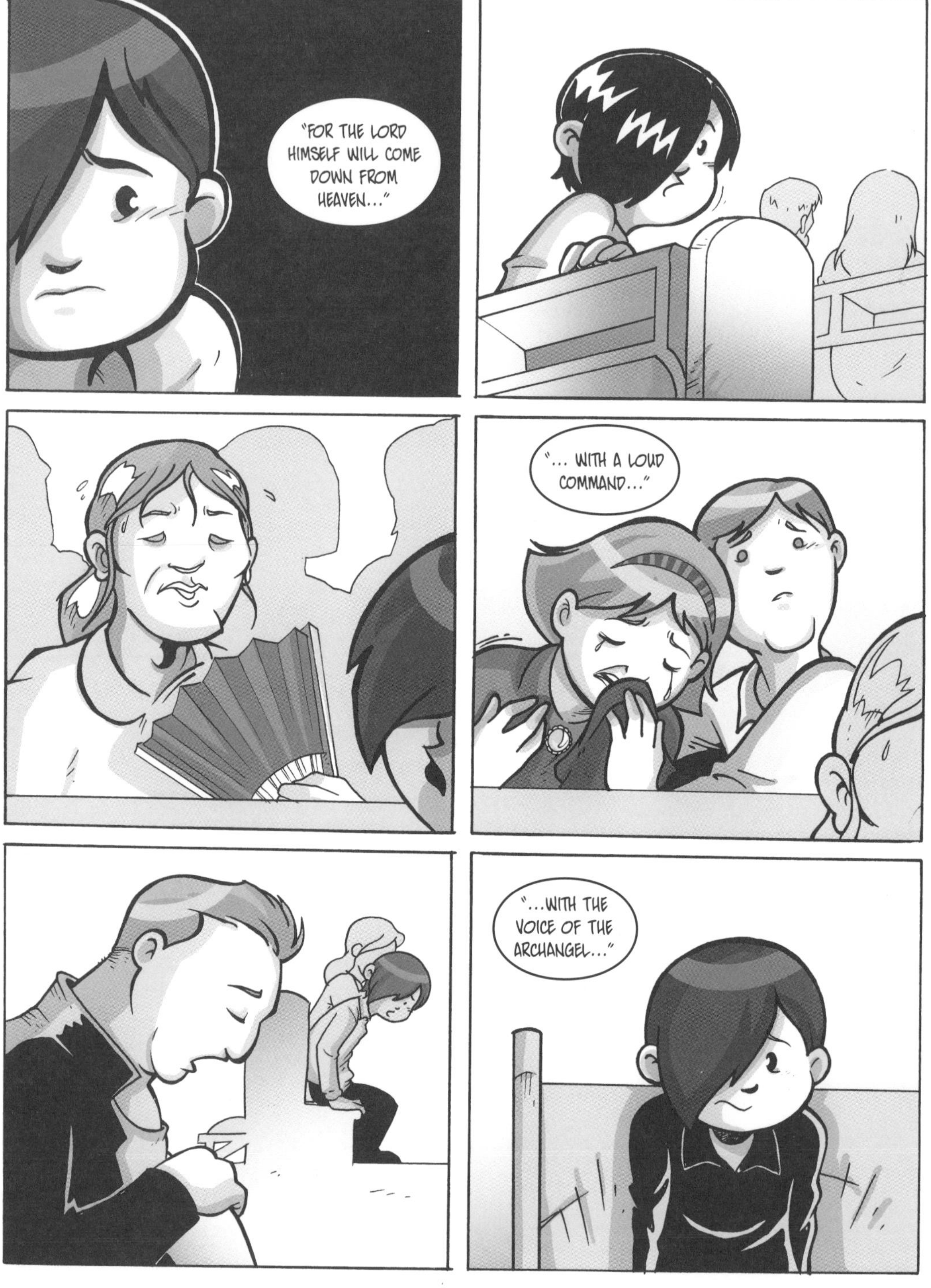
"FOR THE LORD HIMSELF WILL COME DOWN FROM HEAVEN..."
"... WITH A LOUD COMMAND..."
"...WITH THE VOICE OF THE ARCHANGEL..."

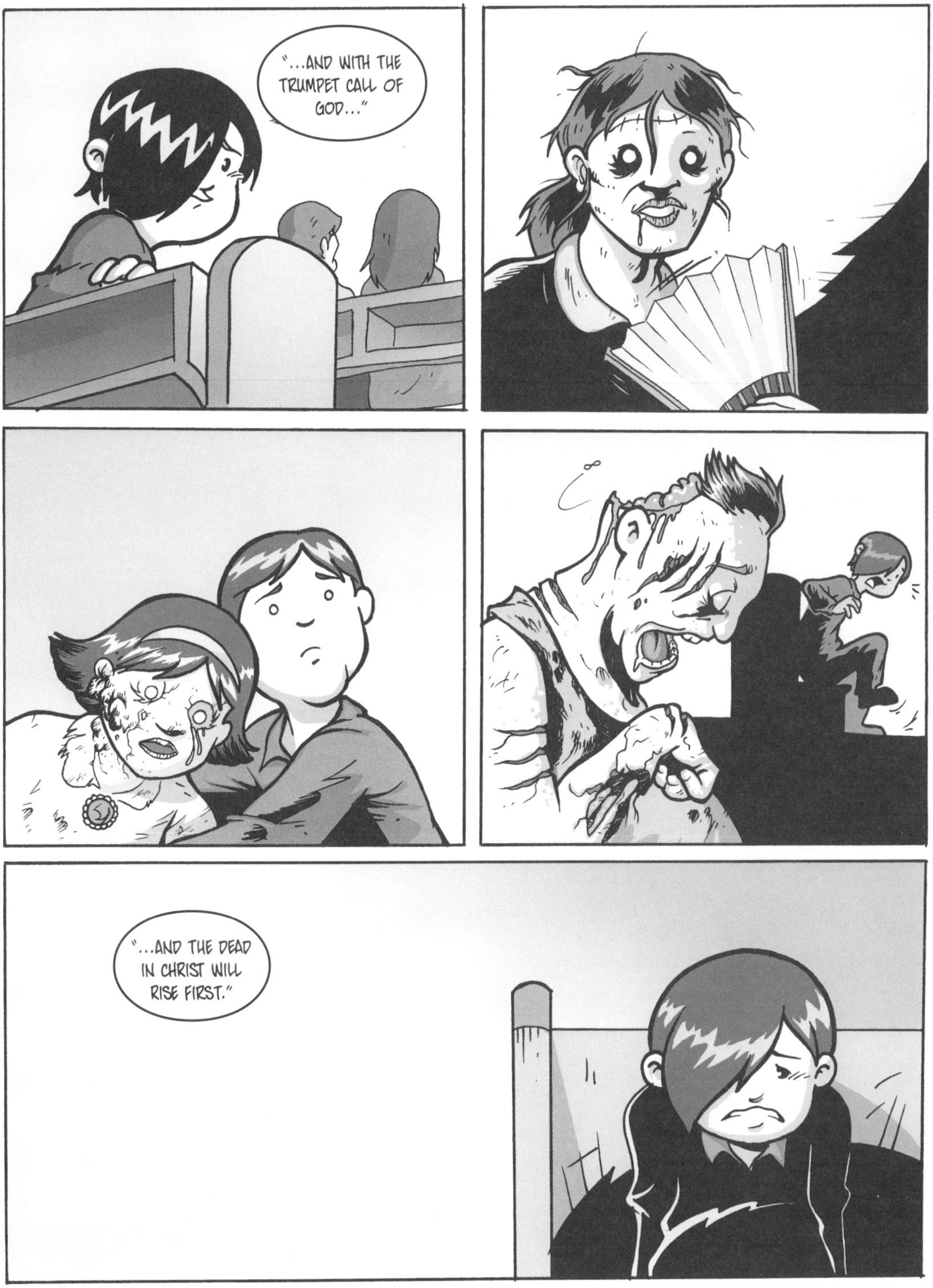
"...AND WITH THE TRUMPET CALL OF GOD..."
"...AND THE DEAD IN CHRIST WILL RISE FIRST."

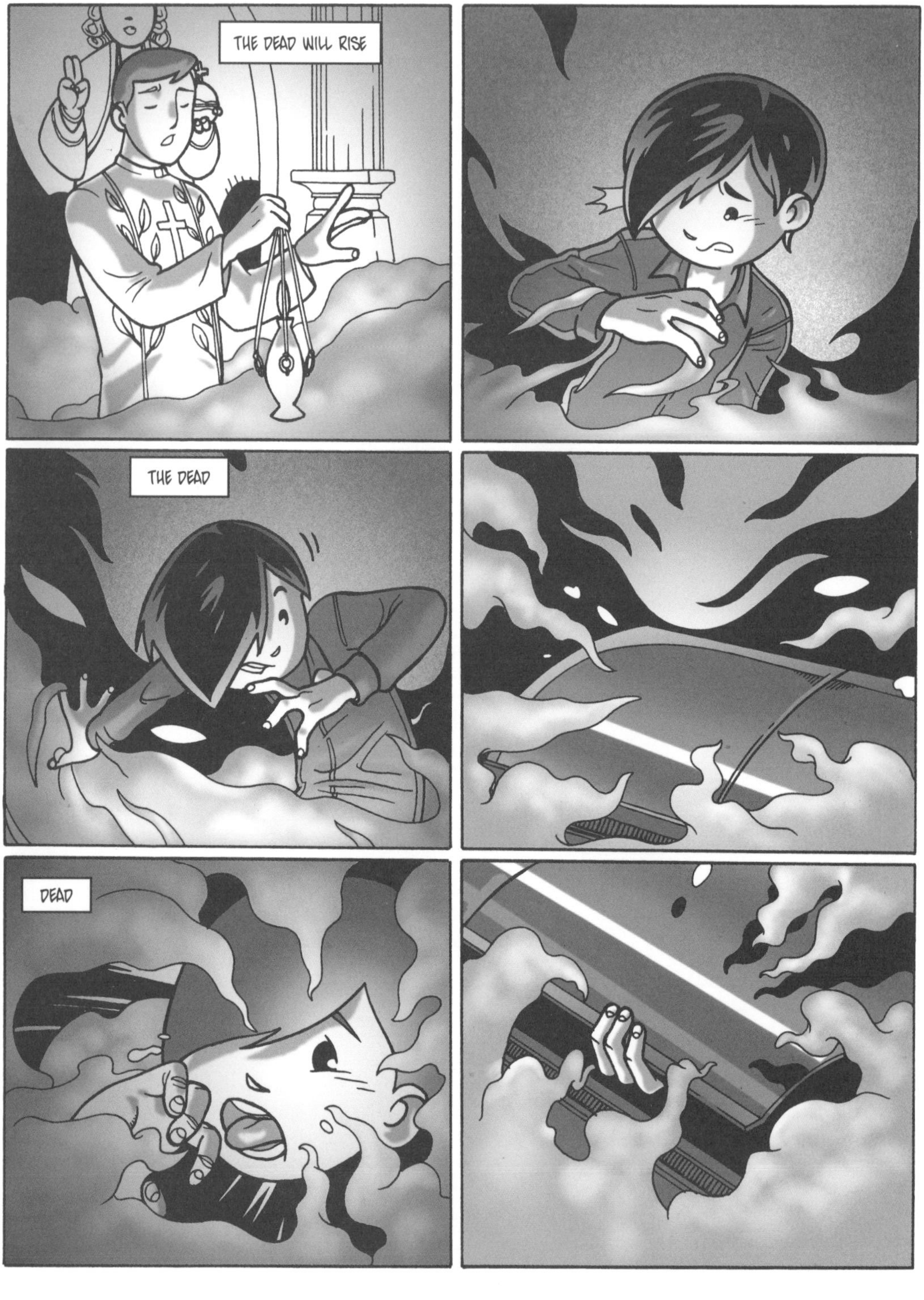
THE DEAD WILL RISE
THE DEAD
DEAD

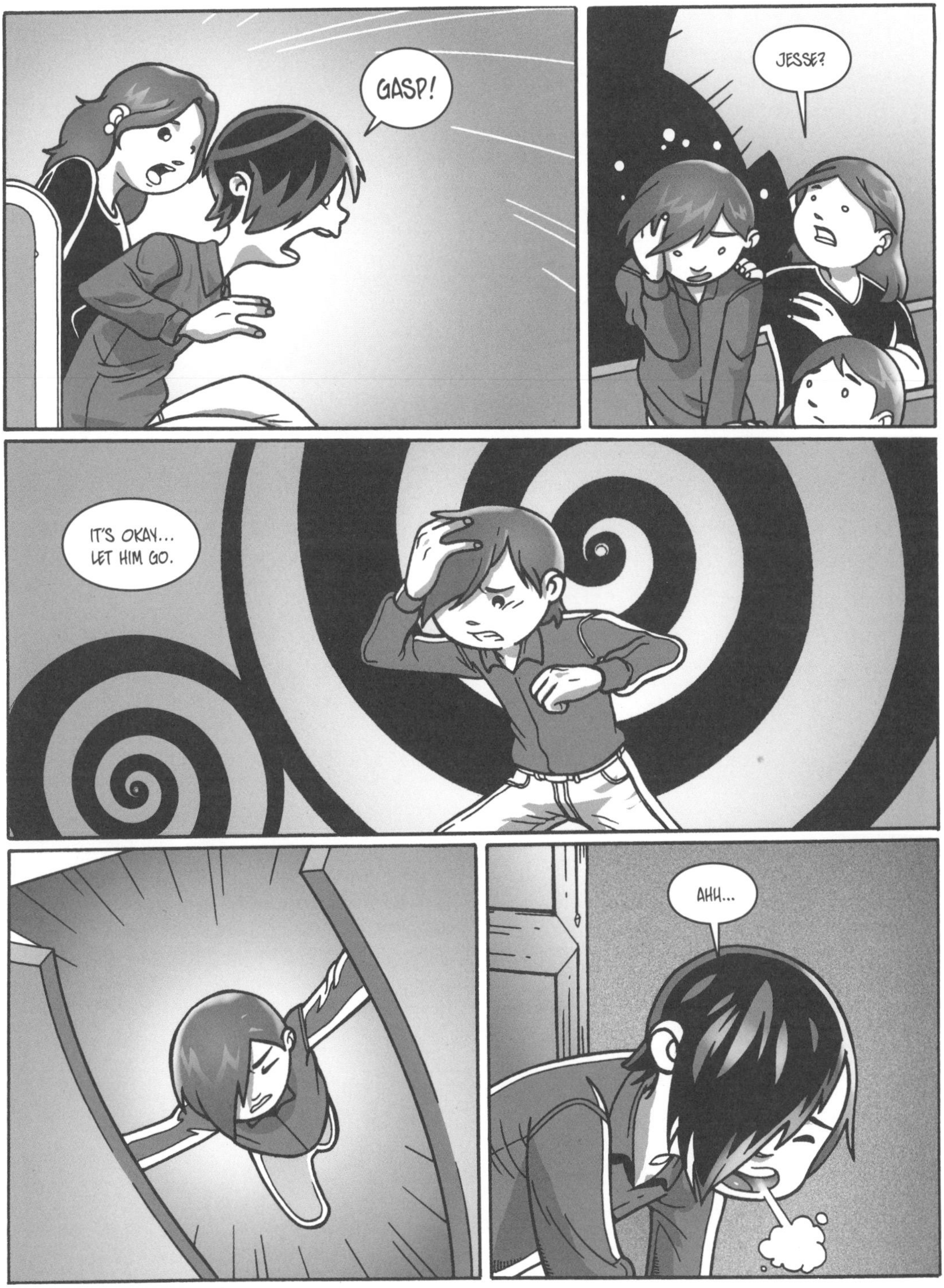
GASP!
JESSE?
IT'S OKAY... LET HIM GO.
AHH...

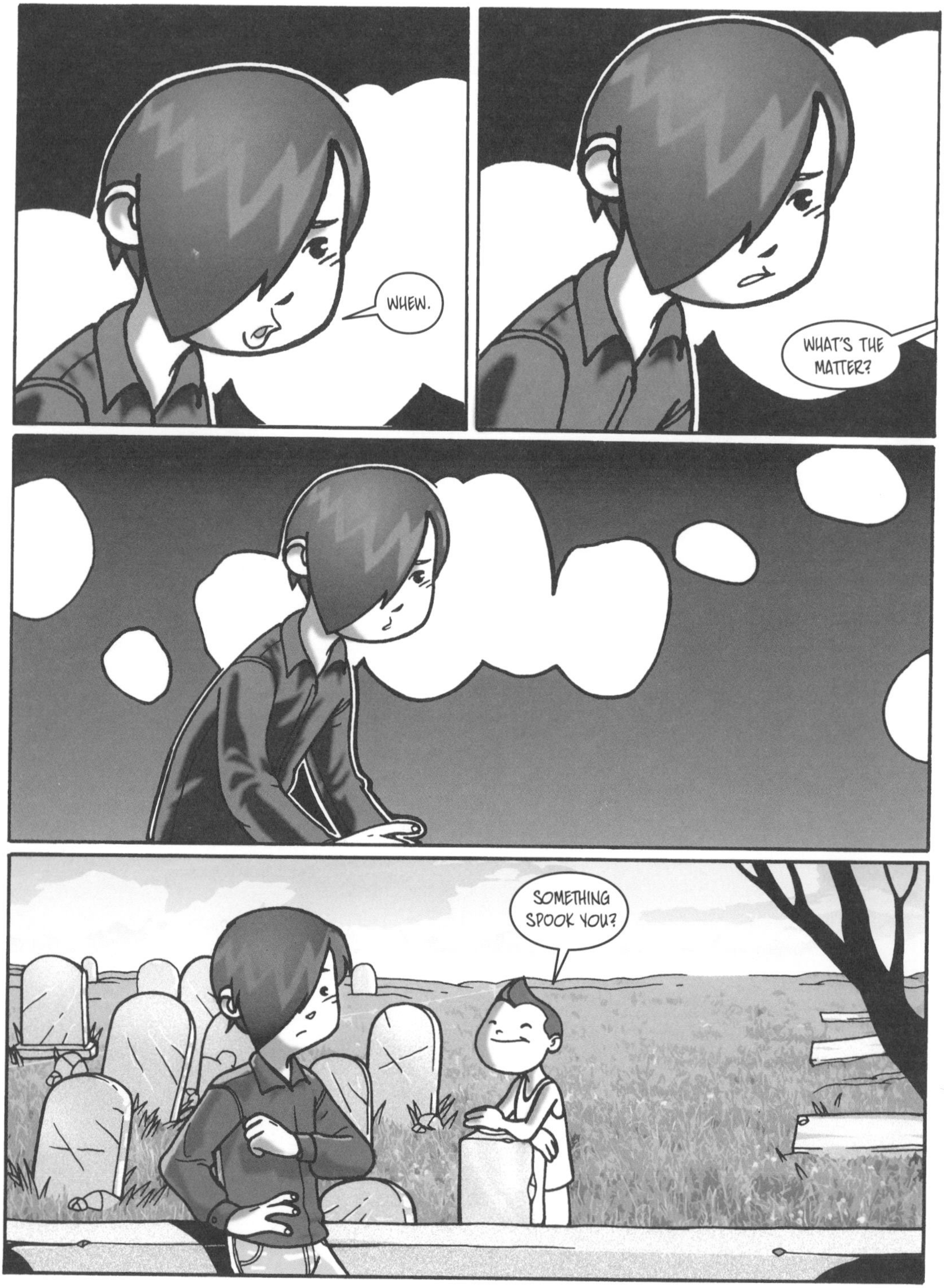
WHEW.
WHAT'S THE MATTER?
SOMETHING SPOOK YOU?

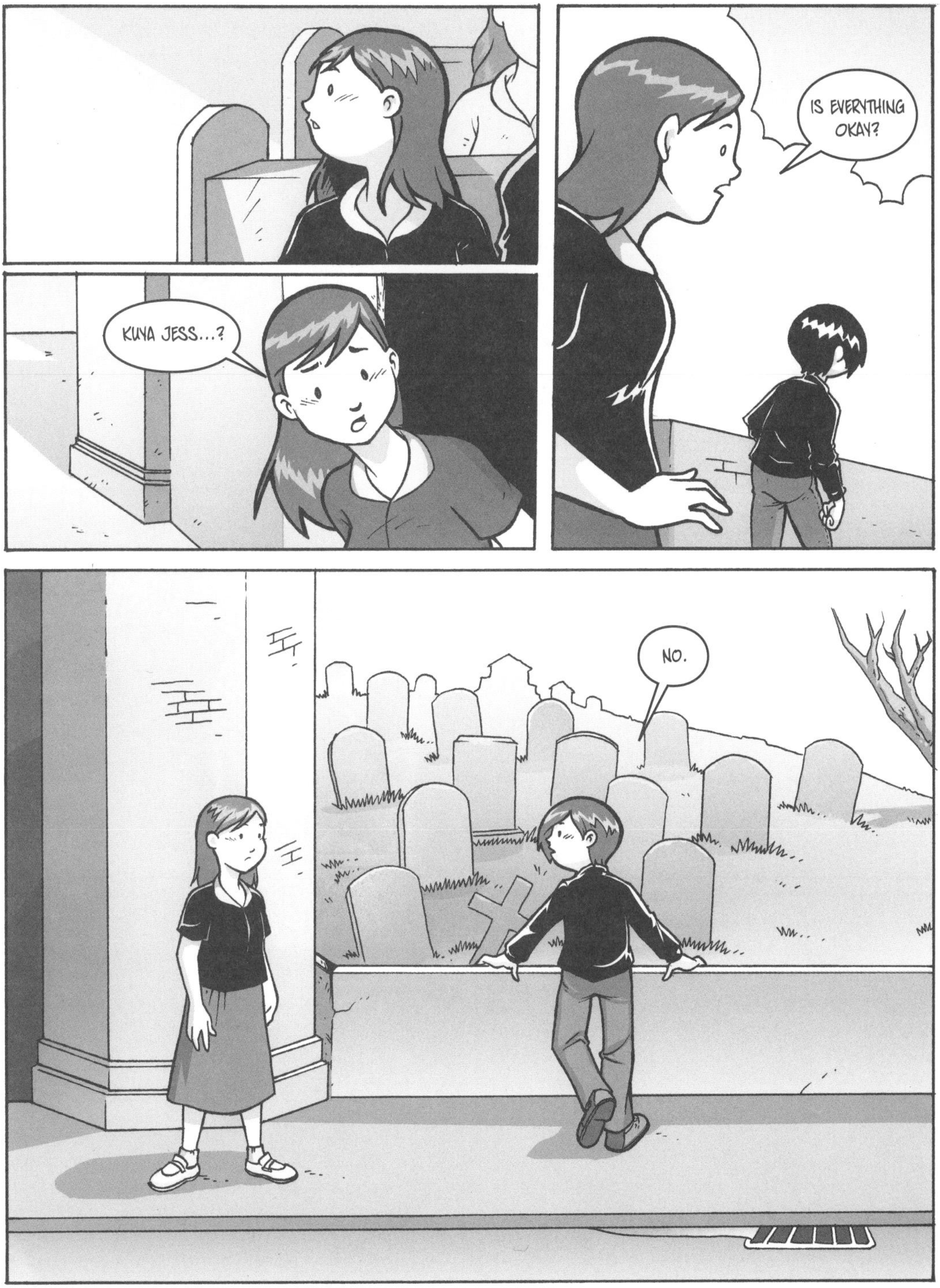
IS EVERYTHING OKAY?
KUYA JESS...?
NO.

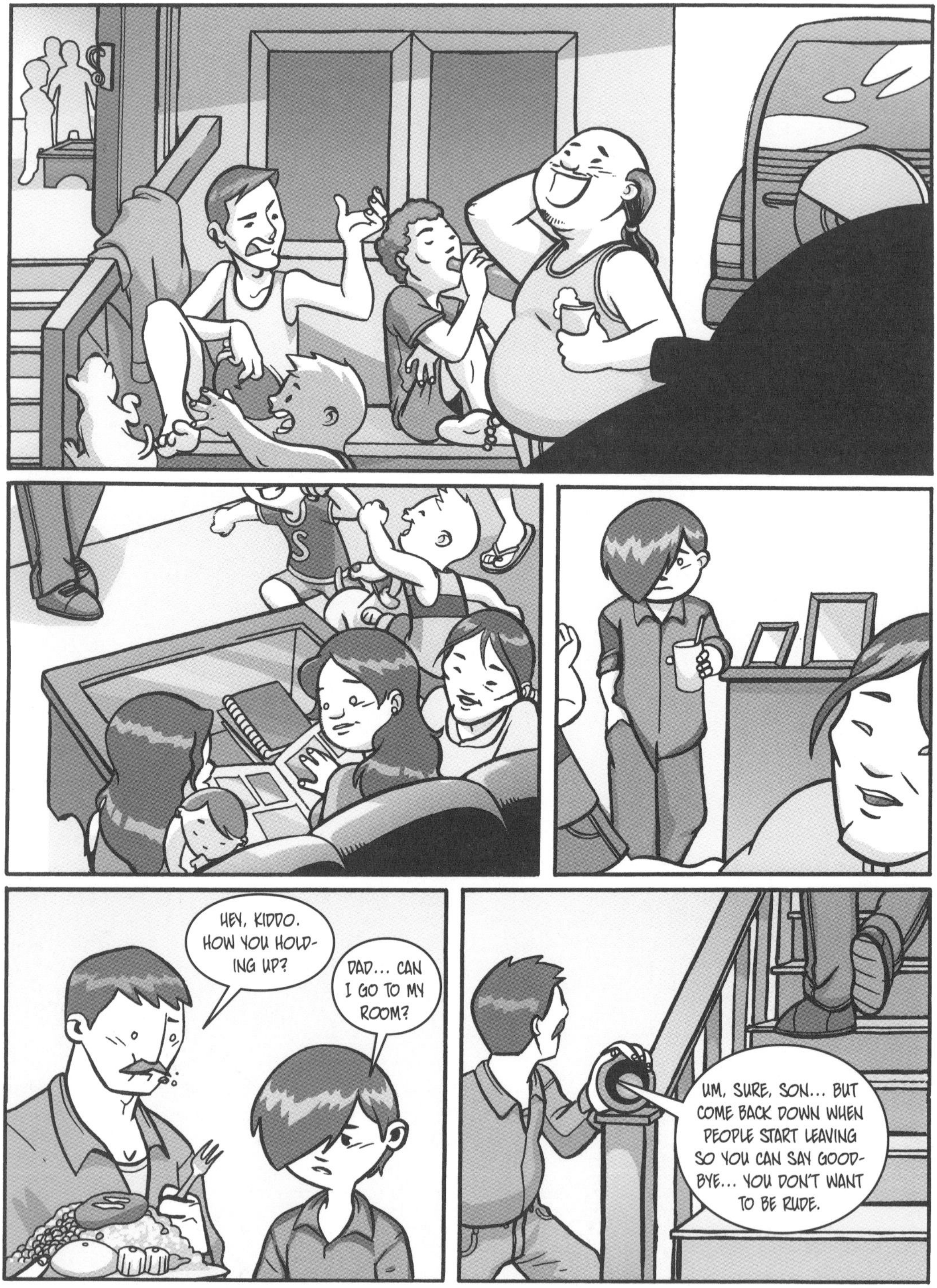
HEY, KIDDO. HOW YOU HOLDING UP?
DAD... CAN I GO TO MY ROOM?
UM, SURE, SON... BUT COME BACK DOWN WHEN PEOPLE START LEAVING SO YOU CAN SAY GOOD-BYE... YOU DON'T WANT TO BE RUDE.

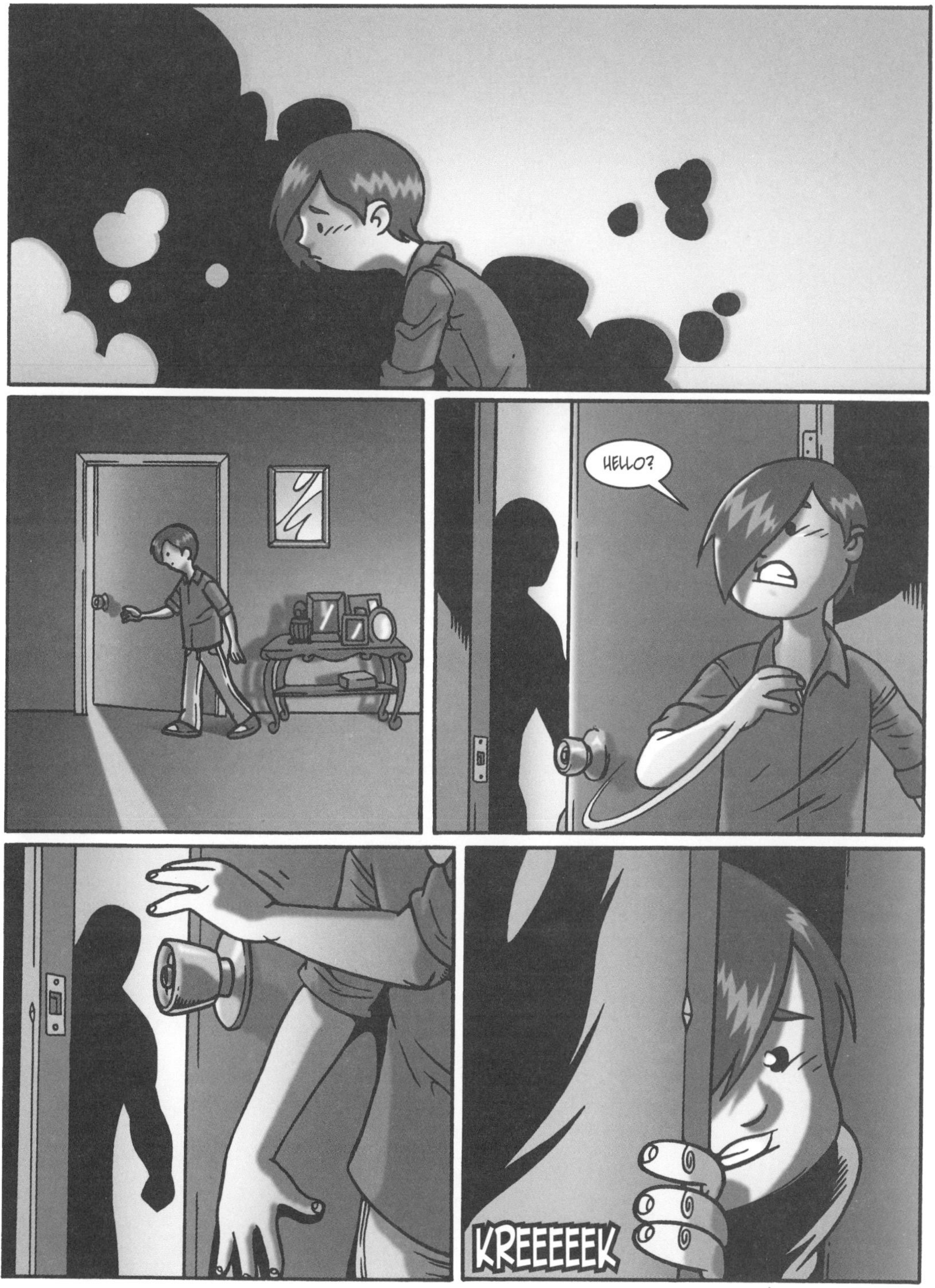
HELLO?
KREEEEEK

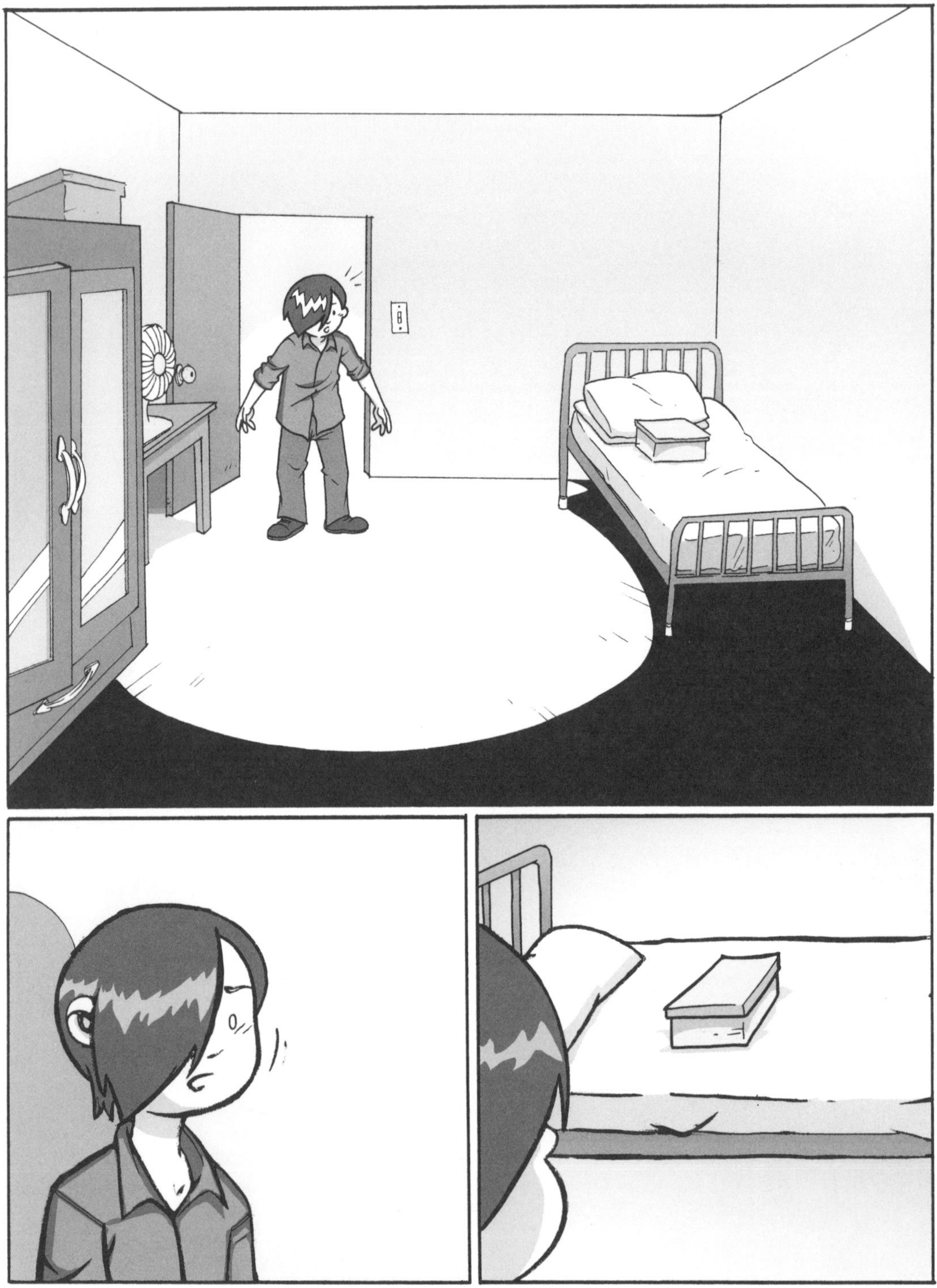

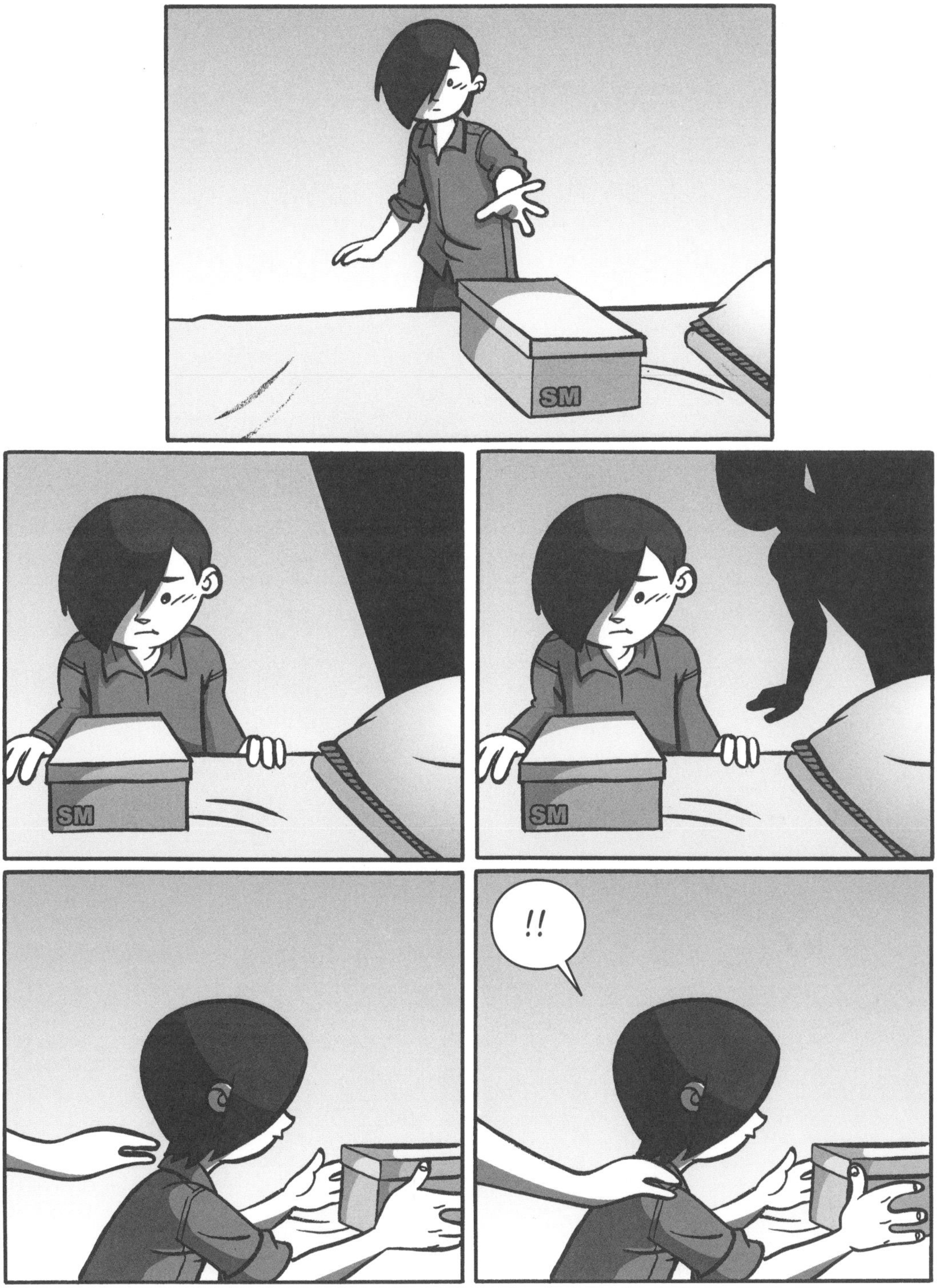
SM
SM
SM
!!

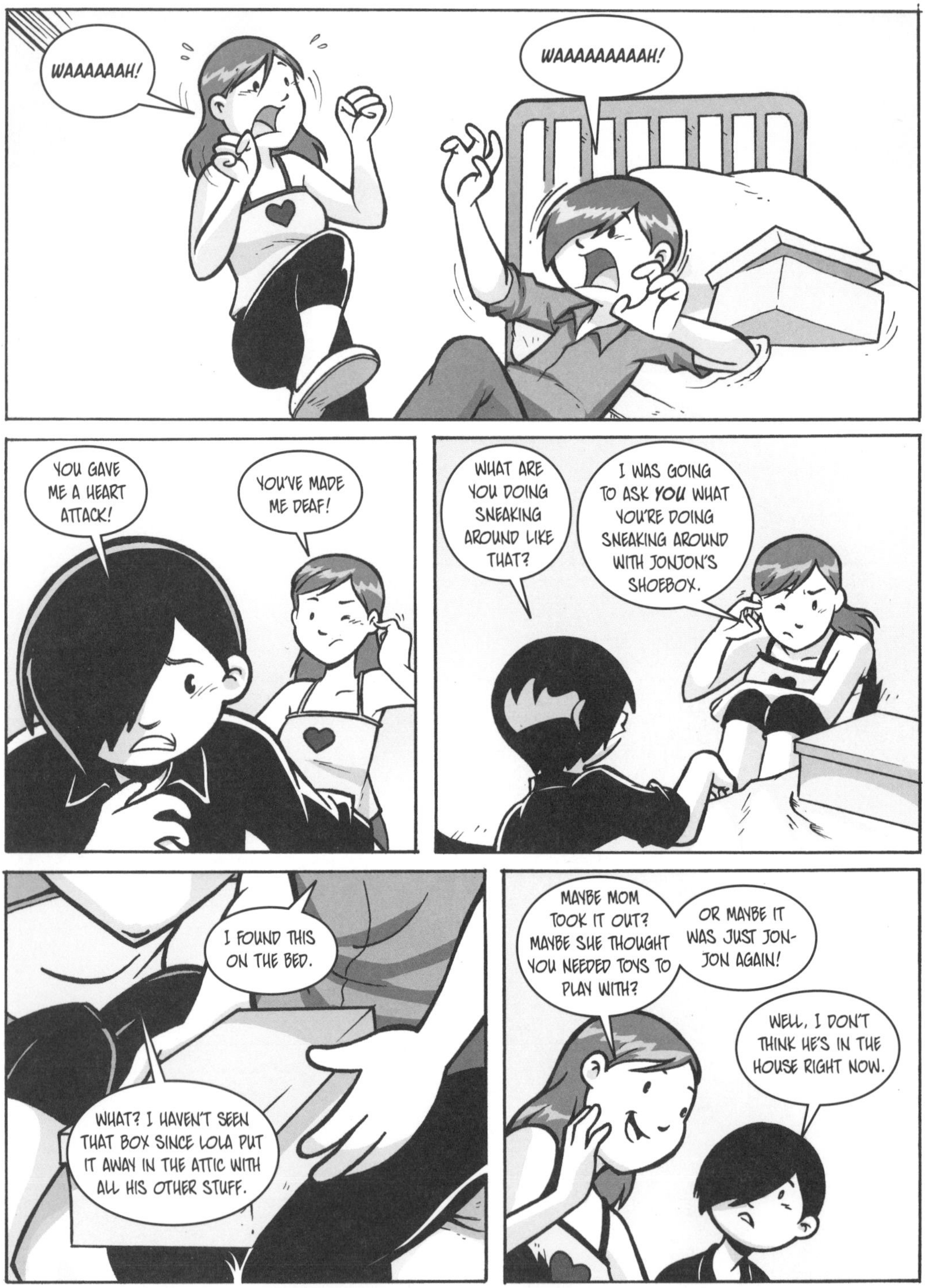
WAAAAAAH!
WAAAAAAAAAH!
YOU GAVE ME A HEART ATTACK!
YOU'VE MADE ME DEAF!
WHAT ARE YOU DOING SNEAKING AROUND LIKE THAT?
I WAS GOING TO ASK YOU WHAT YOU'RE DOING SNEAKING AROUND WITH JONJON'S SHOEBOX.
I FOUND THIS ON THE BED.
WHAT? I HAVEN'T SEEN THAT BOX SINCE LOLA PUT IT AWAY IN THE ATTIC WITH ALL HIS OTHER STUFF.
MAYBE MOM TOOK IT OUT? MAYBE SHE THOUGHT YOU NEEDED TOYS TO PLAY WITH?
OR MAYBE IT WAS JUST JON-JON AGAIN!
WELL, I DON'T THINK HE'S IN THE HOUSE RIGHT NOW.

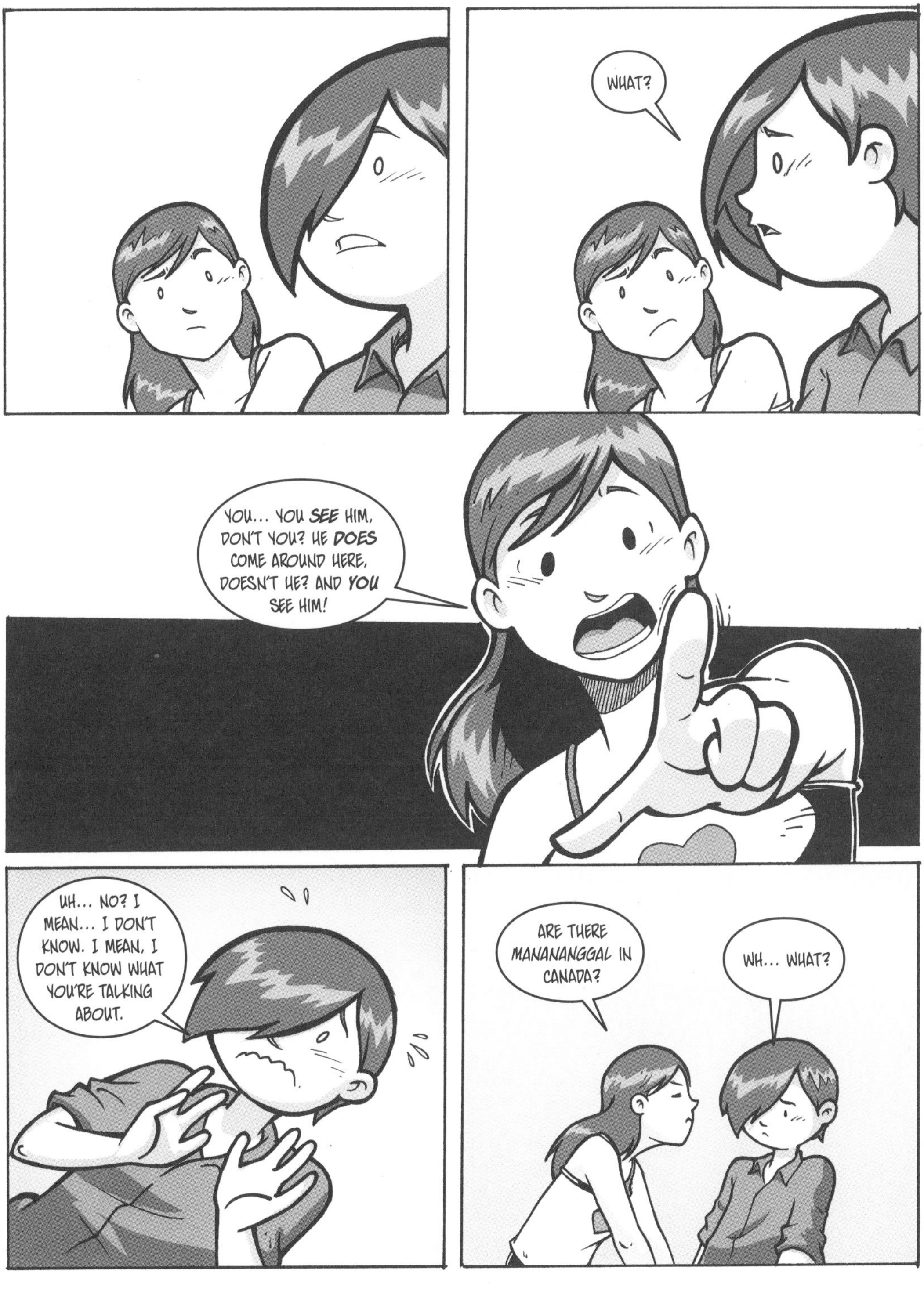
WHAT?
YOU... YOU **SEE** HIM, DON'T YOU? HE **DOES** COME AROUND HERE, DOESN'T HE? AND **YOU** SEE HIM!
UH... NO? I MEAN... I DON'T KNOW. I MEAN, I DON'T KNOW WHAT YOU'RE TALKING ABOUT.
ARE THERE *MANANANGGAL* IN CANADA?
WH... WHAT?

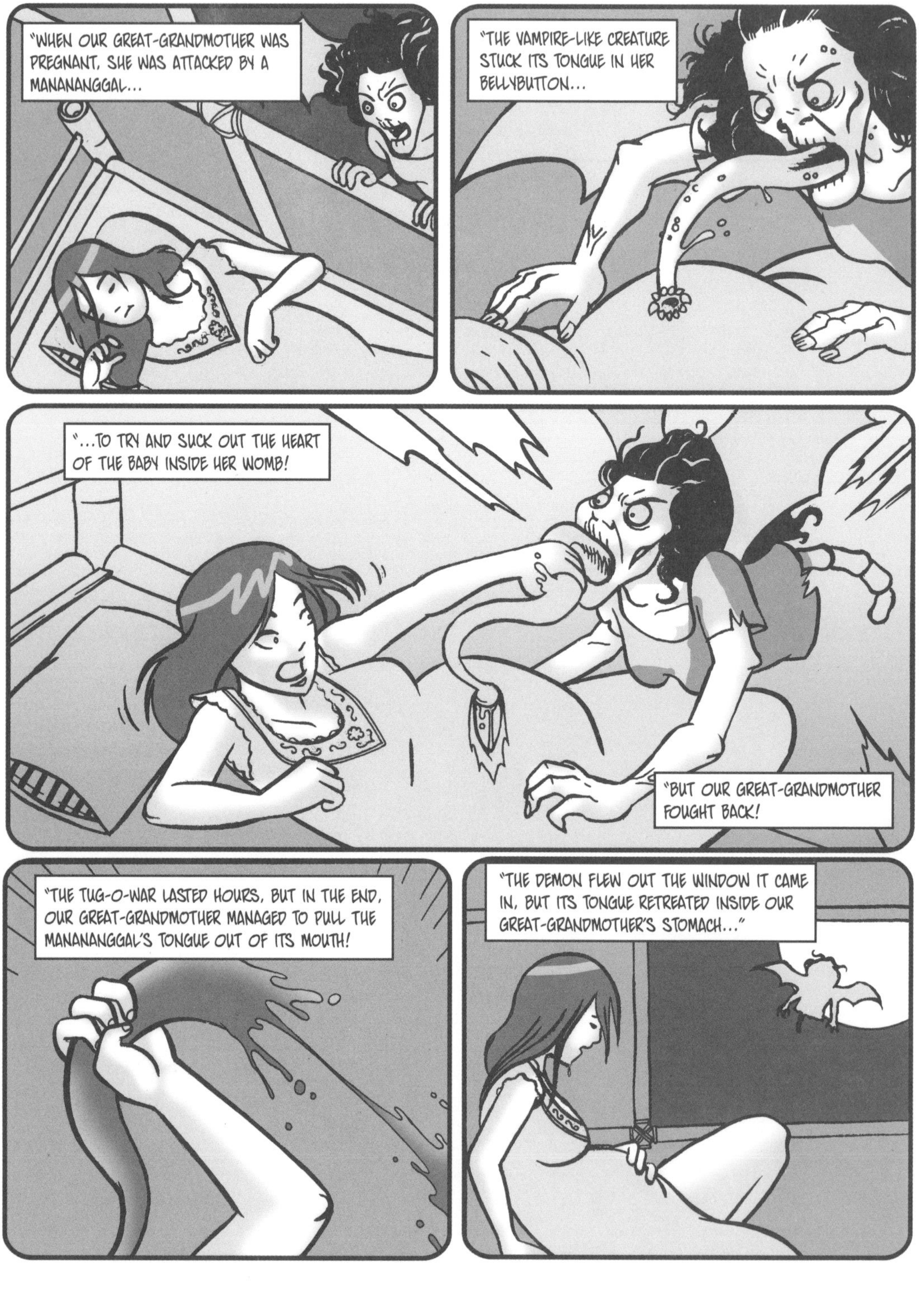
"WHEN OUR GREAT-GRANDMOTHER WAS PREGNANT, SHE WAS ATTACKED BY A MANANANGGAL...
"THE VAMPIRE-LIKE CREATURE STUCK ITS TONGUE IN HER BELLYBUTTON...
"...TO TRY AND SUCK OUT THE HEART OF THE BABY INSIDE HER WOMB!
"BUT OUR GREAT-GRANDMOTHER FOUGHT BACK!
"THE TUG-O-WAR LASTED HOURS, BUT IN THE END, OUR GREAT-GRANDMOTHER MANAGED TO PULL THE MANANANGGAL'S TONGUE OUT OF ITS MOUTH!
"THE DEMON FLEW OUT THE WINDOW IT CAME IN, BUT ITS TONGUE RETREATED INSIDE OUR GREAT-GRANDMOTHER'S STOMACH..."

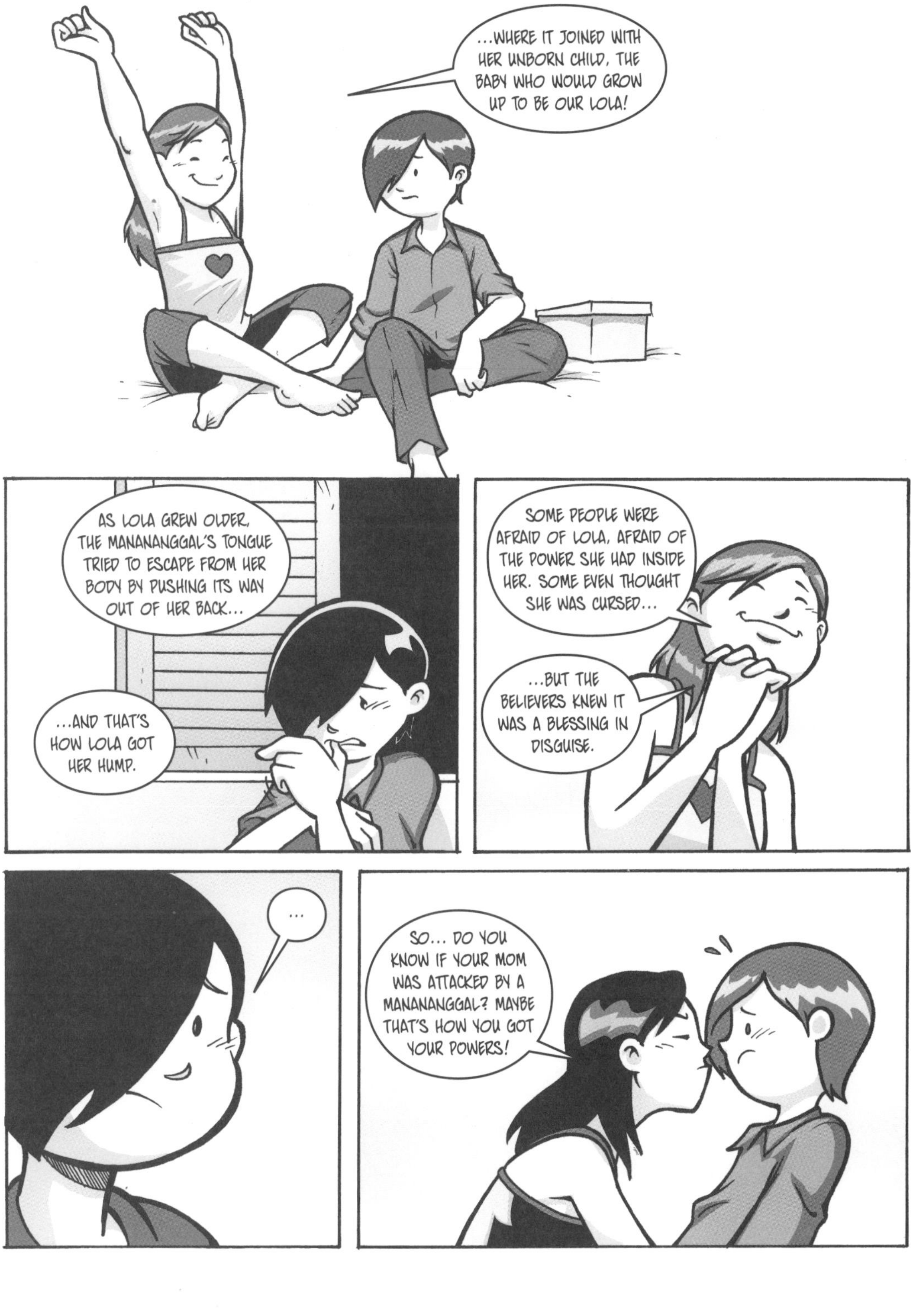
...WHERE IT JOINED WITH HER UNBORN CHILD, THE BABY WHO WOULD GROW UP TO BE OUR LOLA!
AS LOLA GREW OLDER, THE MANANANGGAL'S TONGUE TRIED TO ESCAPE FROM HER BODY BY PUSHING ITS WAY OUT OF HER BACK...
...AND THAT'S HOW LOLA GOT HER HUMP.
SOME PEOPLE WERE AFRAID OF LOLA, AFRAID OF THE POWER SHE HAD INSIDE HER. SOME EVEN THOUGHT SHE WAS CURSED...
...BUT THE BELIEVERS KNEW IT WAS A BLESSING IN DISGUISE.
...
SO... DO YOU KNOW IF YOUR MOM WAS ATTACKED BY A MANANANGGAL? MAYBE THAT'S HOW YOU GOT YOUR POWERS!

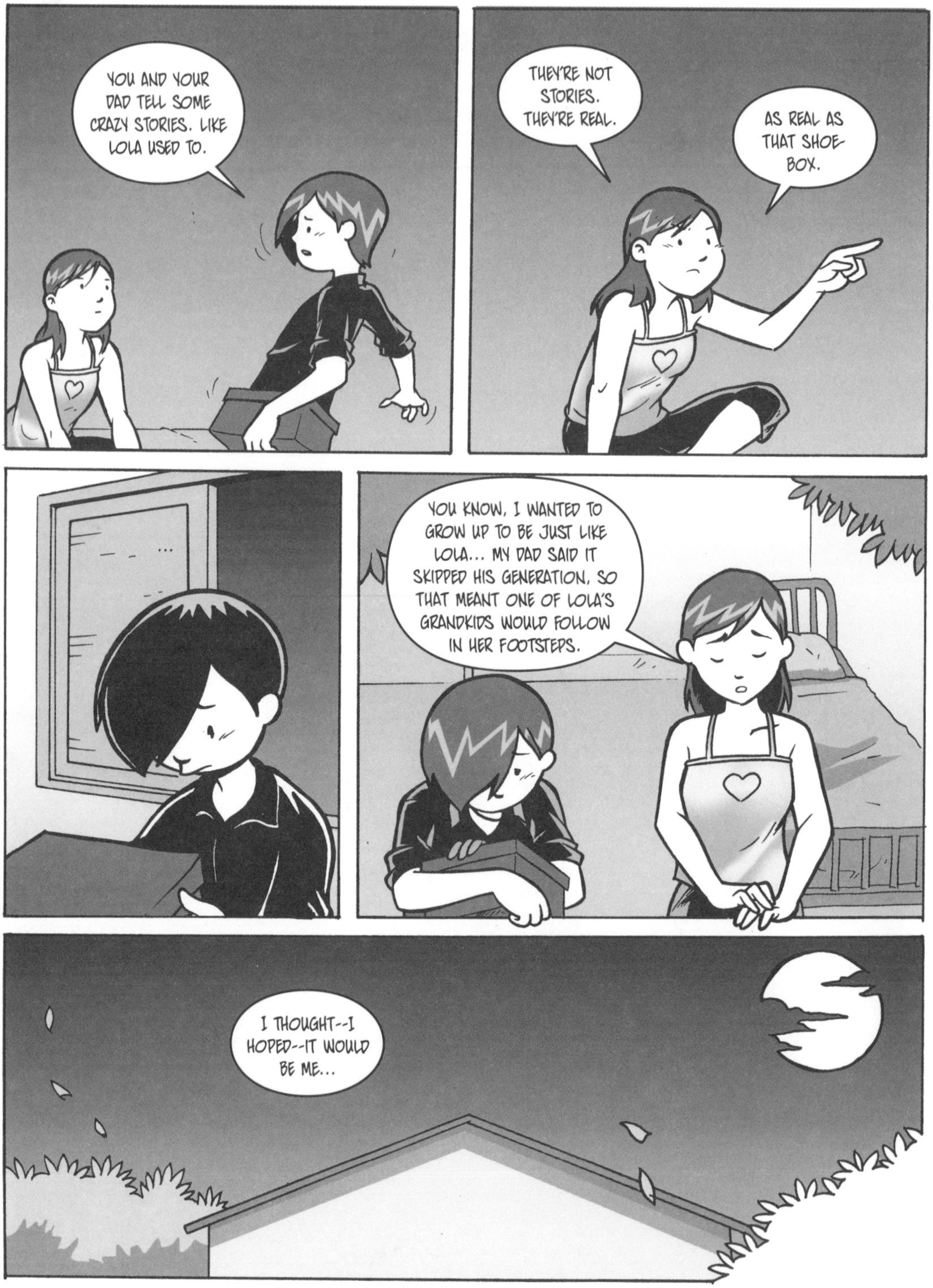
YOU AND YOUR DAD TELL SOME CRAZY STORIES. LIKE LOLA USED TO.
THEY'RE NOT STORIES. THEY'RE REAL.
AS REAL AS THAT SHOE-BOX.
...
YOU KNOW, I WANTED TO GROW UP TO BE JUST LIKE LOLA... MY DAD SAID IT SKIPPED HIS GENERATION, SO THAT MEANT ONE OF LOLA'S GRANDKIDS WOULD FOLLOW IN HER FOOTSTEPS.
I THOUGHT--I HOPED--IT WOULD BE ME...

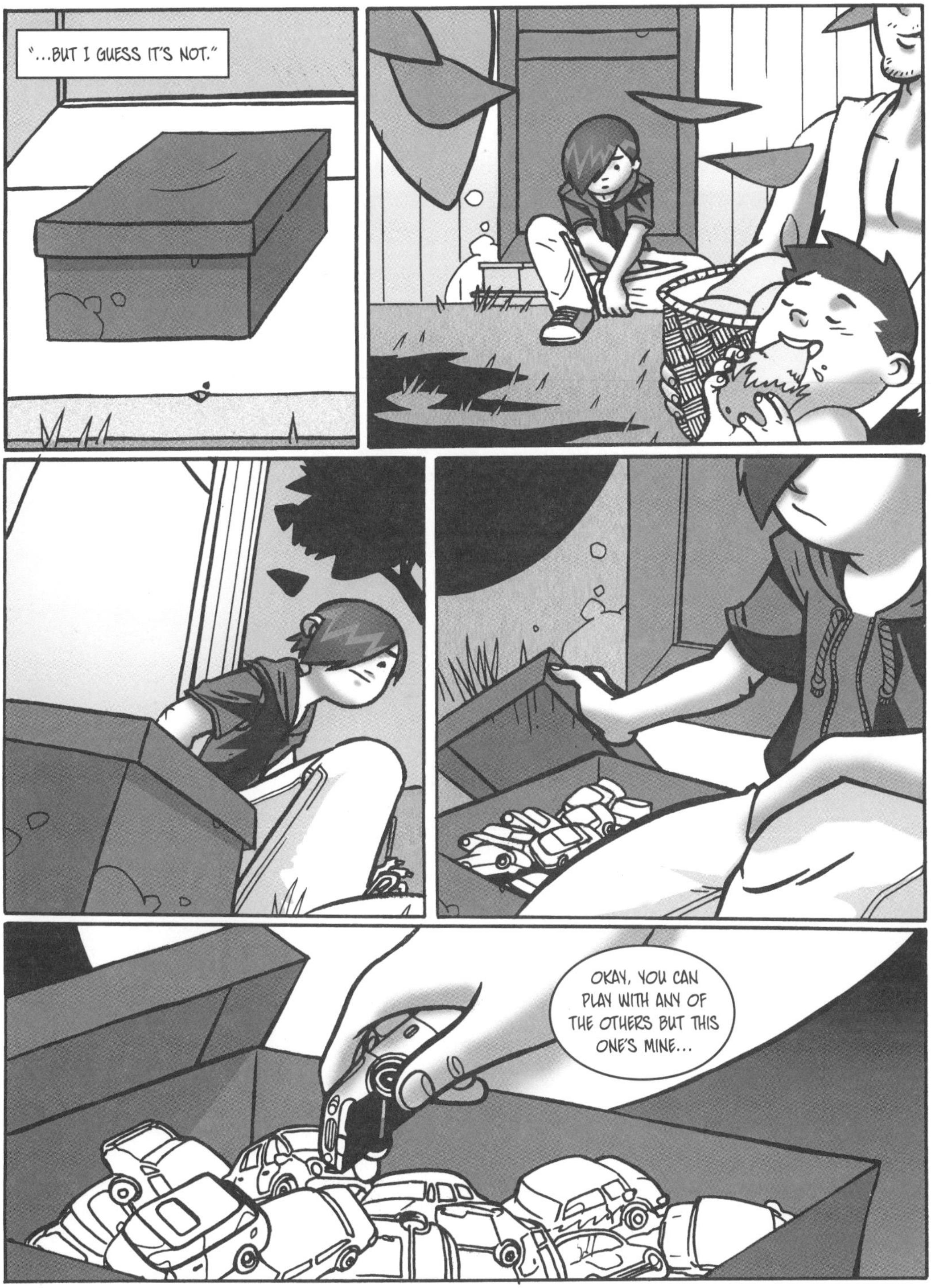
"...BUT I GUESS IT'S NOT."
OKAY, YOU CAN PLAY WITH ANY OF THE OTHERS BUT THIS ONE'S MINE...

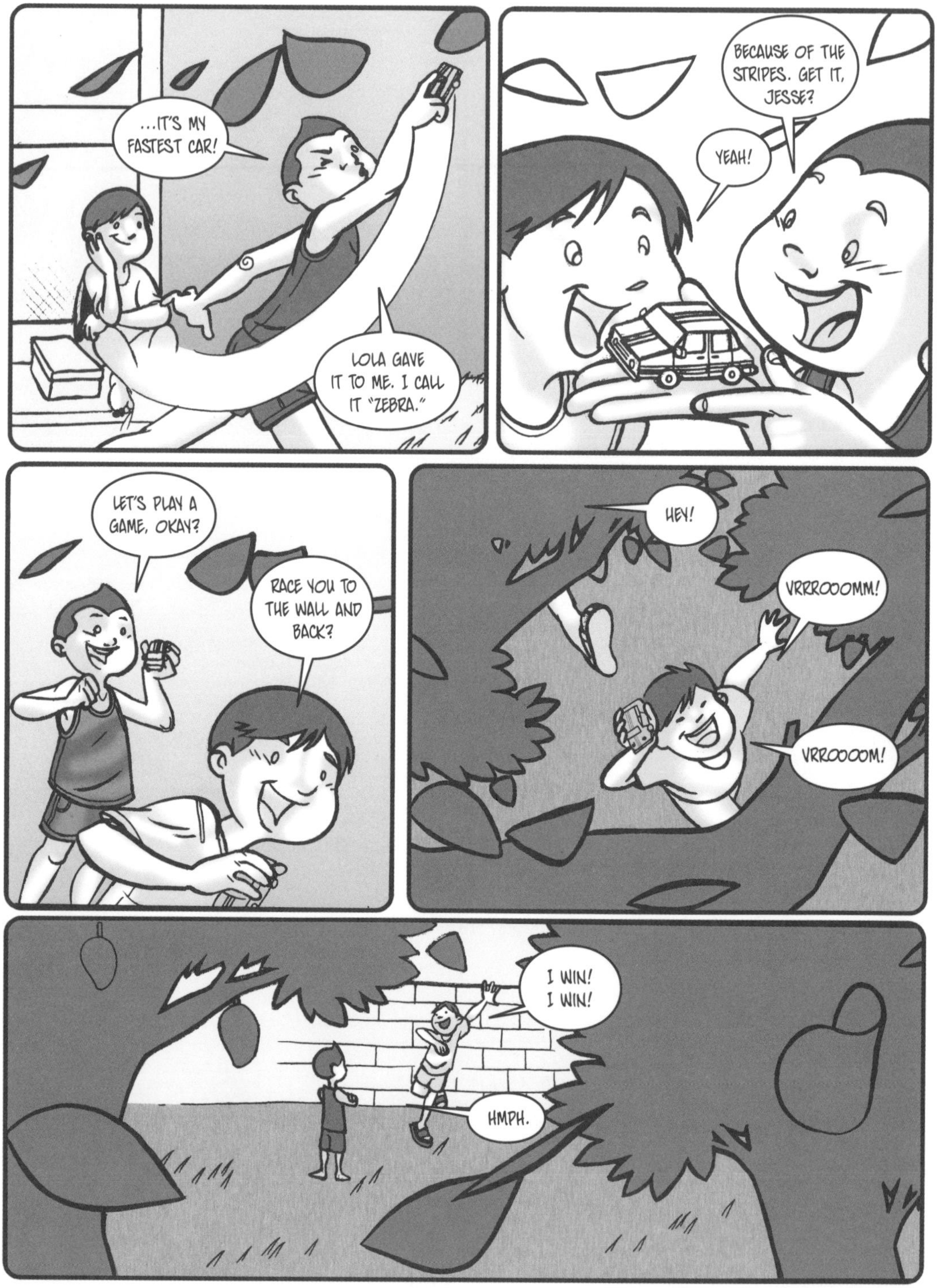
...IT'S MY FASTEST CAR!
LOLA GAVE IT TO ME. I CALL IT "ZEBRA."
BECAUSE OF THE STRIPES. GET IT, JESSE?
YEAH!
LET'S PLAY A GAME, OKAY?
RACE YOU TO THE WALL AND BACK?
HEY!
VRRROOOMM!
VRROOOOM!
I WIN! I WIN!
HMPH.

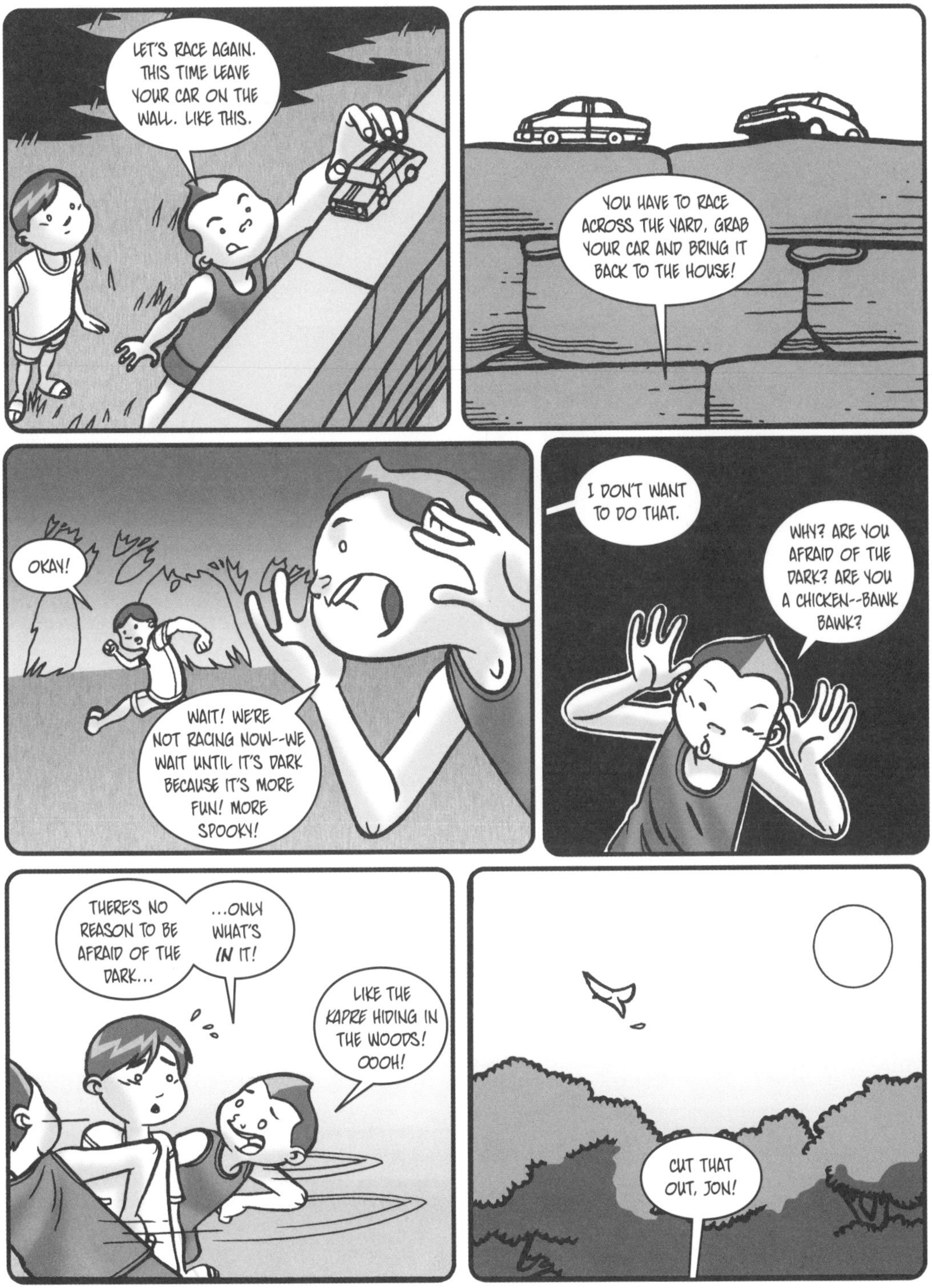
LET'S RACE AGAIN. THIS TIME LEAVE YOUR CAR ON THE WALL. LIKE THIS.
YOU HAVE TO RACE ACROSS THE YARD, GRAB YOUR CAR AND BRING IT BACK TO THE HOUSE!
OKAY!
WAIT! WE'RE NOT RACING NOW--WE WAIT UNTIL IT'S DARK BECAUSE IT'S MORE FUN! MORE SPOOKY!
I DON'T WANT TO DO THAT.
WHY? ARE YOU AFRAID OF THE DARK? ARE YOU A CHICKEN--BAWK BAWK?
THERE'S NO REASON TO BE AFRAID OF THE DARK...
...ONLY WHAT'S *IN* IT!
LIKE THE KAPRE HIDING IN THE WOODS! OOOH!
CUT THAT OUT, JON!

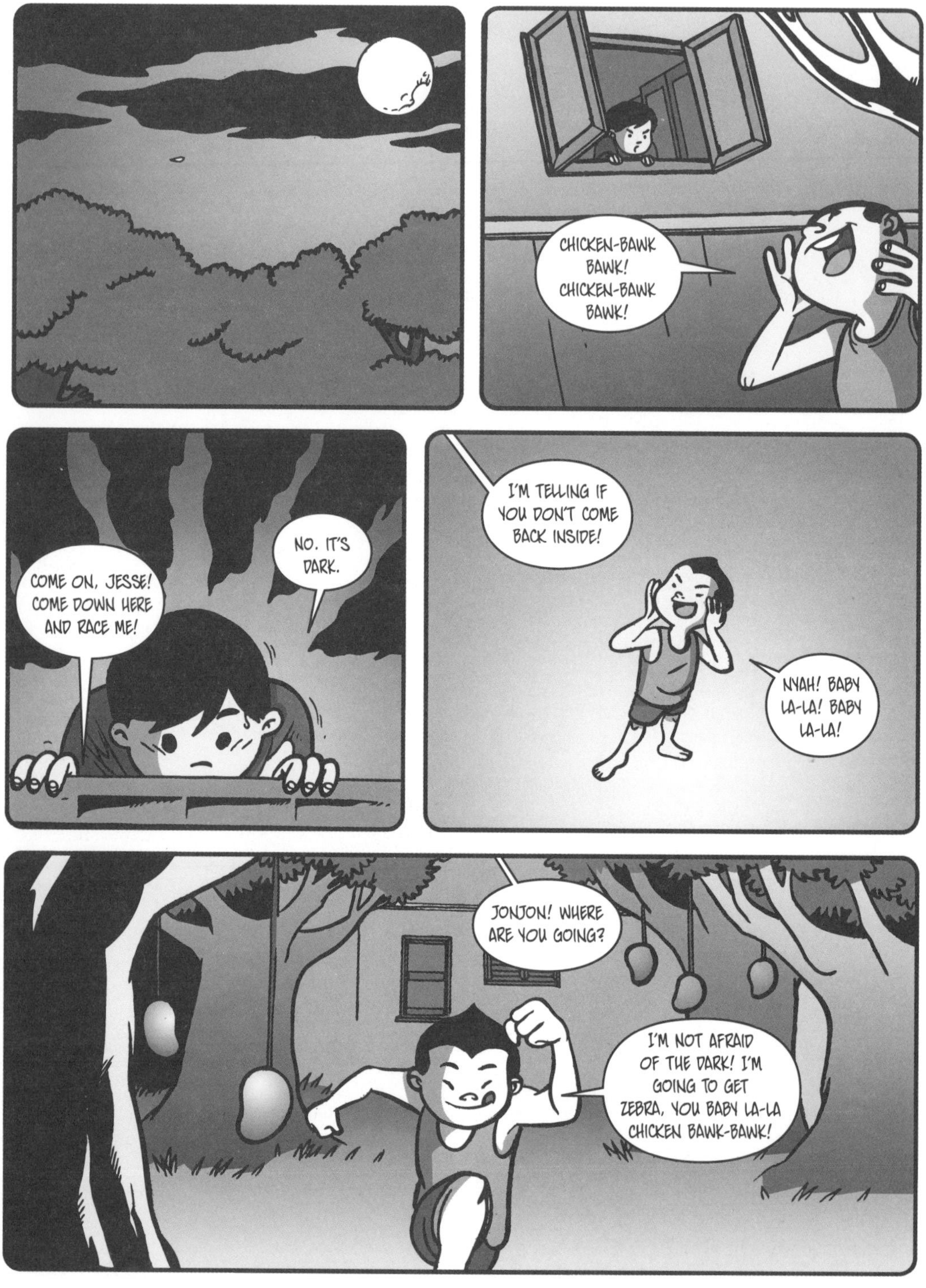
CHICKEN-BAWK BAWK! CHICKEN-BAWK BAWK!
COME ON, JESSE! COME DOWN HERE AND RACE ME!
NO. IT'S DARK.
I'M TELLING IF YOU DON'T COME BACK INSIDE!
NYAH! BABY LA-LA! BABY LA-LA!
JONJON! WHERE ARE YOU GOING?
I'M NOT AFRAID OF THE DARK! I'M GOING TO GET ZEBRA, YOU BABY LA-LA CHICKEN BAWK-BAWK!

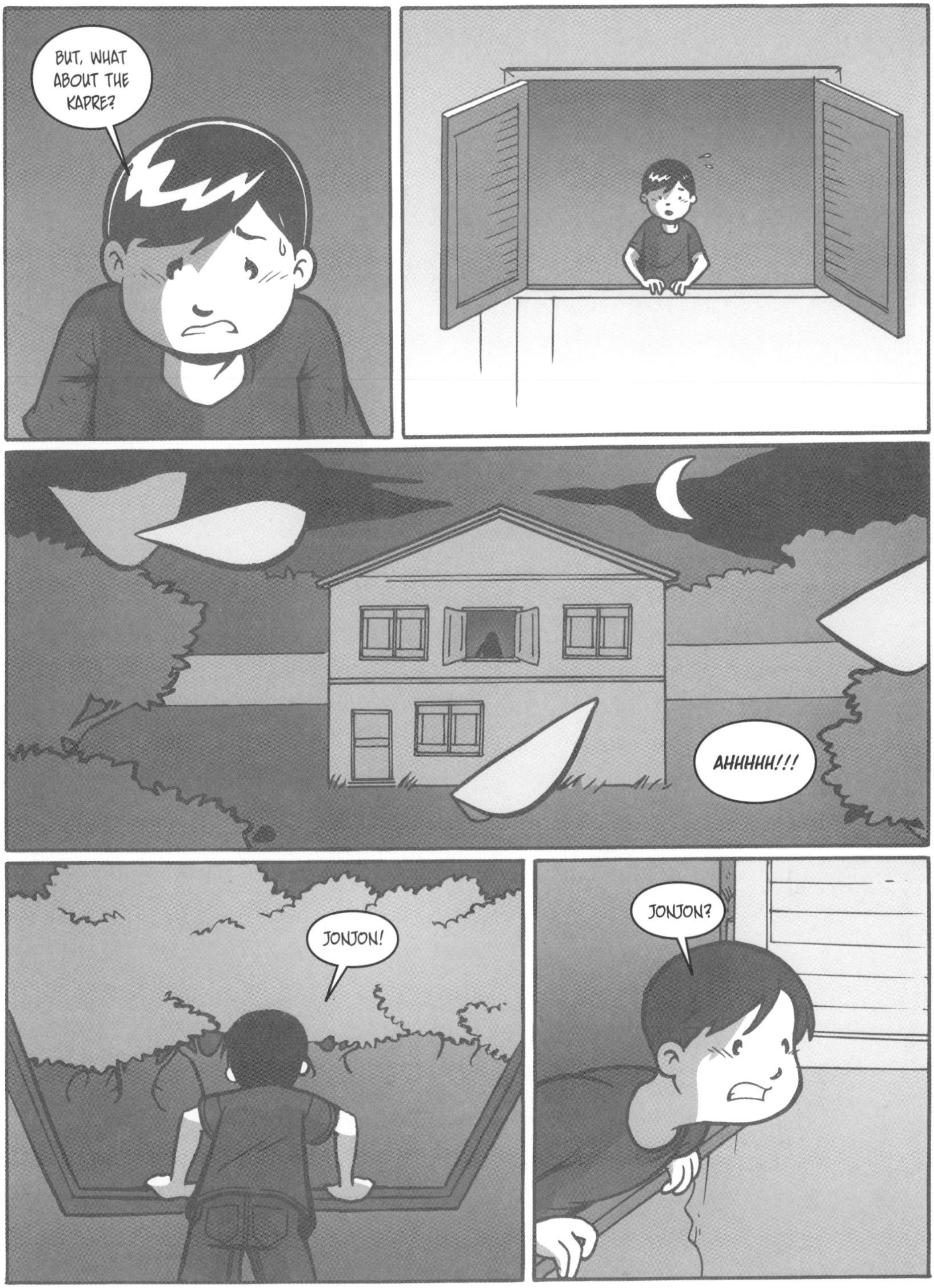
BUT, WHAT ABOUT THE KAPRE?
AHHHHH!!!
JONJON!
JONJON?

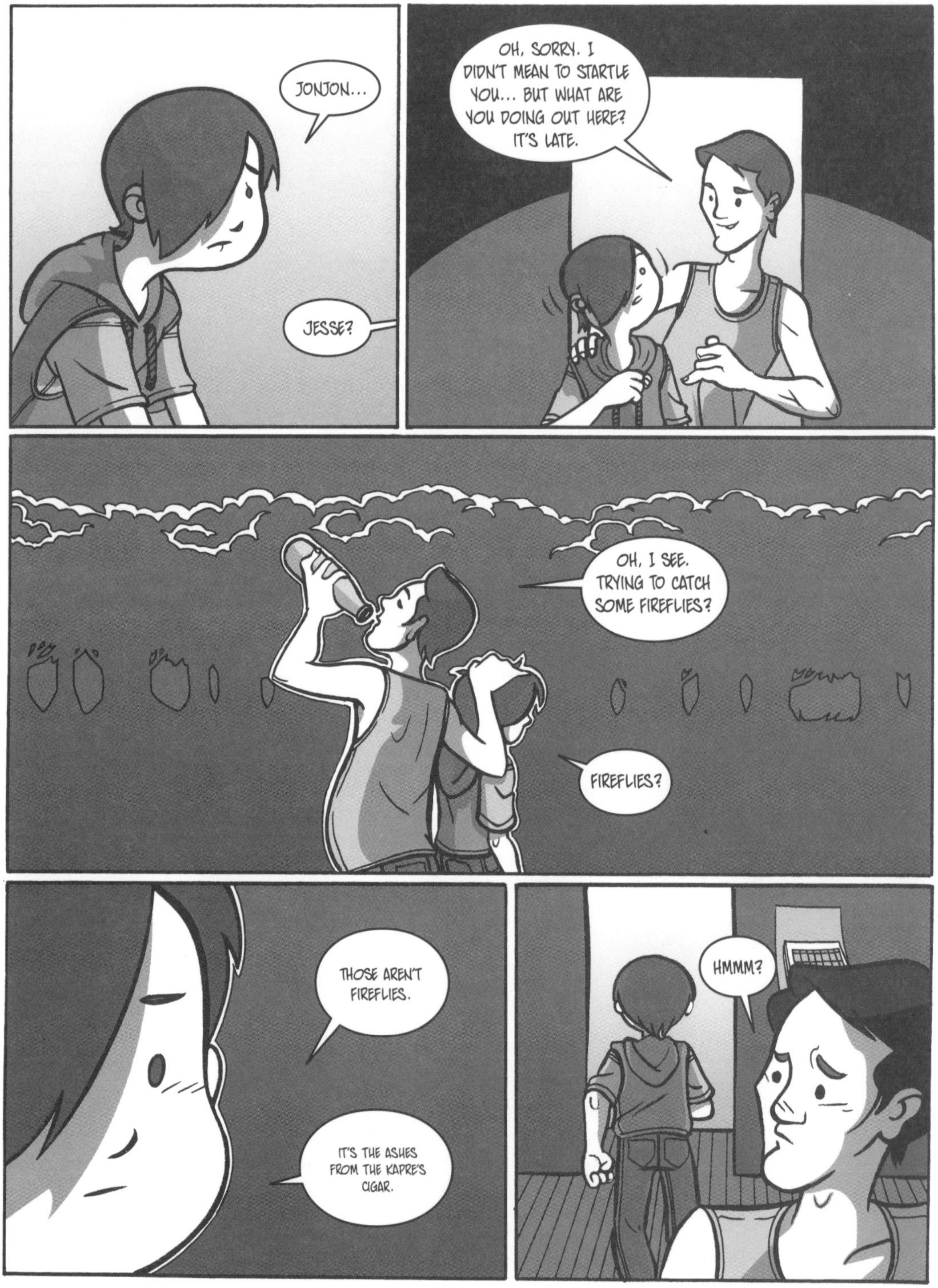
JONJON...
JESSE?
OH, SORRY. I DIDN'T MEAN TO STARTLE YOU... BUT WHAT ARE YOU DOING OUT HERE? IT'S LATE.
OH, I SEE. TRYING TO CATCH SOME FIREFLIES?
FIREFLIES?
THOSE AREN'T FIREFLIES.
IT'S THE ASHES FROM THE KAPRE'S CIGAR.
HMMM?

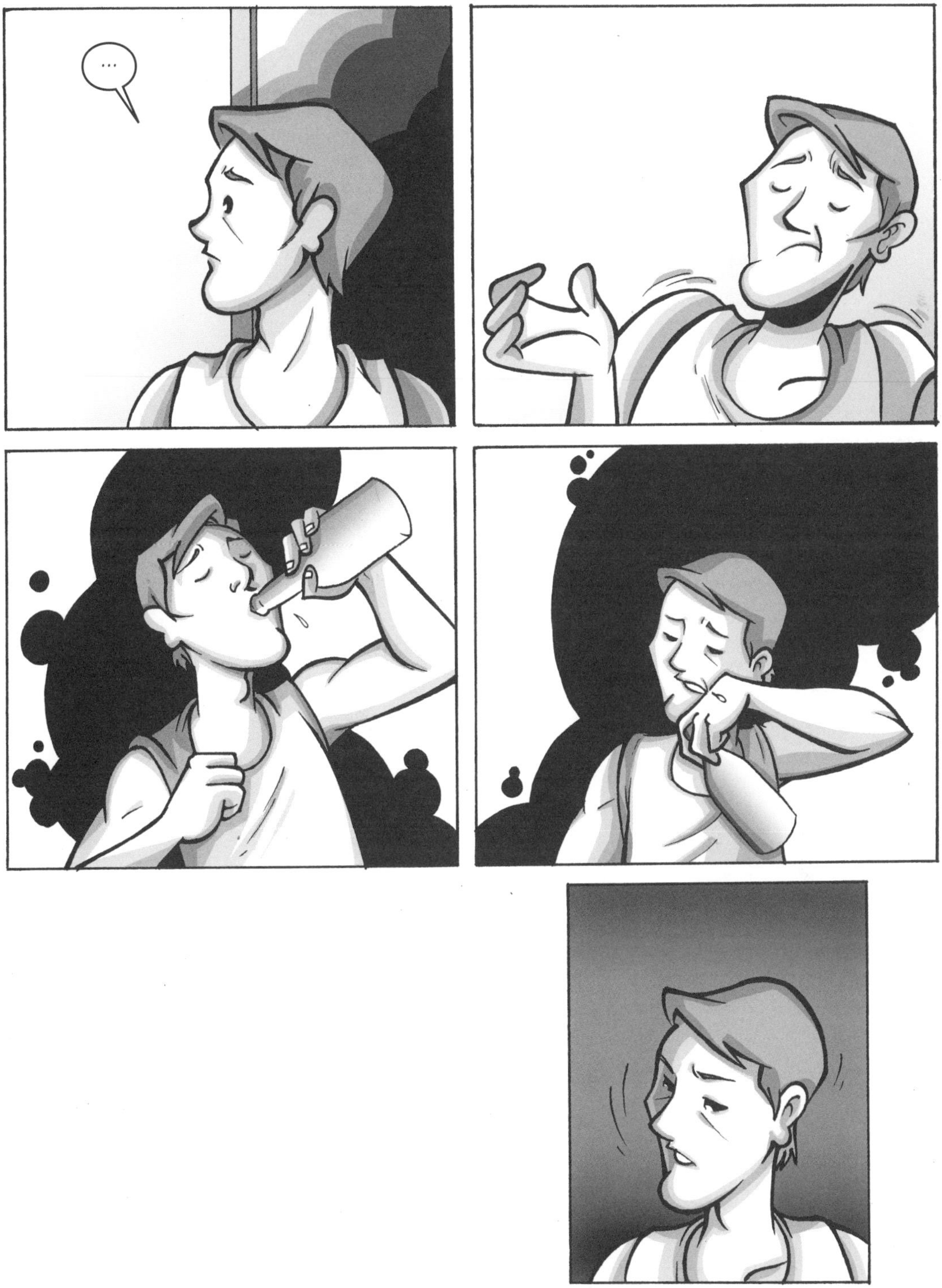
...

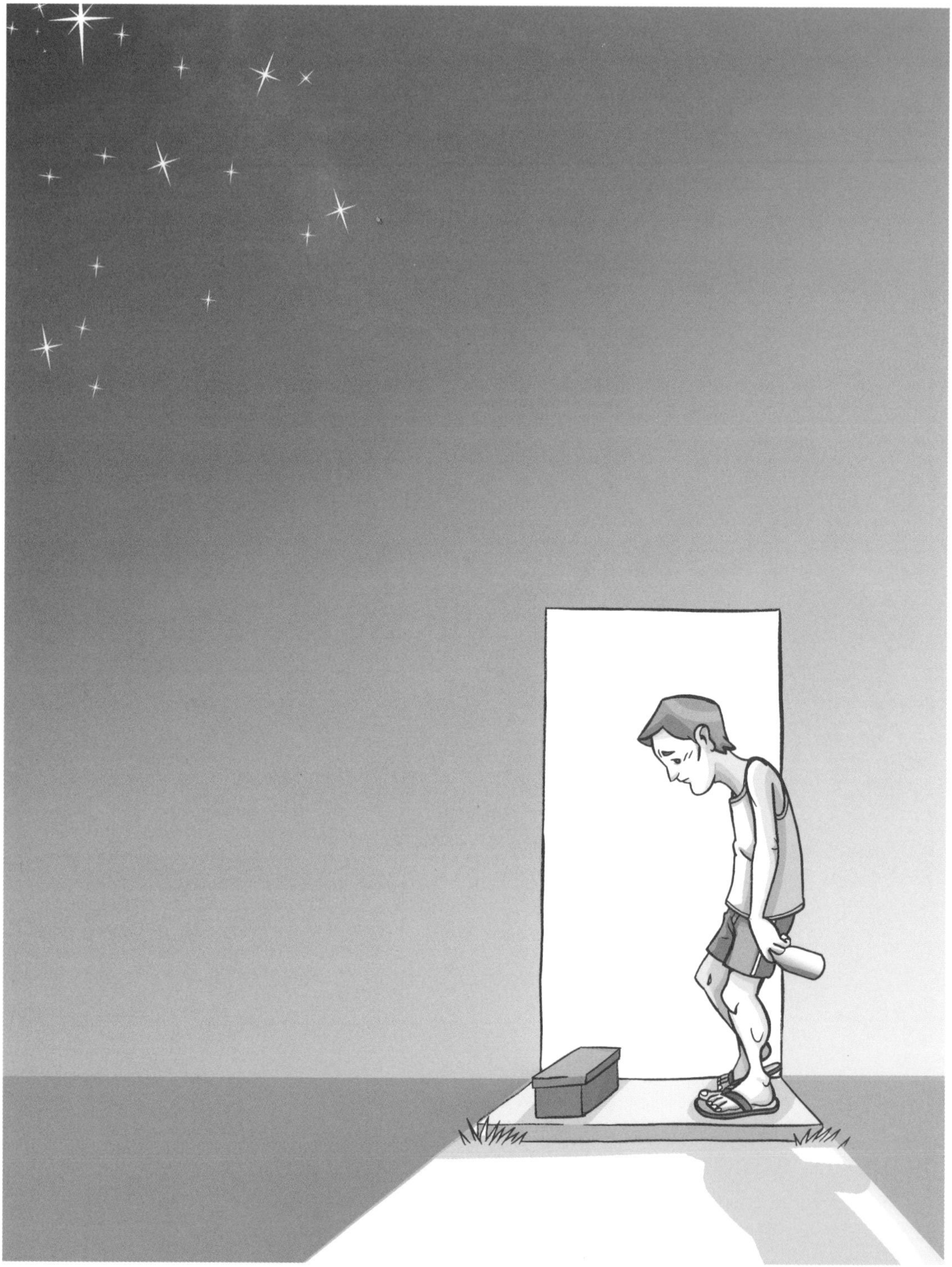

ACT

III

LOLA

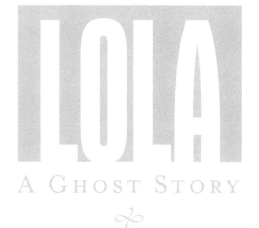

A Ghost Story

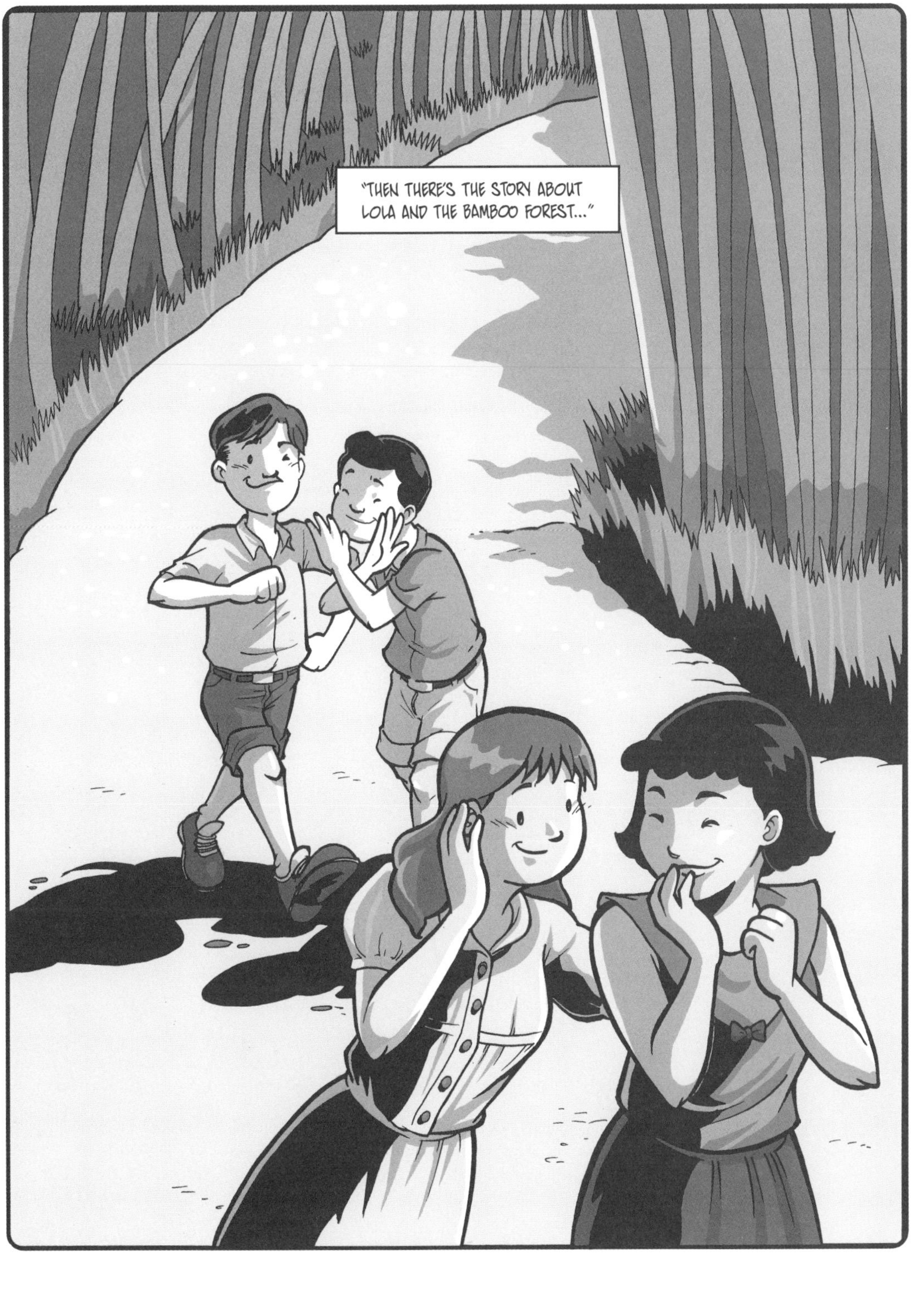
"THEN THERE'S THE STORY ABOUT
LOLA AND THE BAMBOO FOREST..."

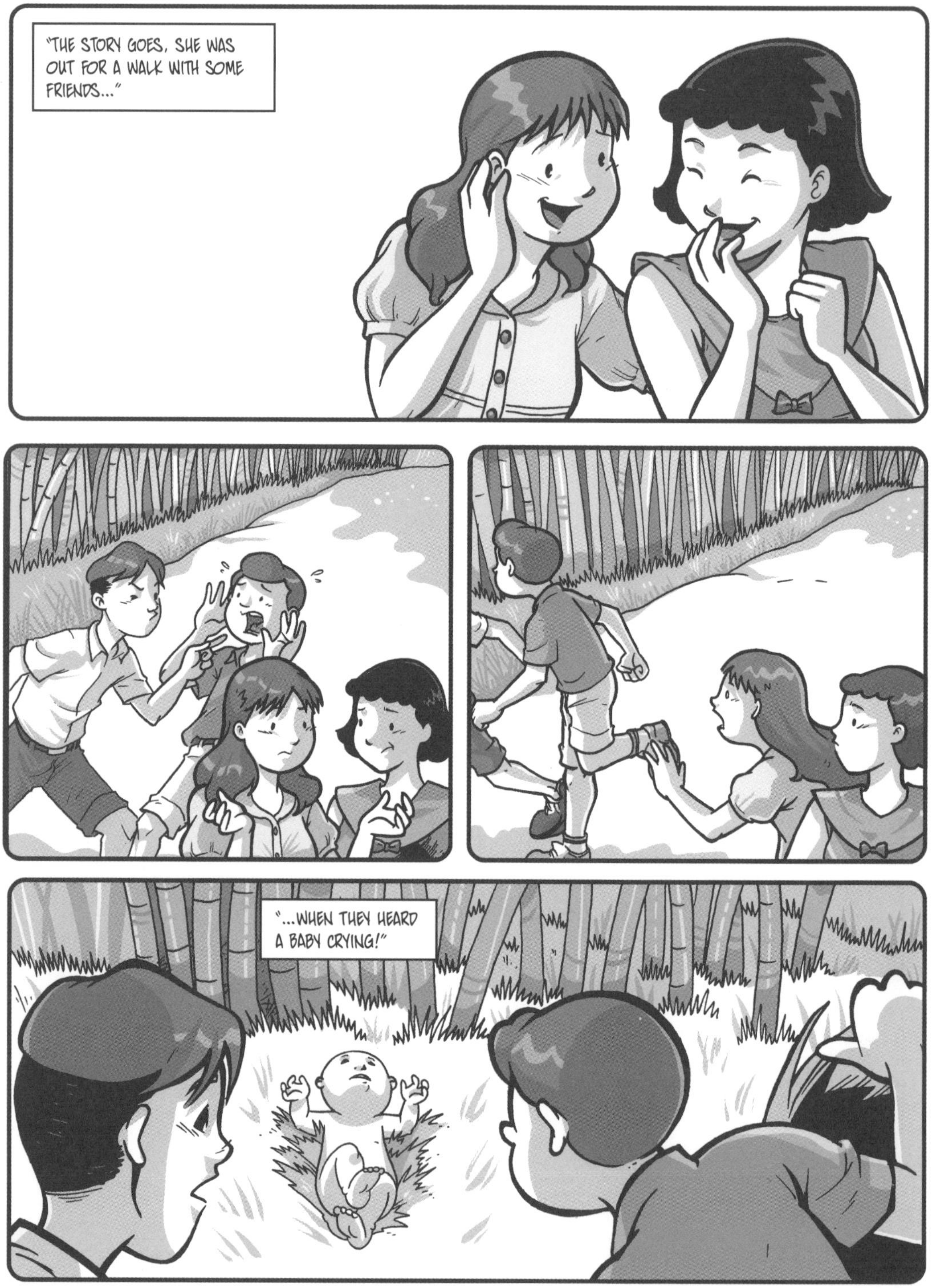
"THE STORY GOES, SHE WAS OUT FOR A WALK WITH SOME FRIENDS..."
"...WHEN THEY HEARD A BABY CRYING!"

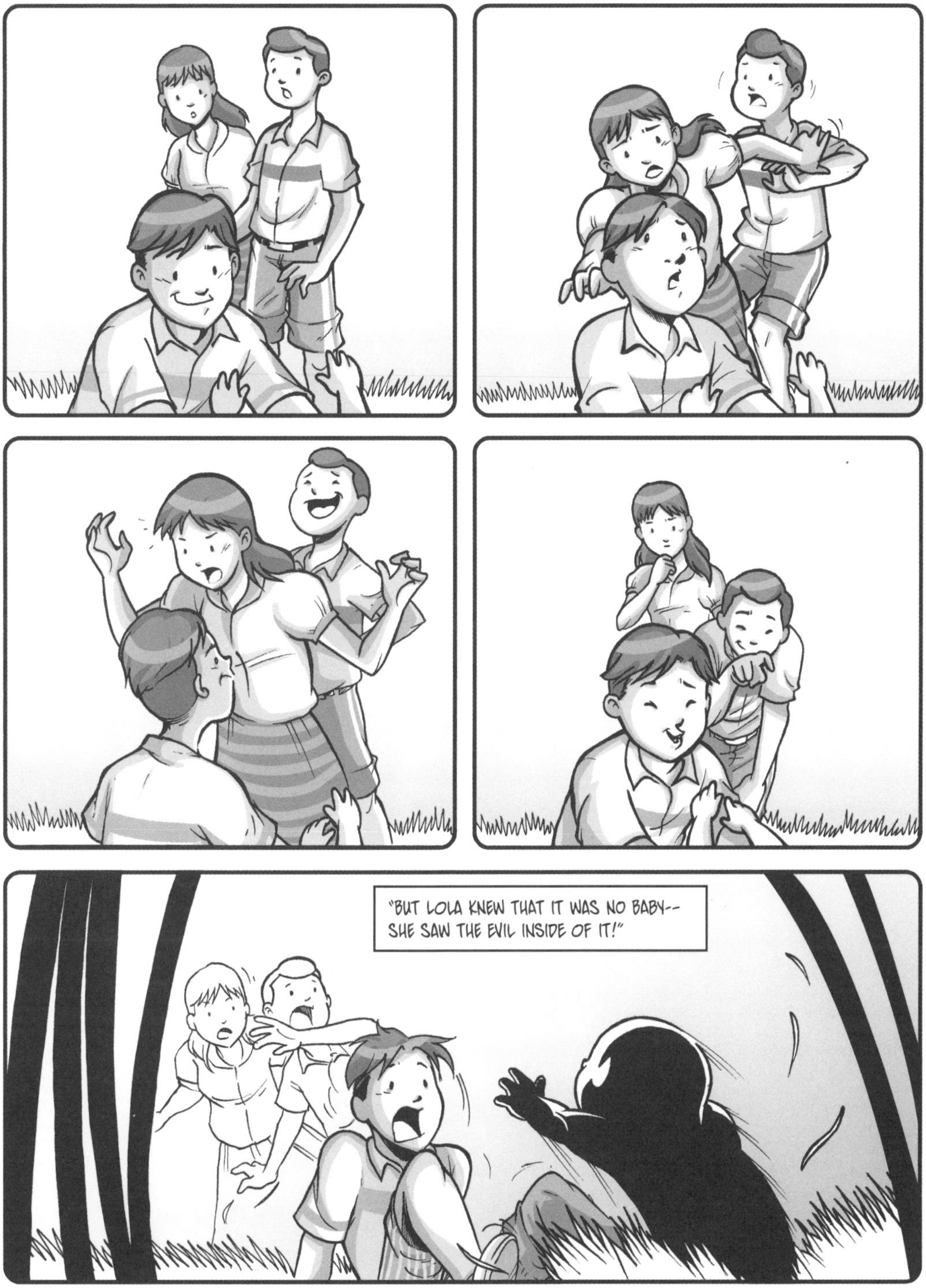
"BUT LOLA KNEW THAT IT WAS NO BABY--
SHE SAW THE EVIL INSIDE OF IT!"

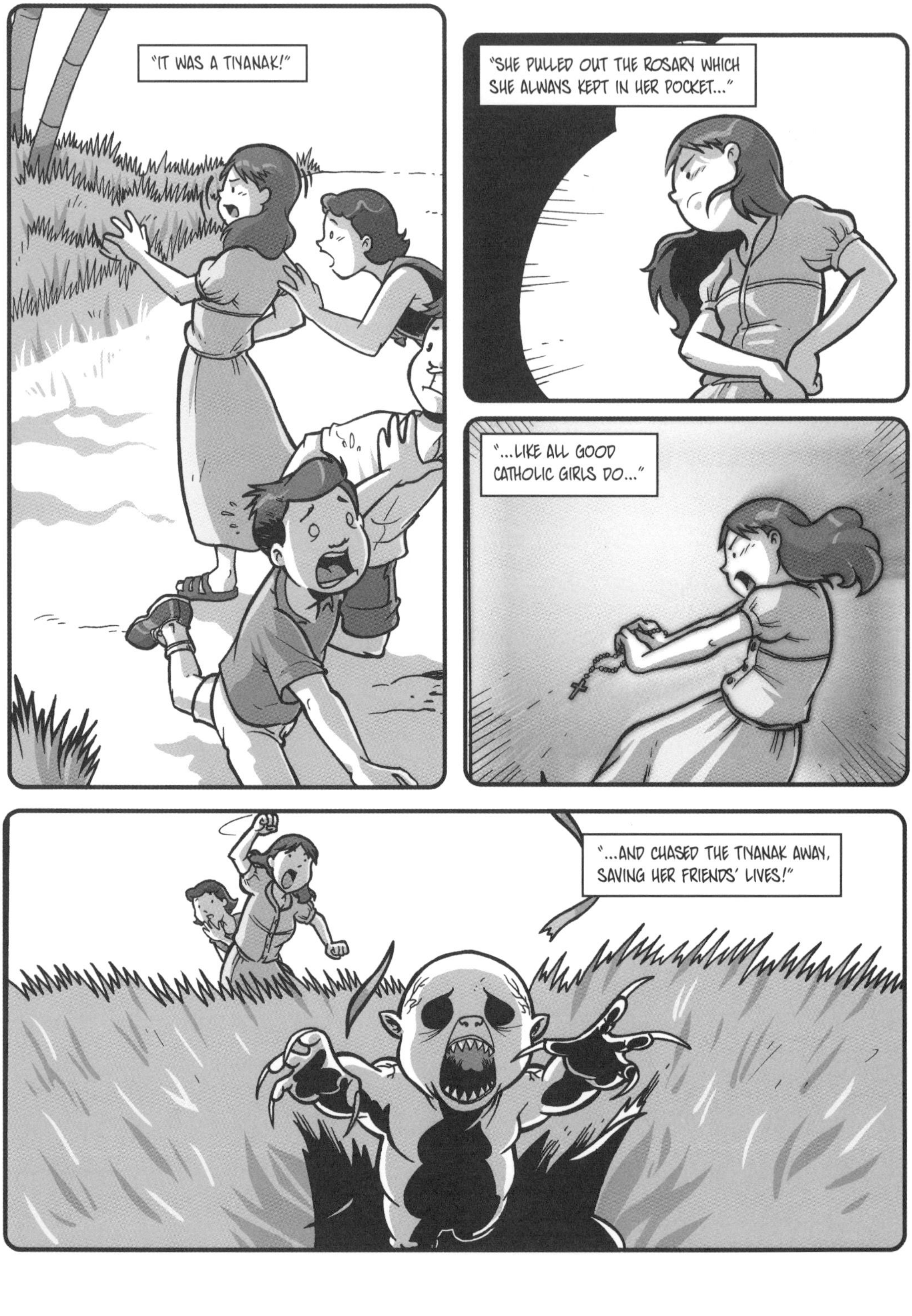
"IT WAS A TIYANAK!"
"SHE PULLED OUT THE ROSARY WHICH SHE ALWAYS KEPT IN HER POCKET..."
"...LIKE ALL GOOD CATHOLIC GIRLS DO..."
"...AND CHASED THE TIYANAK AWAY, SAVING HER FRIENDS' LIVES!"

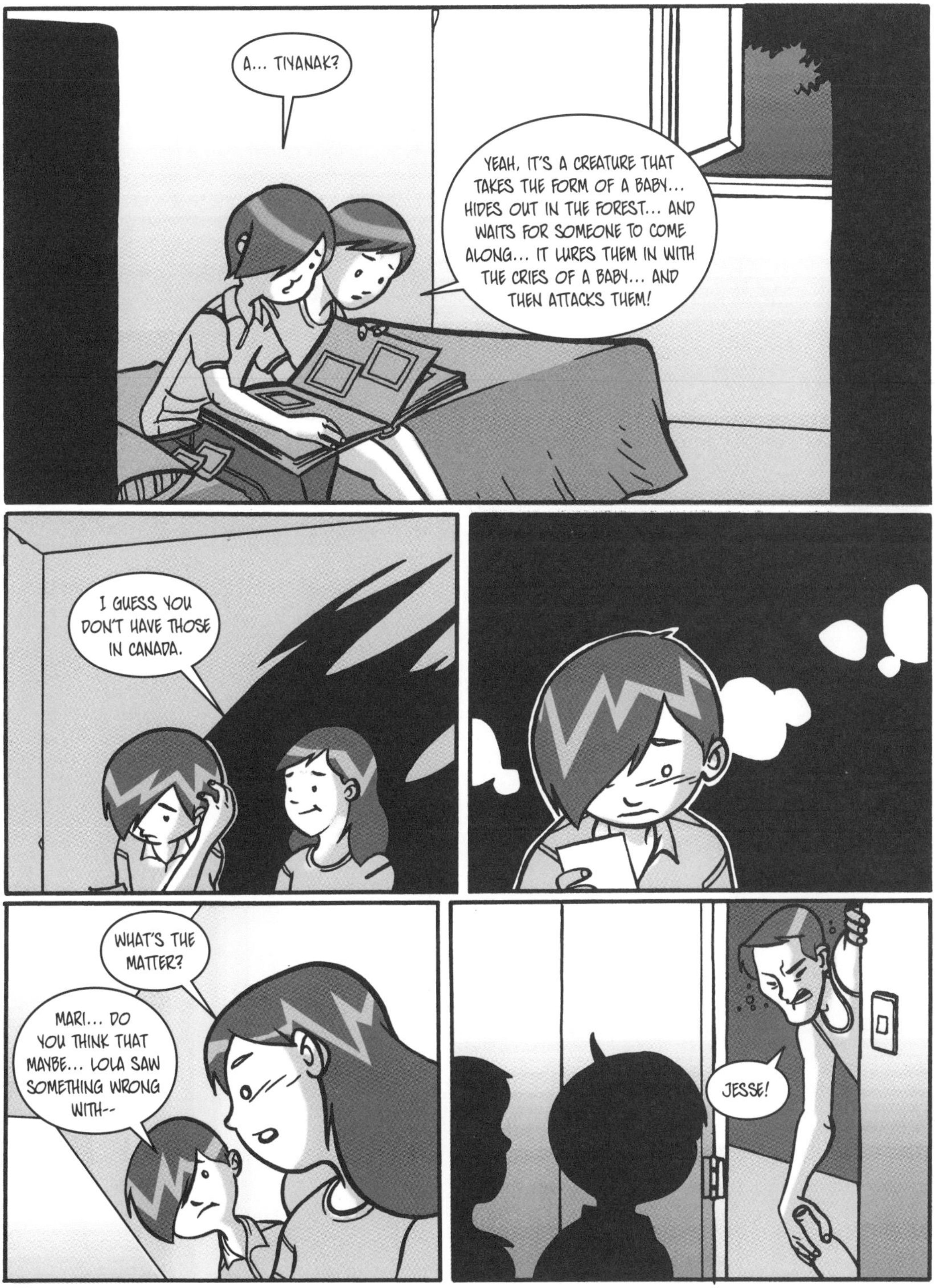
A... TIYANAK?
YEAH, IT'S A CREATURE THAT TAKES THE FORM OF A BABY... HIDES OUT IN THE FOREST... AND WAITS FOR SOMEONE TO COME ALONG... IT LURES THEM IN WITH THE CRIES OF A BABY... AND THEN ATTACKS THEM!
I GUESS YOU DON'T HAVE THOSE IN CANADA.
WHAT'S THE MATTER?
MARI... DO YOU THINK THAT MAYBE... LOLA SAW SOMETHING WRONG WITH--
JESSE!

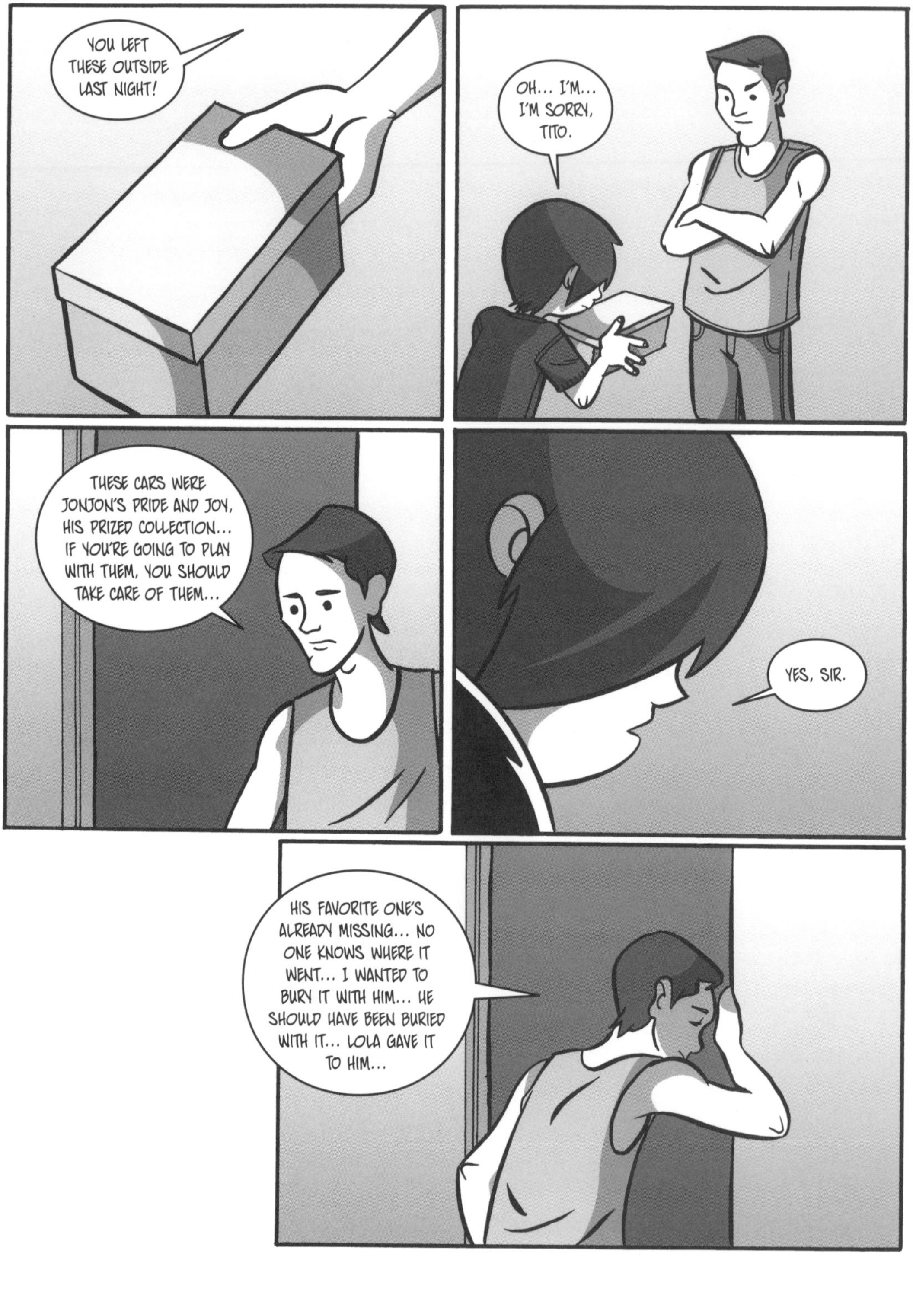
YOU LEFT THESE OUTSIDE LAST NIGHT!
OH... I'M... I'M SORRY, TITO.
THESE CARS WERE JONJON'S PRIDE AND JOY, HIS PRIZED COLLECTION... IF YOU'RE GOING TO PLAY WITH THEM, YOU SHOULD TAKE CARE OF THEM...
YES, SIR.
HIS FAVORITE ONE'S ALREADY MISSING... NO ONE KNOWS WHERE IT WENT... I WANTED TO BURY IT WITH HIM... HE SHOULD HAVE BEEN BURIED WITH IT... LOLA GAVE IT TO HIM...

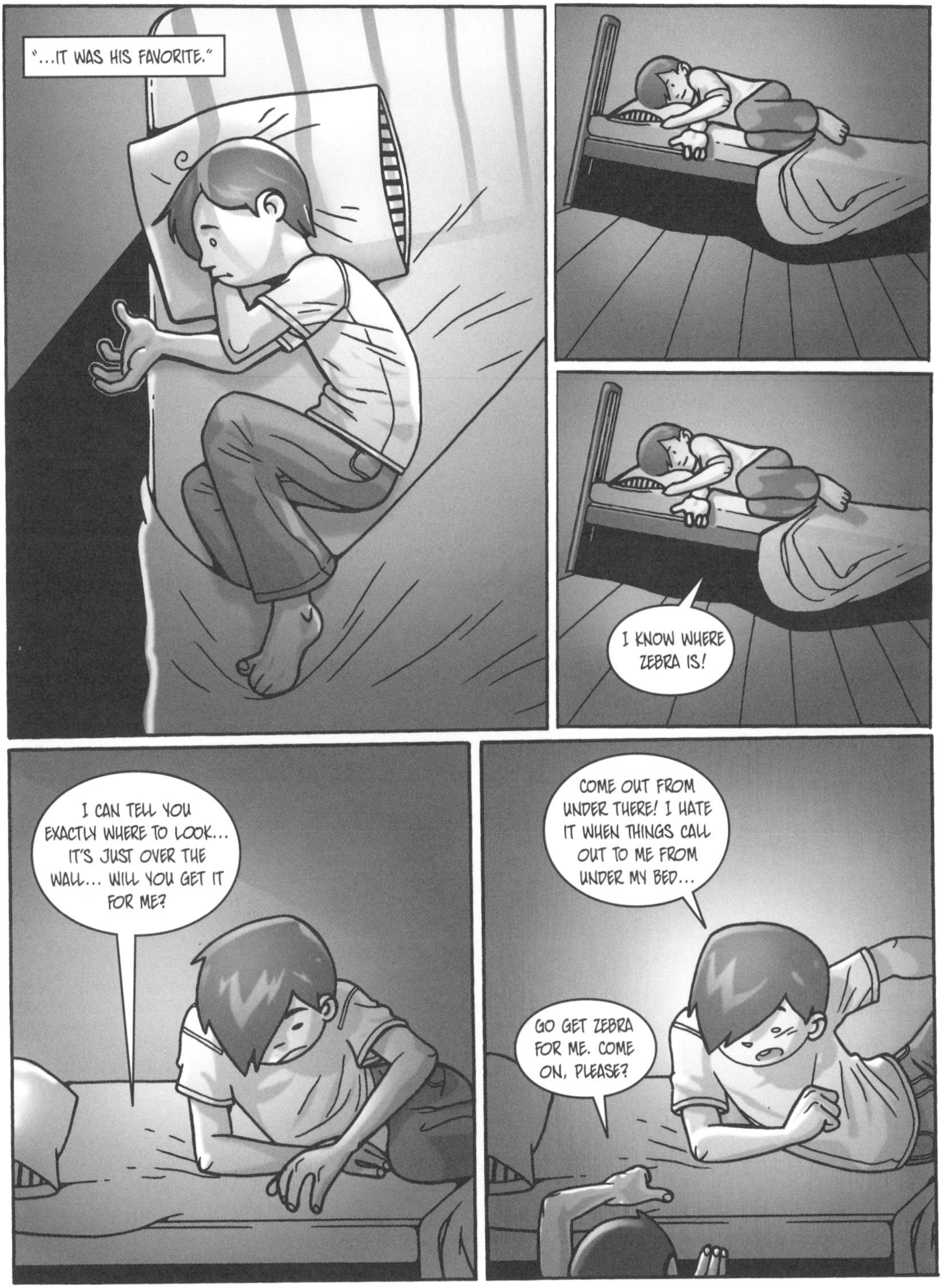
"...IT WAS HIS FAVORITE."
I KNOW WHERE ZEBRA IS!
I CAN TELL YOU EXACTLY WHERE TO LOOK... IT'S JUST OVER THE WALL... WILL YOU GET IT FOR ME?
COME OUT FROM UNDER THERE! I HATE IT WHEN THINGS CALL OUT TO ME FROM UNDER MY BED...
GO GET ZEBRA FOR ME. COME ON, PLEASE?

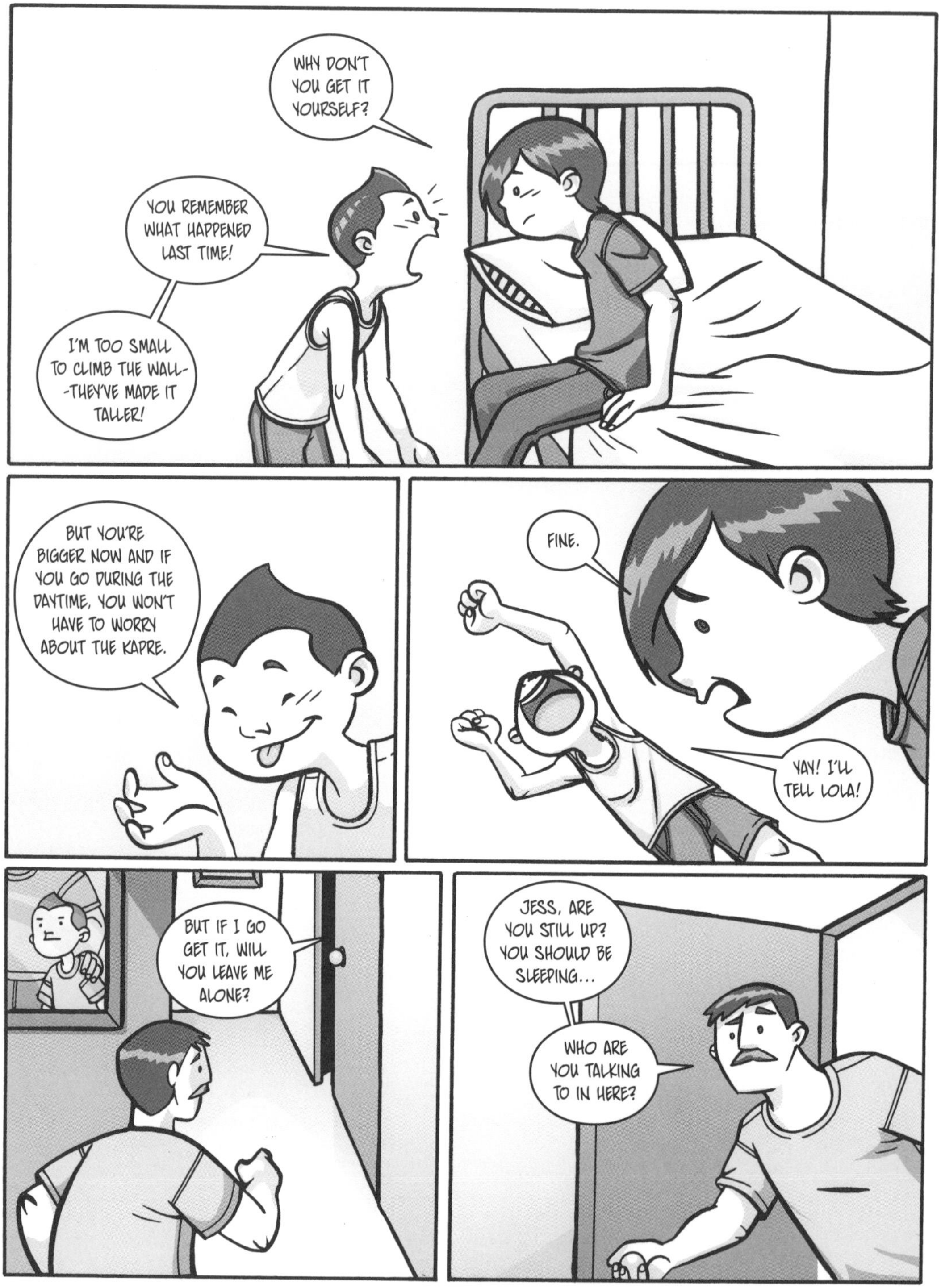
WHY DON'T YOU GET IT YOURSELF?
YOU REMEMBER WHAT HAPPENED LAST TIME!
I'M TOO SMALL TO CLIMB THE WALL- -THEY'VE MADE IT TALLER!
BUT YOU'RE BIGGER NOW AND IF YOU GO DURING THE DAYTIME, YOU WON'T HAVE TO WORRY ABOUT THE KAPRE.
FINE.
YAY! I'LL TELL LOLA!
BUT IF I GO GET IT, WILL YOU LEAVE ME ALONE?
JESS, ARE YOU STILL UP? YOU SHOULD BE SLEEPING...
WHO ARE YOU TALKING TO IN HERE?

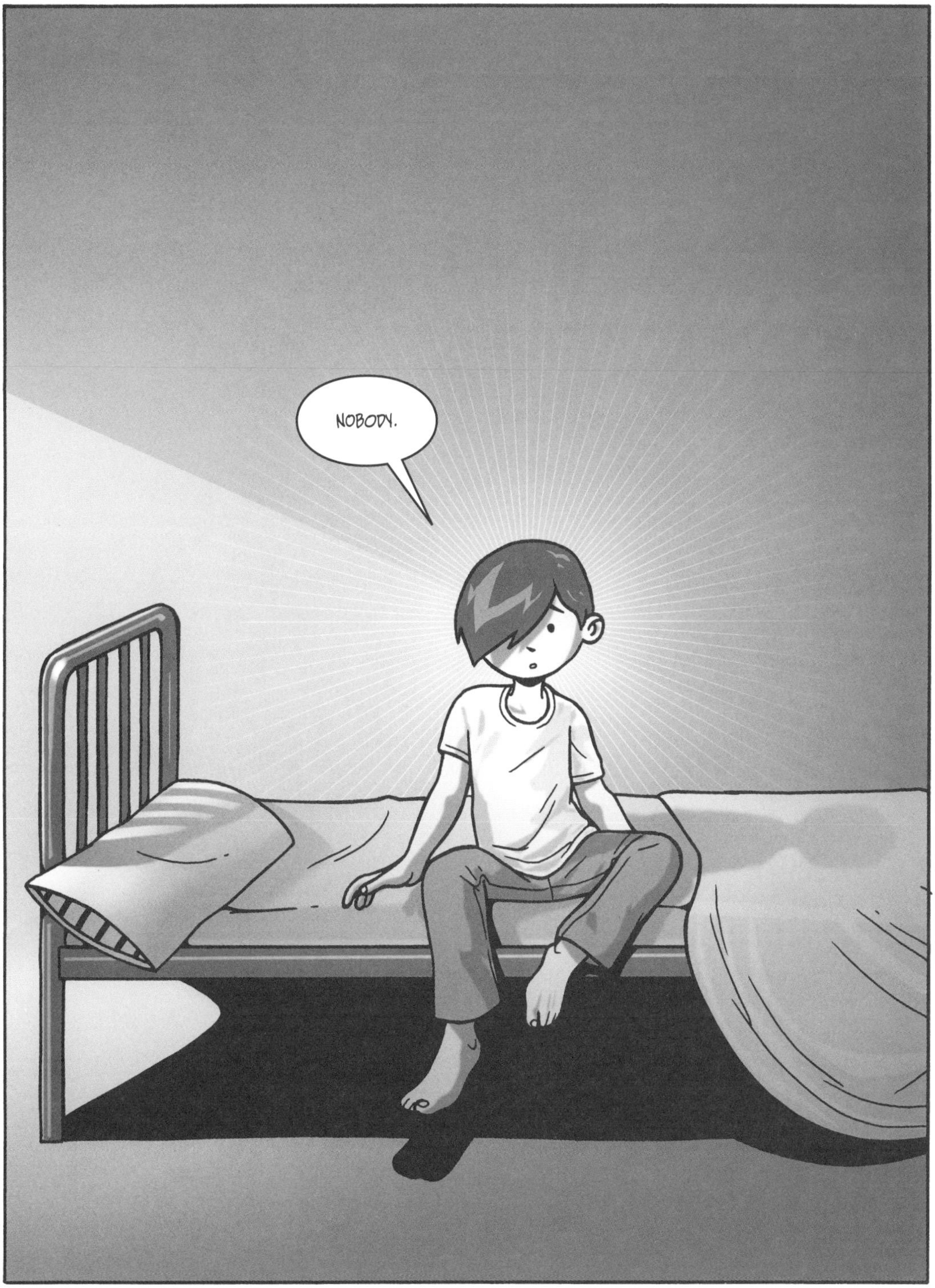
NOBODY.

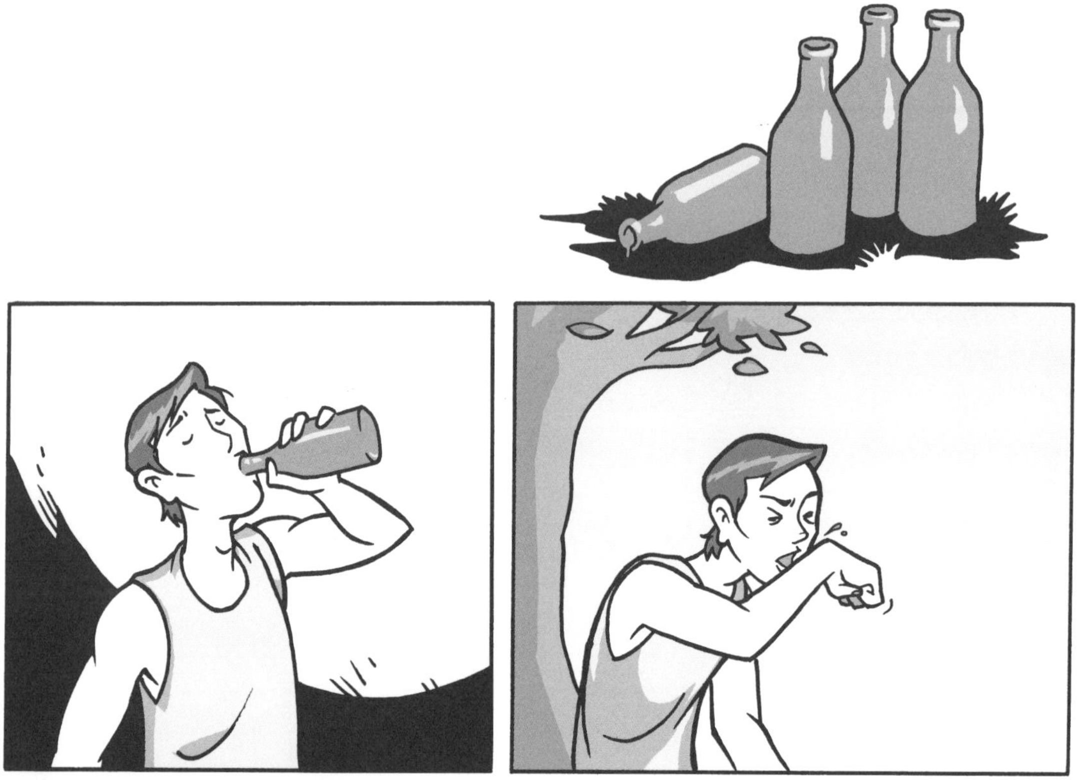
STUPID WALL...

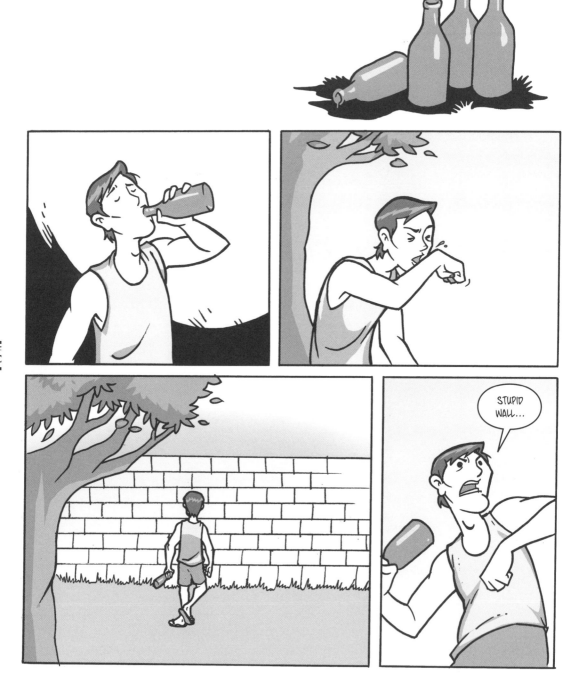

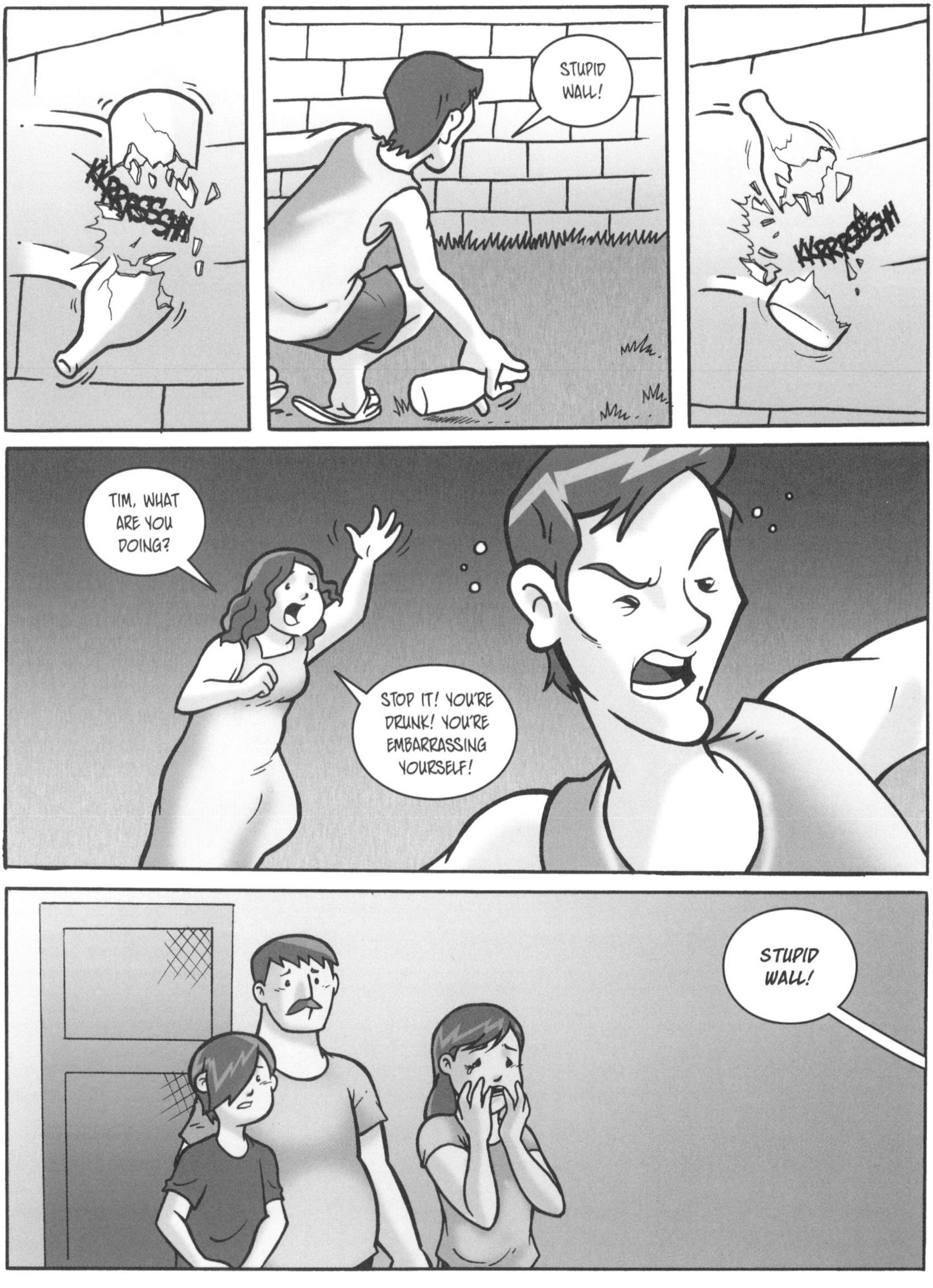
KKRRRSSSHH
STUPID WALL!
KKRRRSSSHH
TIM, WHAT ARE YOU DOING?
STOP IT! YOU'RE DRUNK! YOU'RE EMBARRASSING YOURSELF!
STUPID WALL!

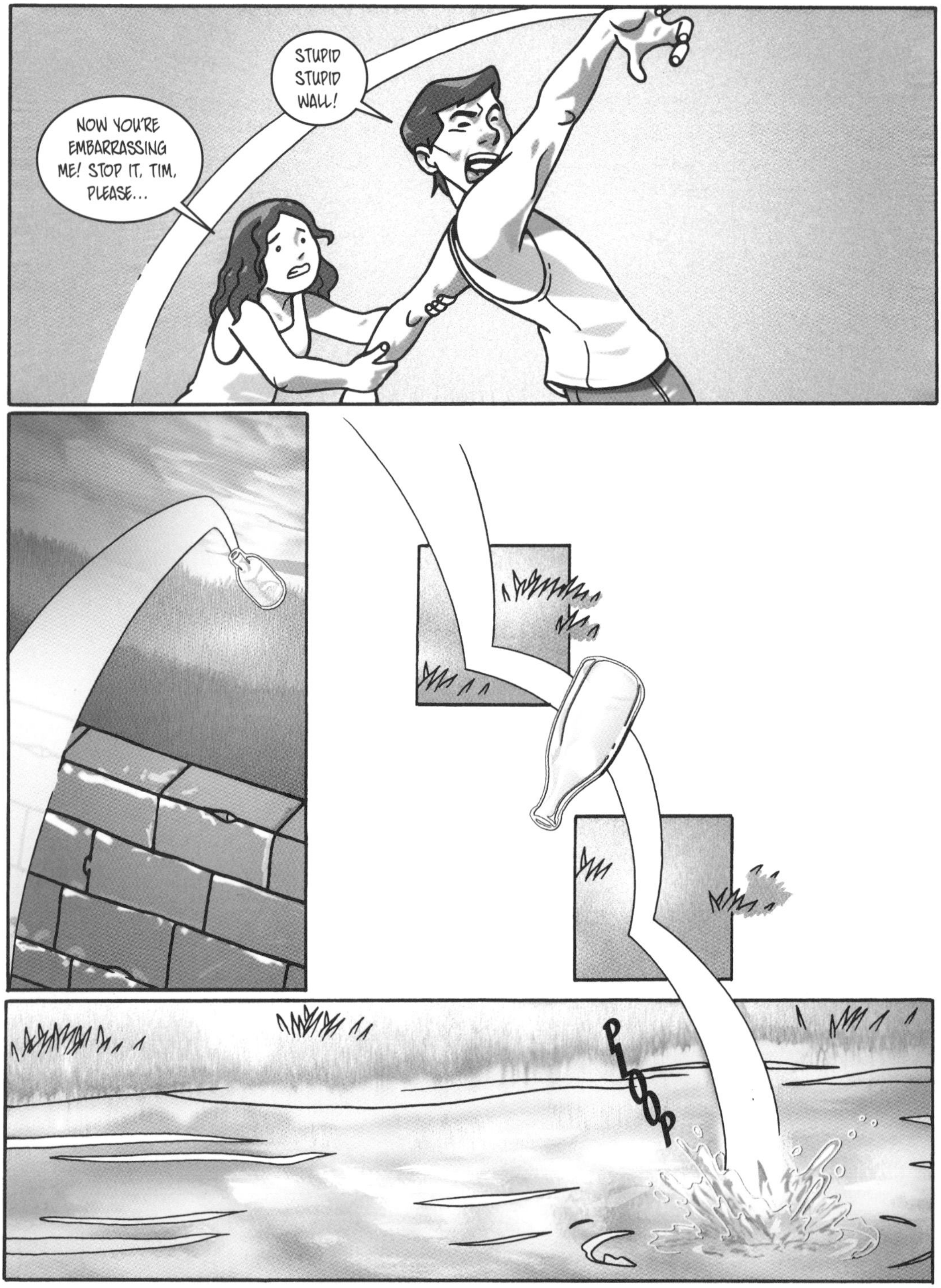
NOW YOU'RE EMBARRASSING ME! STOP IT, TIM, PLEASE...
STUPID STUPID WALL!
PLOOP

LOLA A GHOST STORY

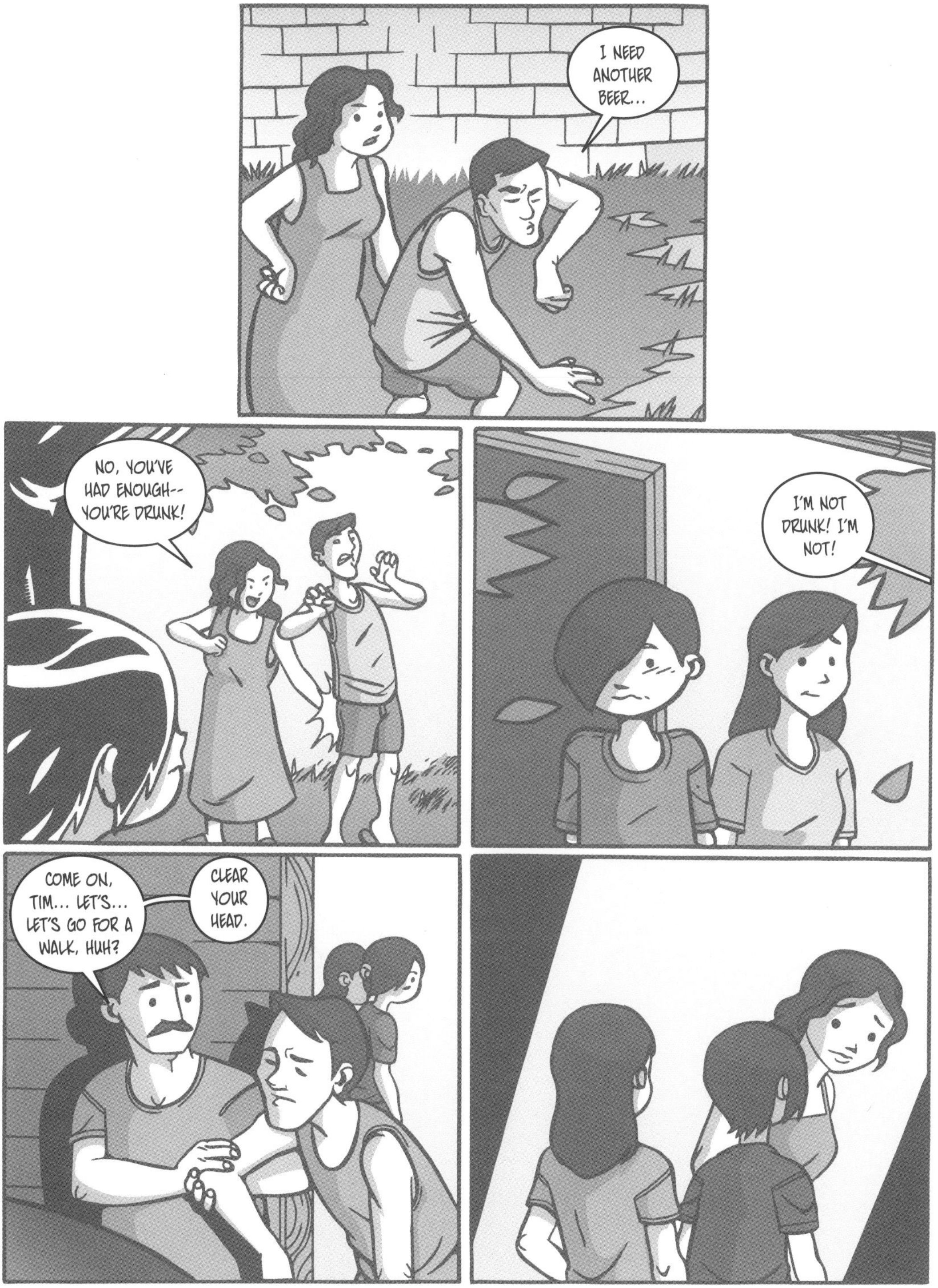
I NEED ANOTHER BEER...
NO, YOU'VE HAD ENOUGH-- YOU'RE DRUNK!
I'M NOT DRUNK! I'M NOT!
COME ON, TIM... LET'S... LET'S GO FOR A WALK, HUH?
CLEAR YOUR HEAD.

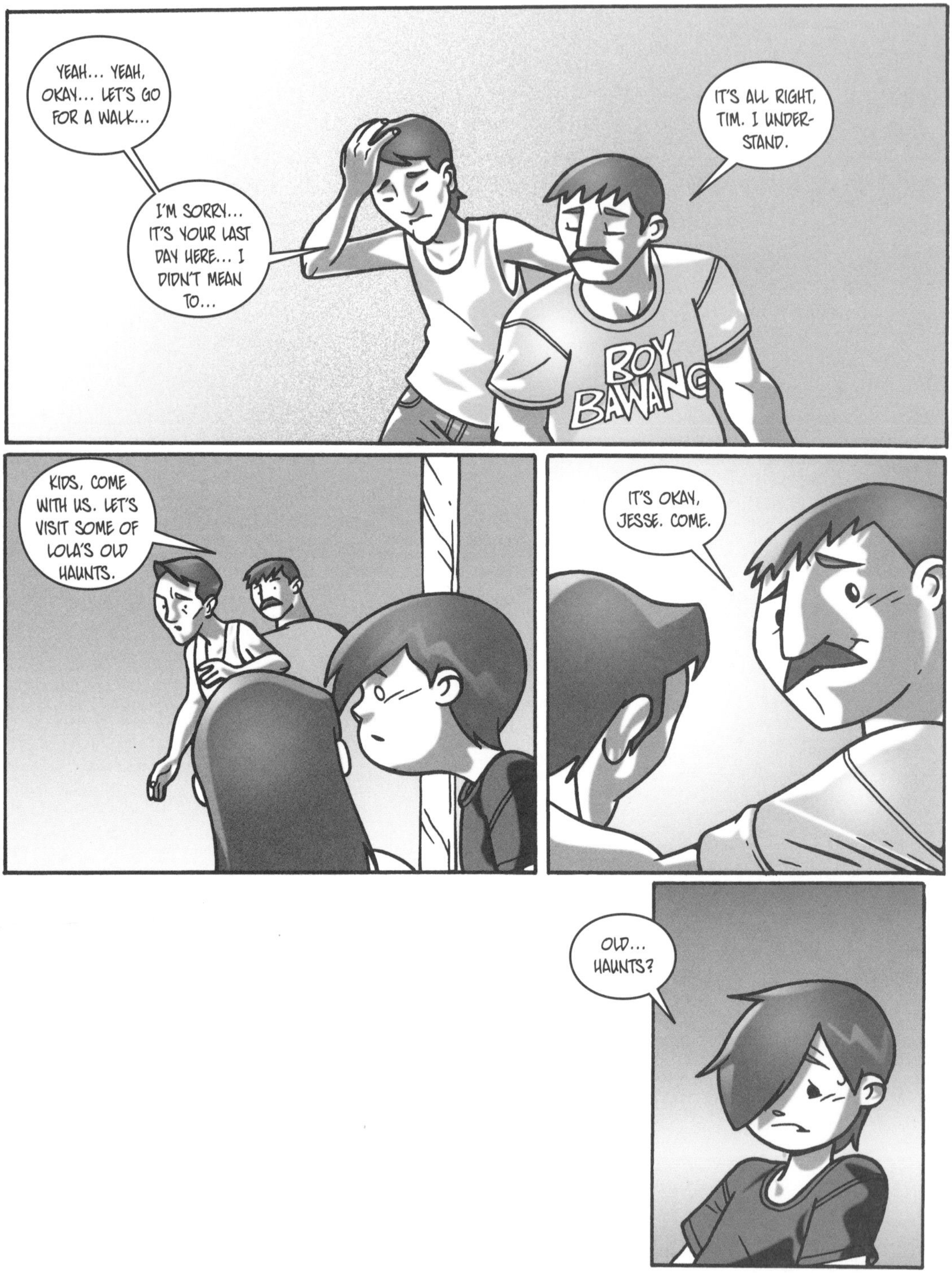
YEAH... YEAH, OKAY... LET'S GO FOR A WALK...
I'M SORRY... IT'S YOUR LAST DAY HERE... I DIDN'T MEAN TO...
IT'S ALL RIGHT, TIM. I UNDER-STAND.
BOY BAWANG
KIDS, COME WITH US. LET'S VISIT SOME OF LOLA'S OLD HAUNTS.
IT'S OKAY, JESSE. COME.
OLD... HAUNTS?

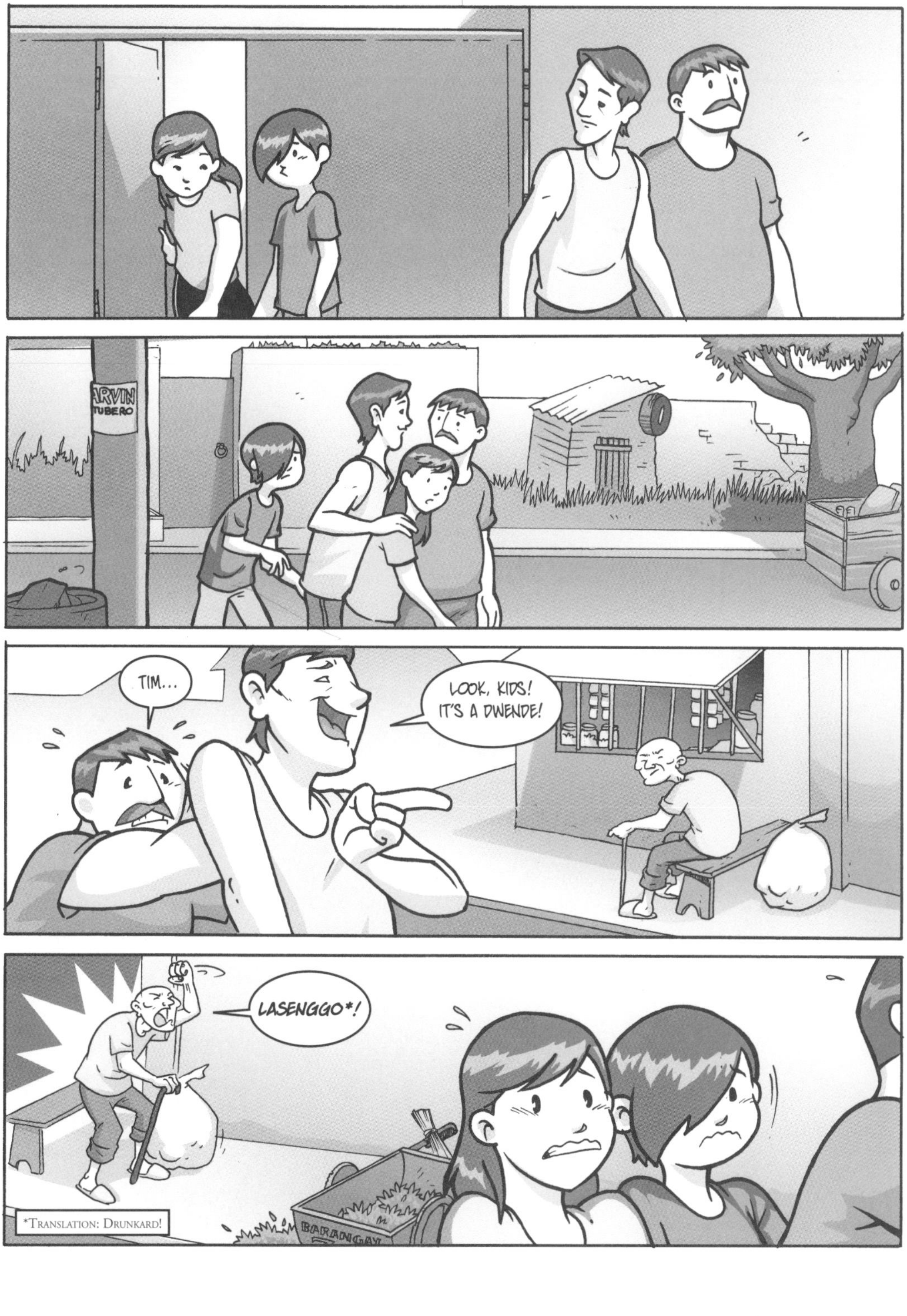
ARVIN
TUBERO
TIM...
LOOK, KIDS! IT'S A DWENDE!
LASENGGO*!
BARANGAY

*Translation: Drunkard!

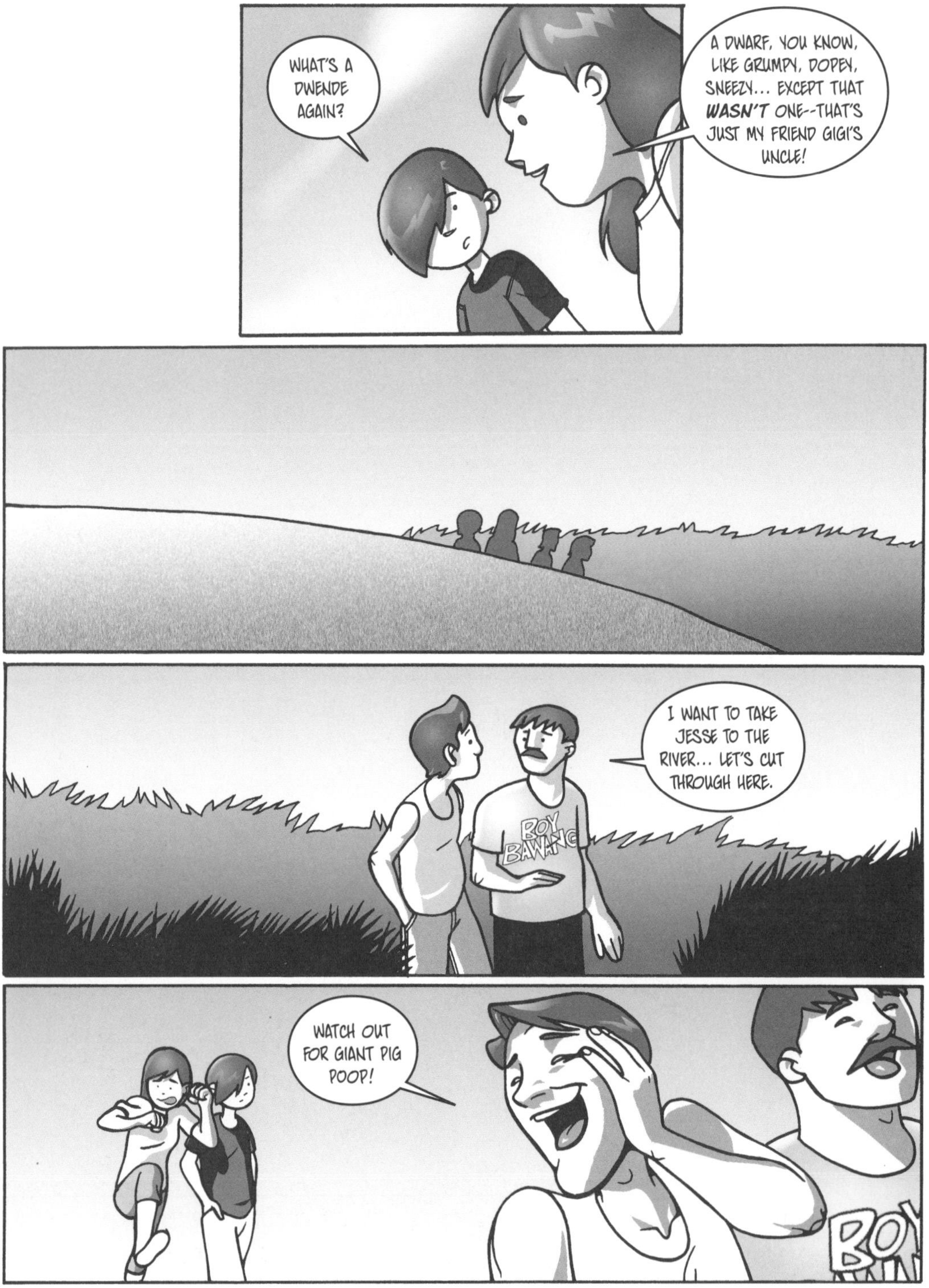
WHAT'S A DWENDE AGAIN?
A DWARF, YOU KNOW, LIKE GRUMPY, DOPEY, SNEEZY... EXCEPT THAT **WASN'T** ONE--THAT'S JUST MY FRIEND GIGI'S UNCLE!
I WANT TO TAKE JESSE TO THE RIVER... LET'S CUT THROUGH HERE.
BOY BAWANG
WATCH OUT FOR GIANT PIG POOP!
BOY

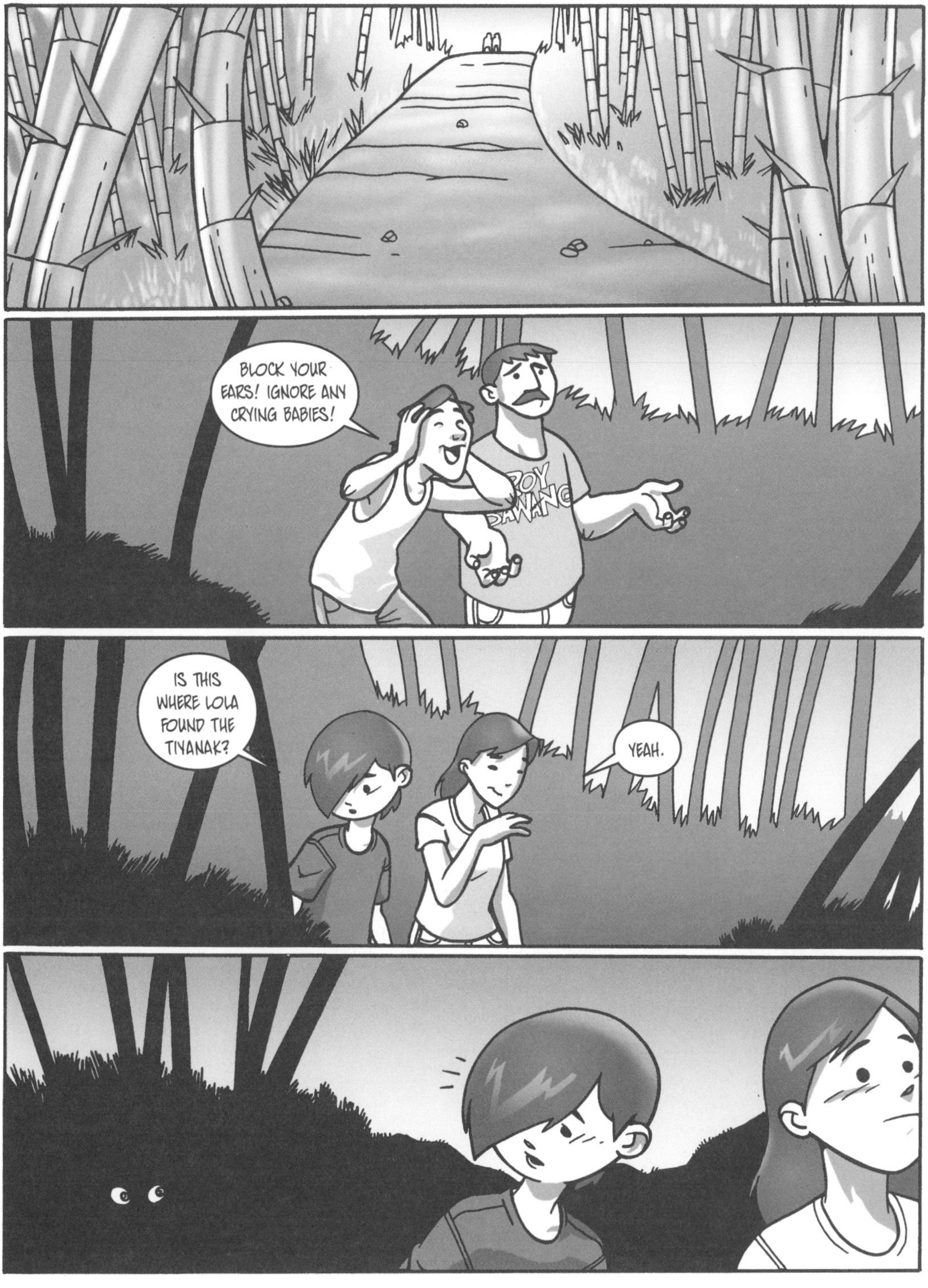
BLOCK YOUR EARS! IGNORE ANY CRYING BABIES!
IS THIS WHERE LOLA FOUND THE TIYANAK?
YEAH.

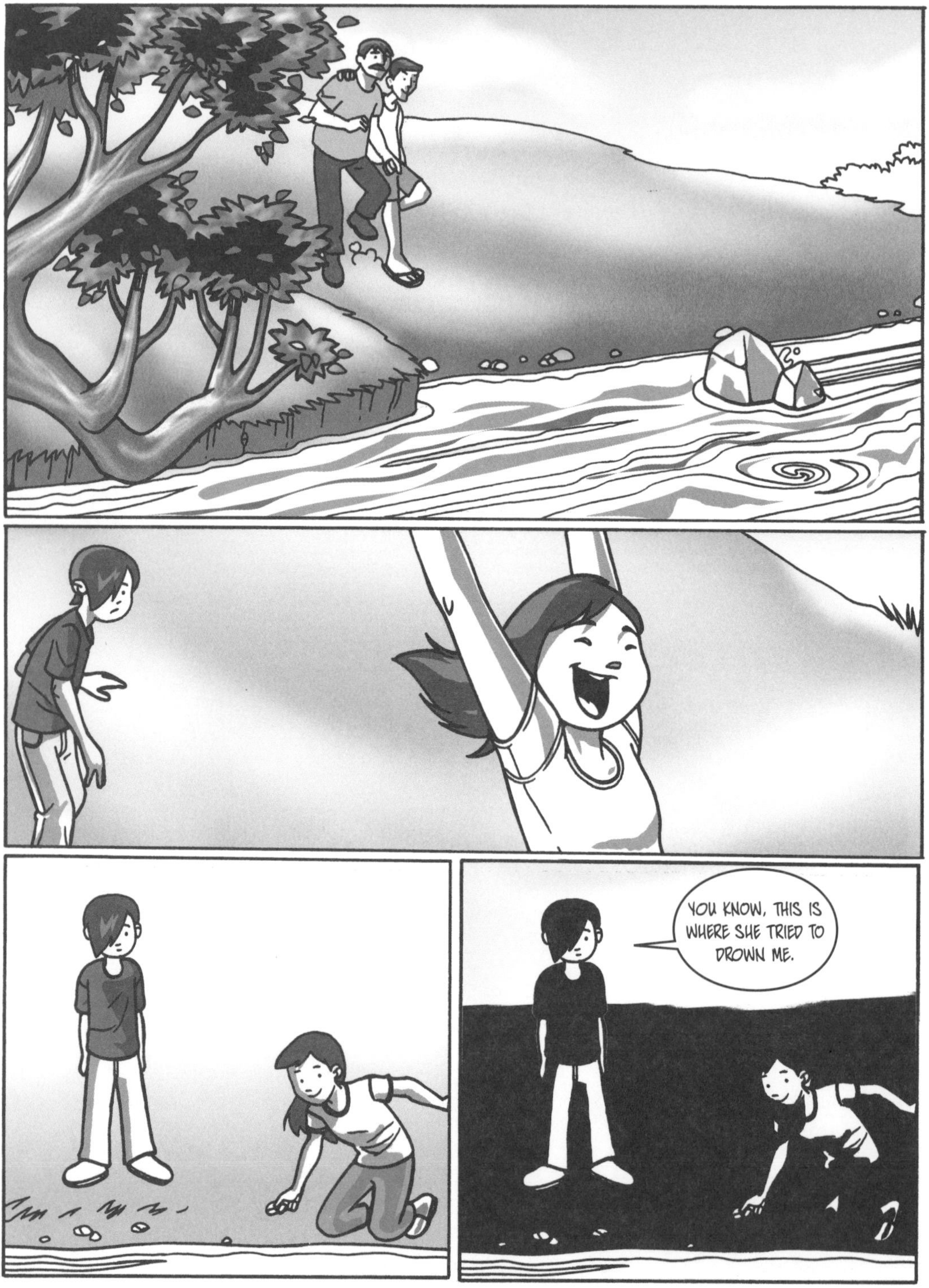
YOU KNOW, THIS IS WHERE SHE TRIED TO DROWN ME.

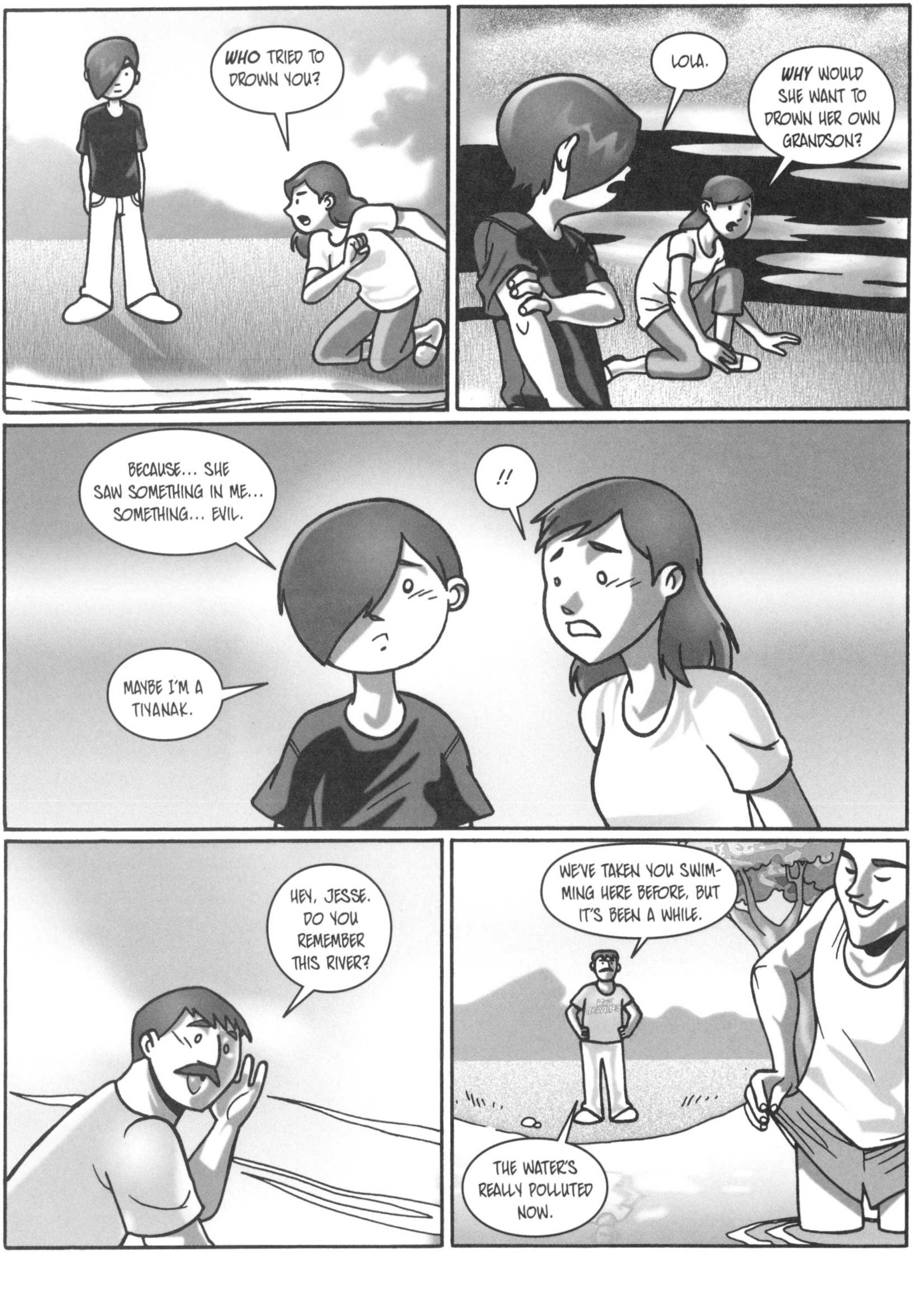
WHO TRIED TO DROWN YOU?
LOLA.
WHY WOULD SHE WANT TO DROWN HER OWN GRANDSON?
BECAUSE... SHE SAW SOMETHING IN ME... SOMETHING... EVIL.
!!
MAYBE I'M A TIYANAK.
HEY, JESSE. DO YOU REMEMBER THIS RIVER?
WE'VE TAKEN YOU SWIM-MING HERE BEFORE, BUT IT'S BEEN A WHILE.
THE WATER'S REALLY POLLUTED NOW.

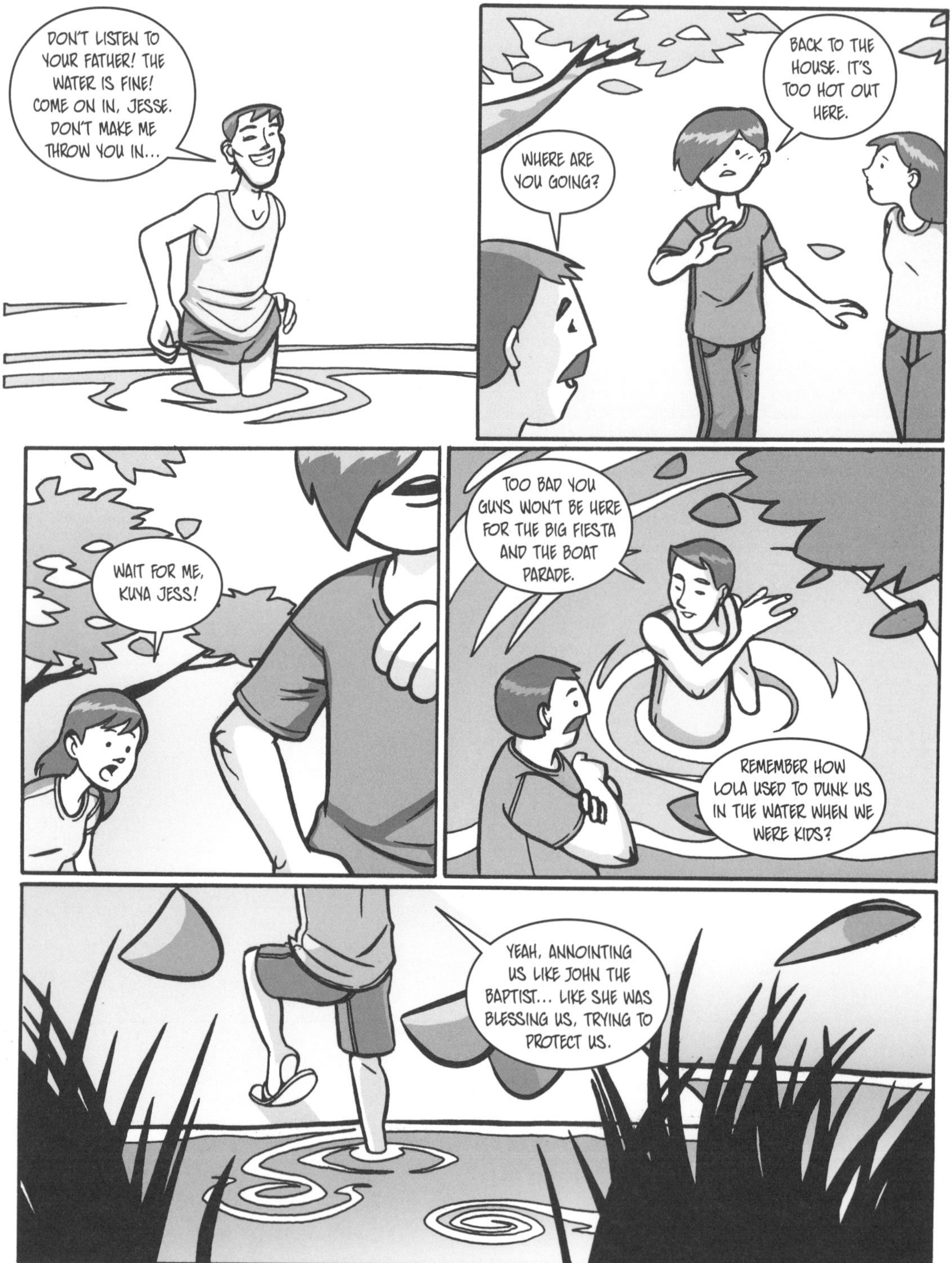
DON'T LISTEN TO YOUR FATHER! THE WATER IS FINE! COME ON IN, JESSE. DON'T MAKE ME THROW YOU IN...
WHERE ARE YOU GOING?
BACK TO THE HOUSE. IT'S TOO HOT OUT HERE.
WAIT FOR ME, KUYA JESS!
TOO BAD YOU GUYS WON'T BE HERE FOR THE BIG FIESTA AND THE BOAT PARADE.
REMEMBER HOW LOLA USED TO DUNK US IN THE WATER WHEN WE WERE KIDS?
YEAH, ANNOINTING US LIKE JOHN THE BAPTIST... LIKE SHE WAS BLESSING US, TRYING TO PROTECT US.

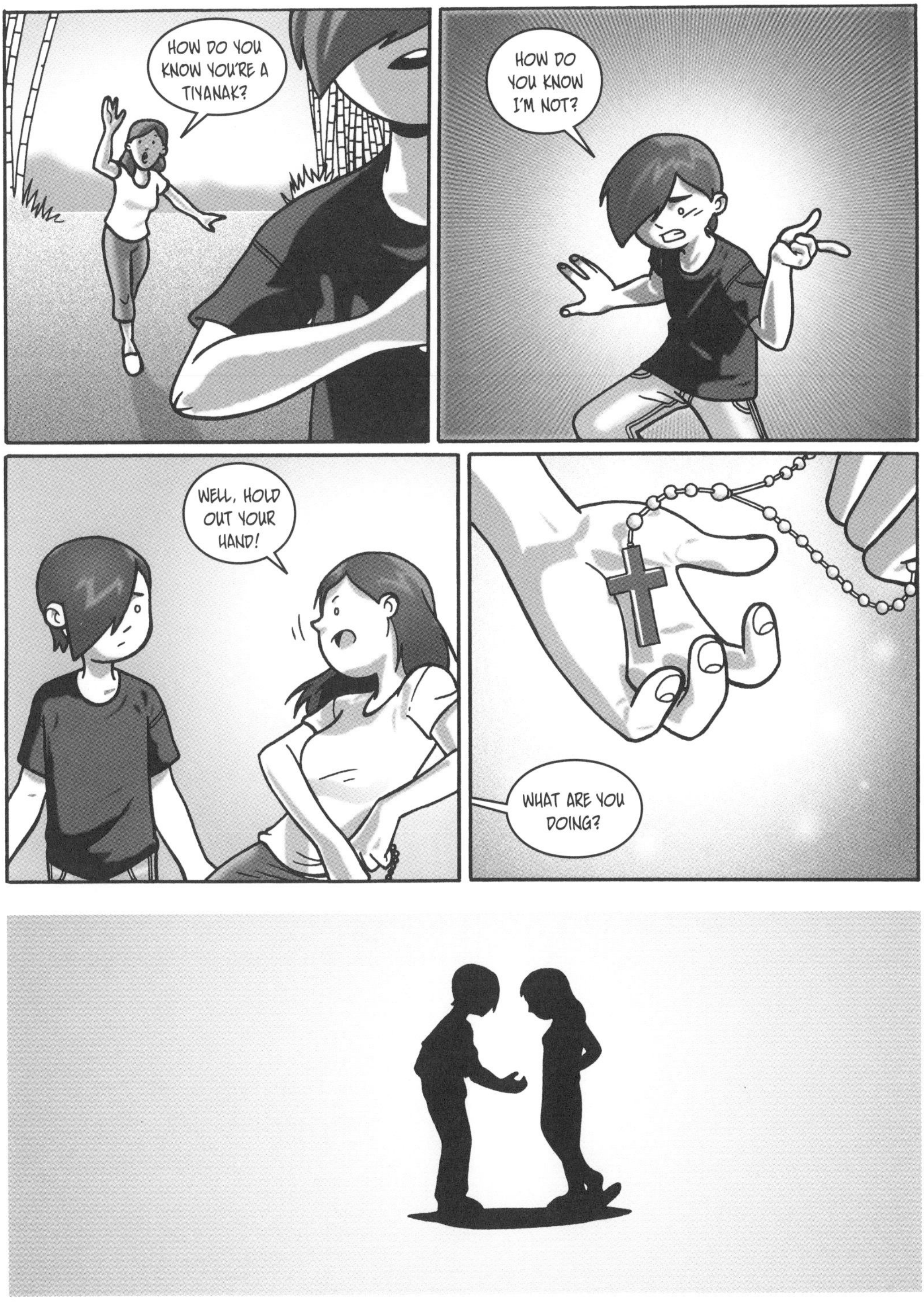
HOW DO YOU KNOW YOU'RE A TIYANAK?
HOW DO YOU KNOW I'M NOT?
WELL, HOLD OUT YOUR HAND!
WHAT ARE YOU DOING?

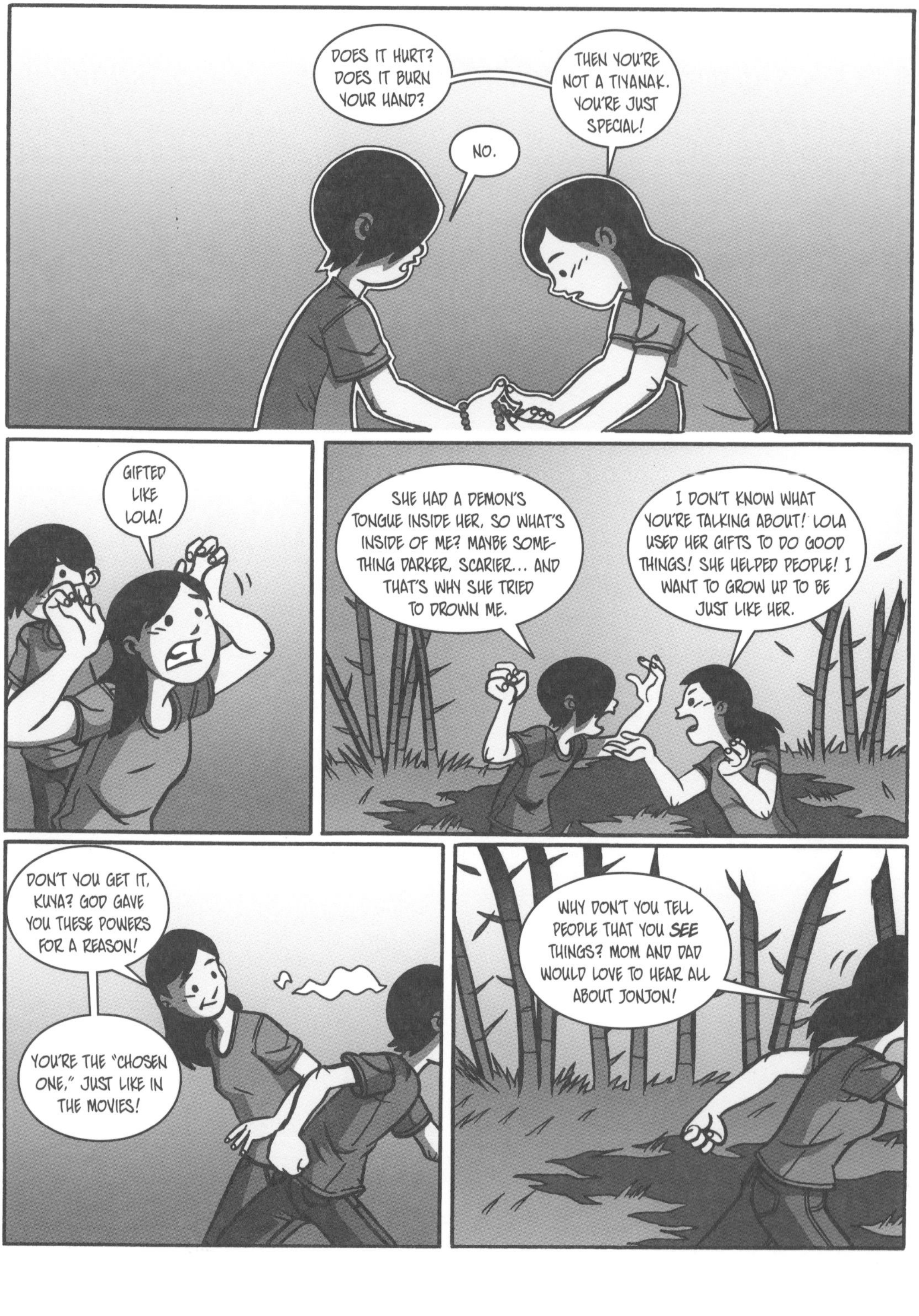
DOES IT HURT? DOES IT BURN YOUR HAND?
NO.
THEN YOU'RE NOT A TIYANAK. YOU'RE JUST SPECIAL!
GIFTED LIKE LOLA!
SHE HAD A DEMON'S TONGUE INSIDE HER, SO WHAT'S INSIDE OF ME? MAYBE SOME-THING DARKER, SCARIER... AND THAT'S WHY SHE TRIED TO DROWN ME.
I DON'T KNOW WHAT YOU'RE TALKING ABOUT! LOLA USED HER GIFTS TO DO GOOD THINGS! SHE HELPED PEOPLE! I WANT TO GROW UP TO BE JUST LIKE HER.
DON'T YOU GET IT, KUYA? GOD GAVE YOU THESE POWERS FOR A REASON!
YOU'RE THE "CHOSEN ONE," JUST LIKE IN THE MOVIES!
WHY DON'T YOU TELL PEOPLE THAT YOU **SEE** THINGS? MOM AND DAD WOULD LOVE TO HEAR ALL ABOUT JONJON!

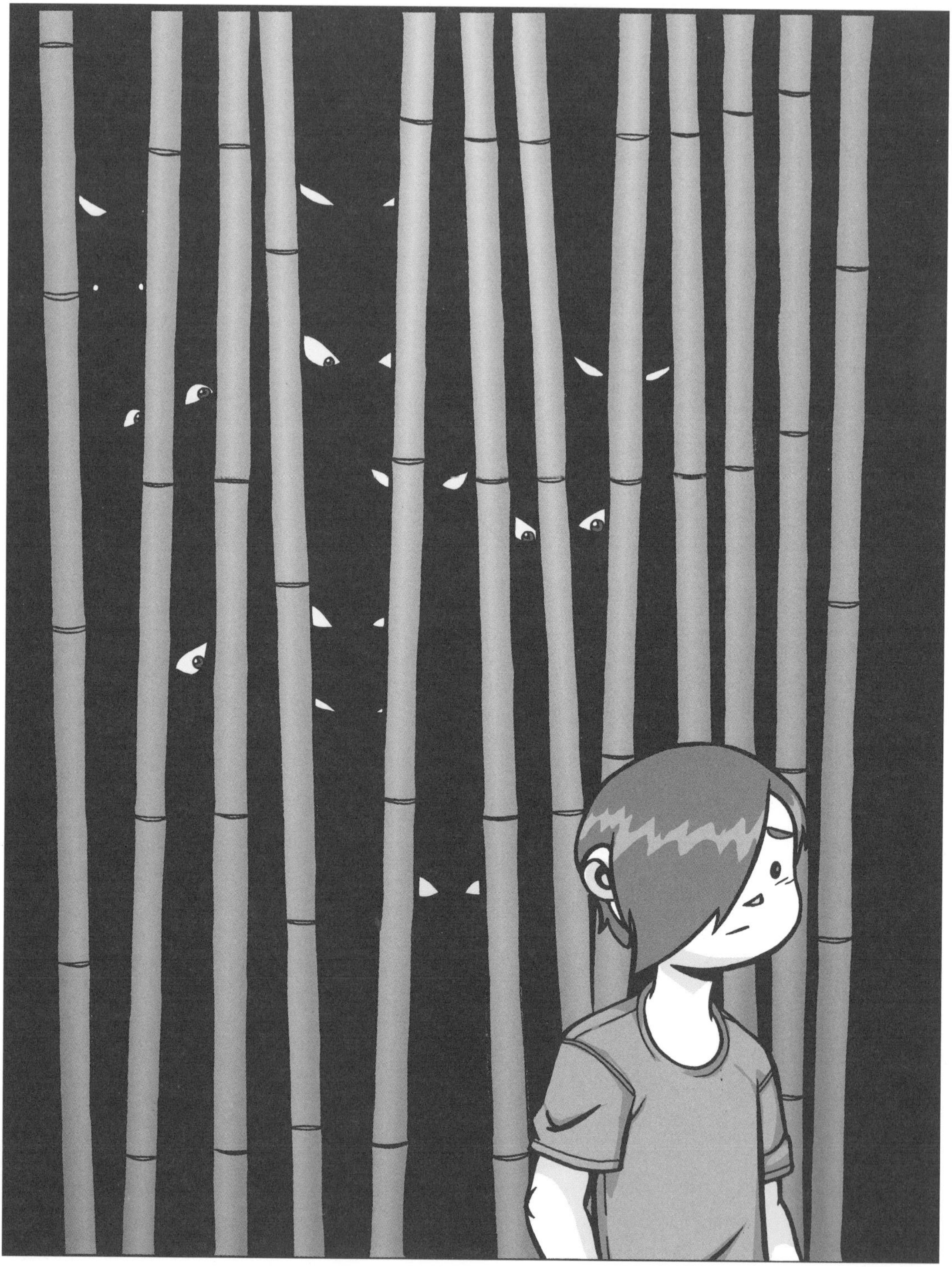

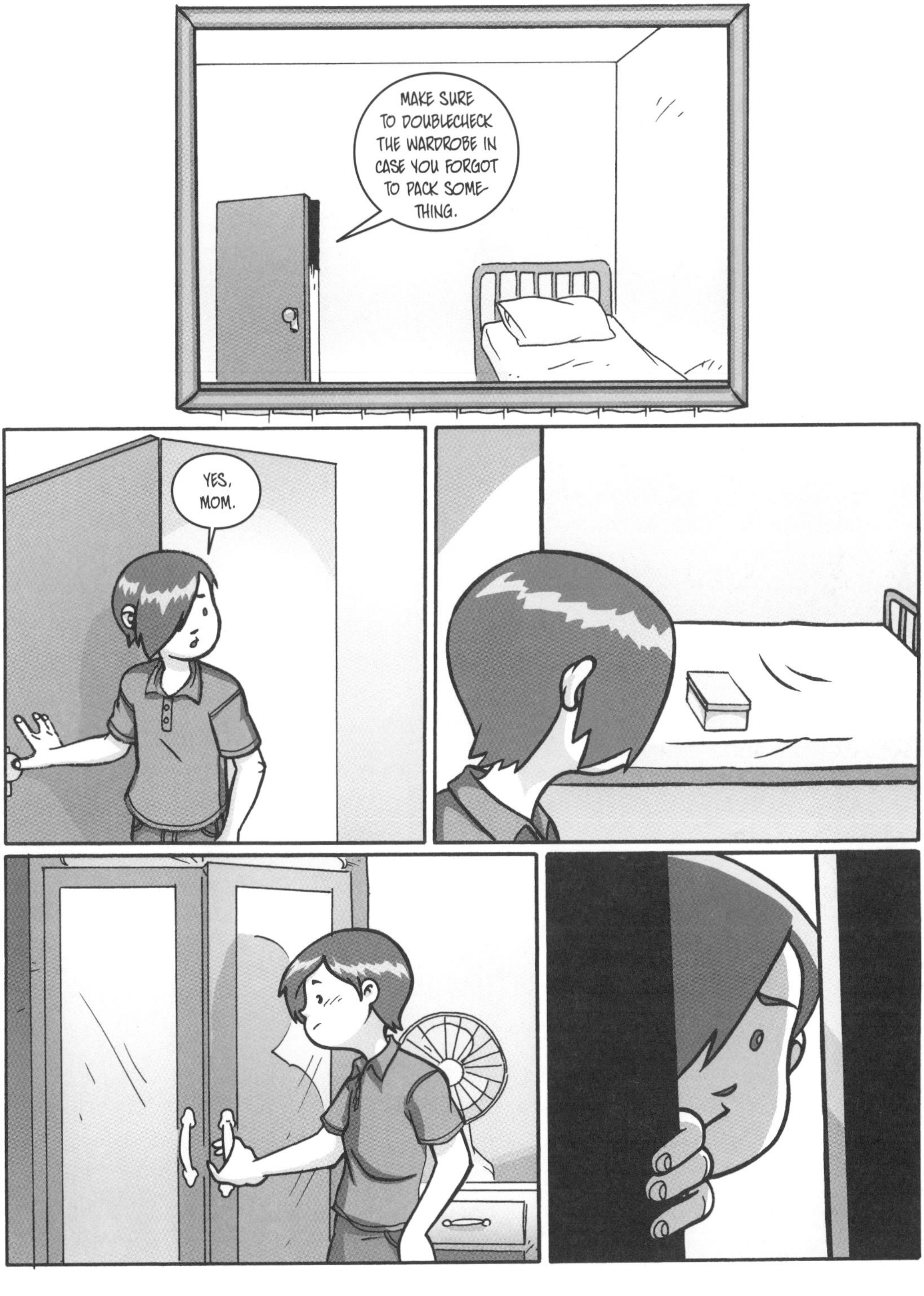
MAKE SURE TO DOUBLECHECK THE WARDROBE IN CASE YOU FORGOT TO PACK SOME-THING.
YES, MOM.

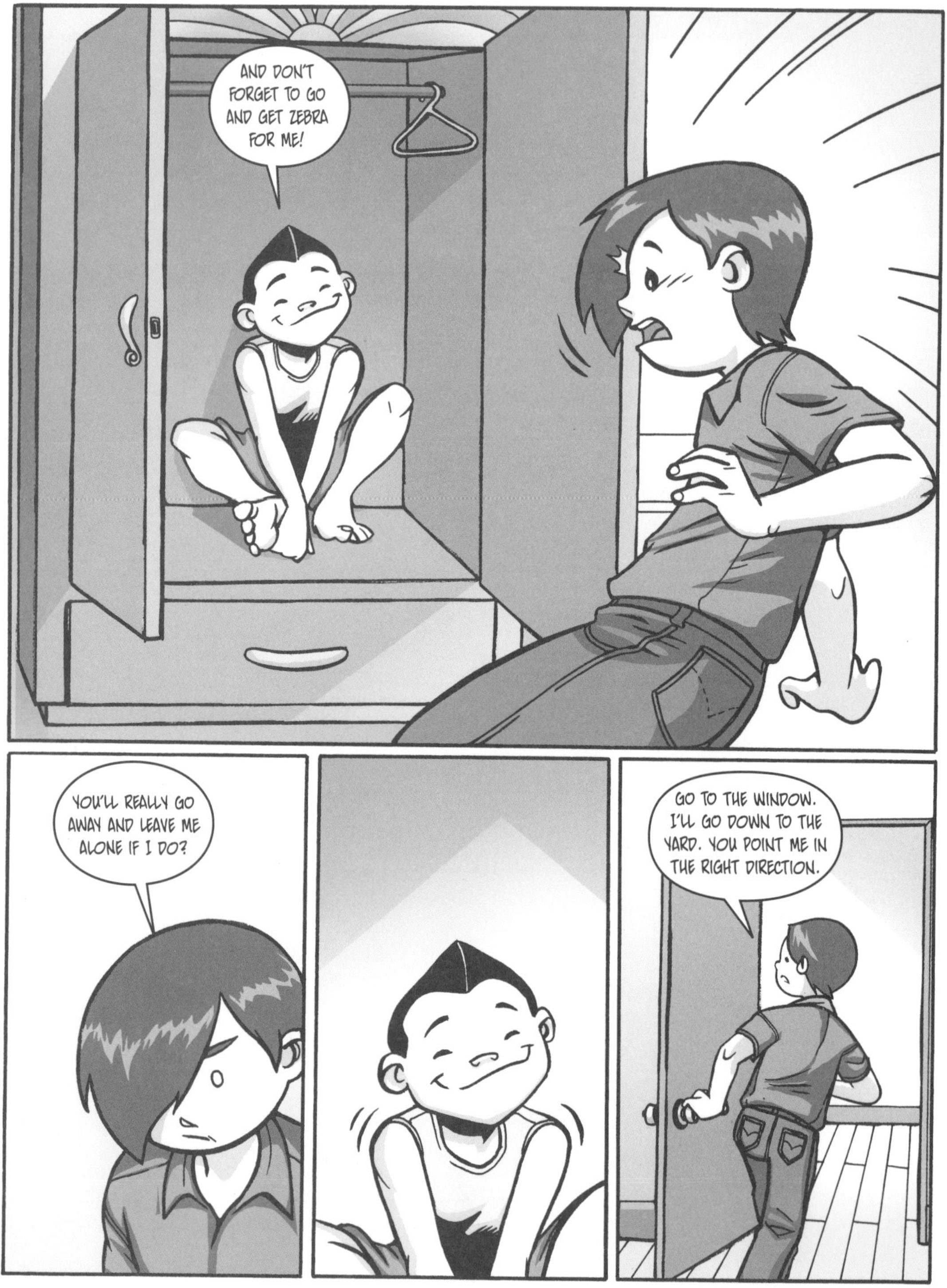
AND DON'T FORGET TO GO AND GET ZEBRA FOR ME!
YOU'LL REALLY GO AWAY AND LEAVE ME ALONE IF I DO?
GO TO THE WINDOW. I'LL GO DOWN TO THE YARD. YOU POINT ME IN THE RIGHT DIRECTION.

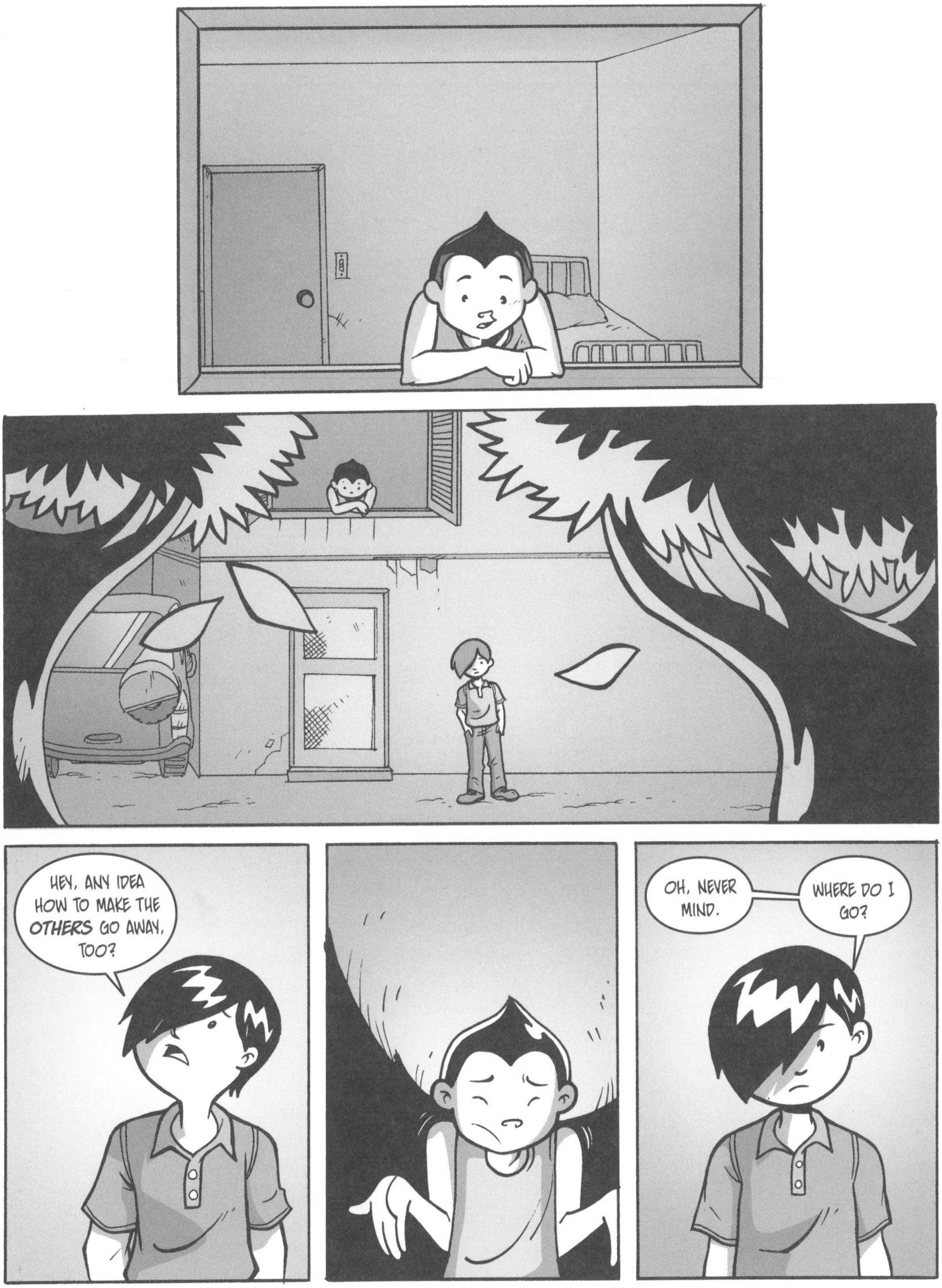
HEY, ANY IDEA HOW TO MAKE THE OTHERS GO AWAY, TOO?
OH, NEVER MIND.
WHERE DO I GO?

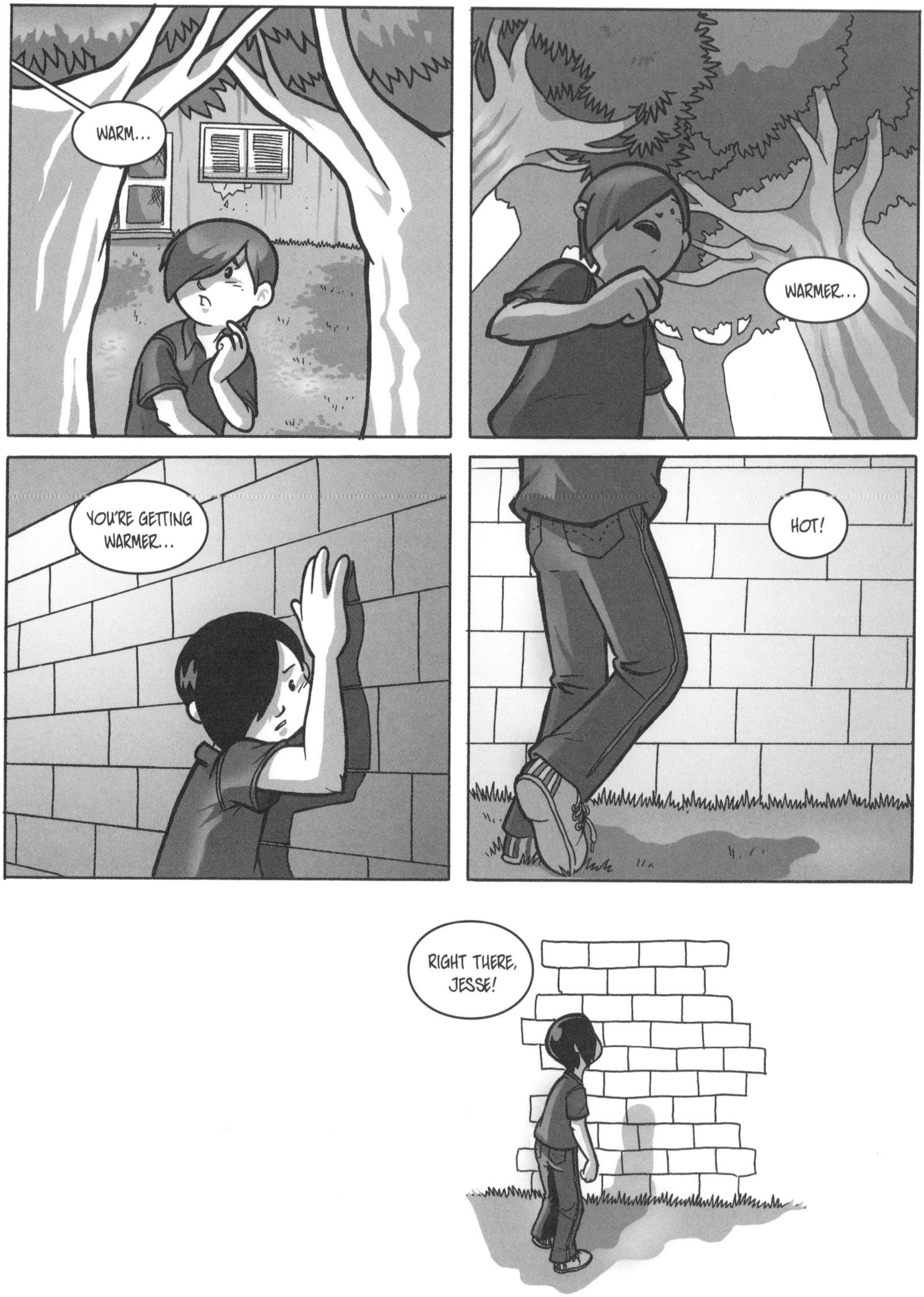
WARM...
WARMER...
YOU'RE GETTING WARMER...
HOT!
RIGHT THERE, JESSE!

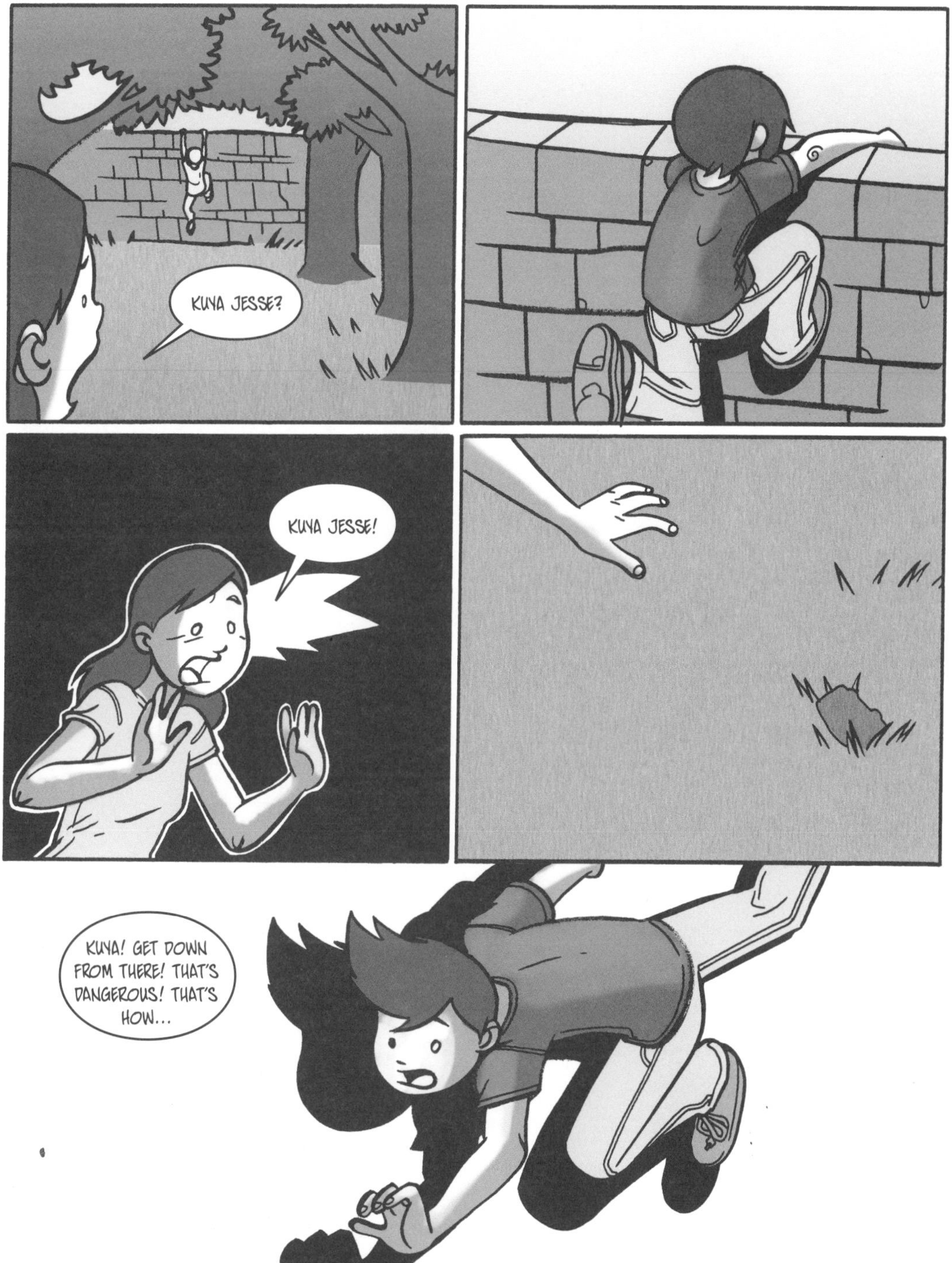
KUYA JESSE?
KUYA JESSE!
KUYA! GET DOWN FROM THERE! THAT'S DANGEROUS! THAT'S HOW...

Lola A Ghost Story

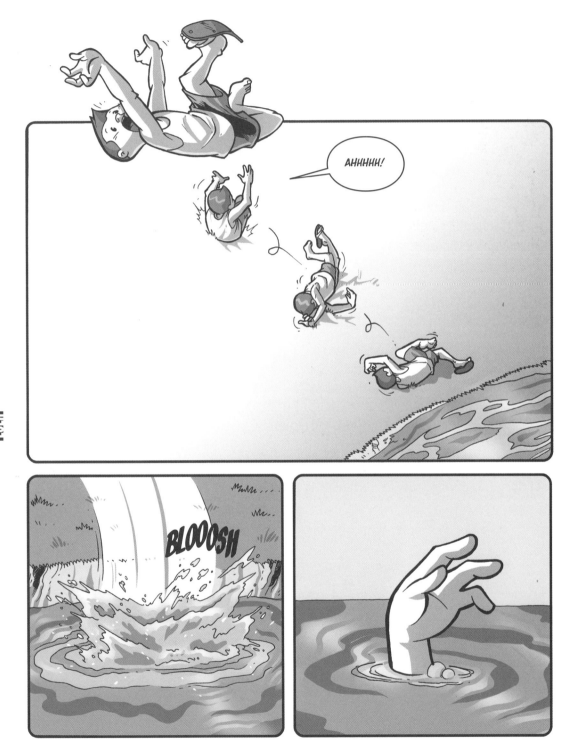

AHHHHH!

BLOOOSH

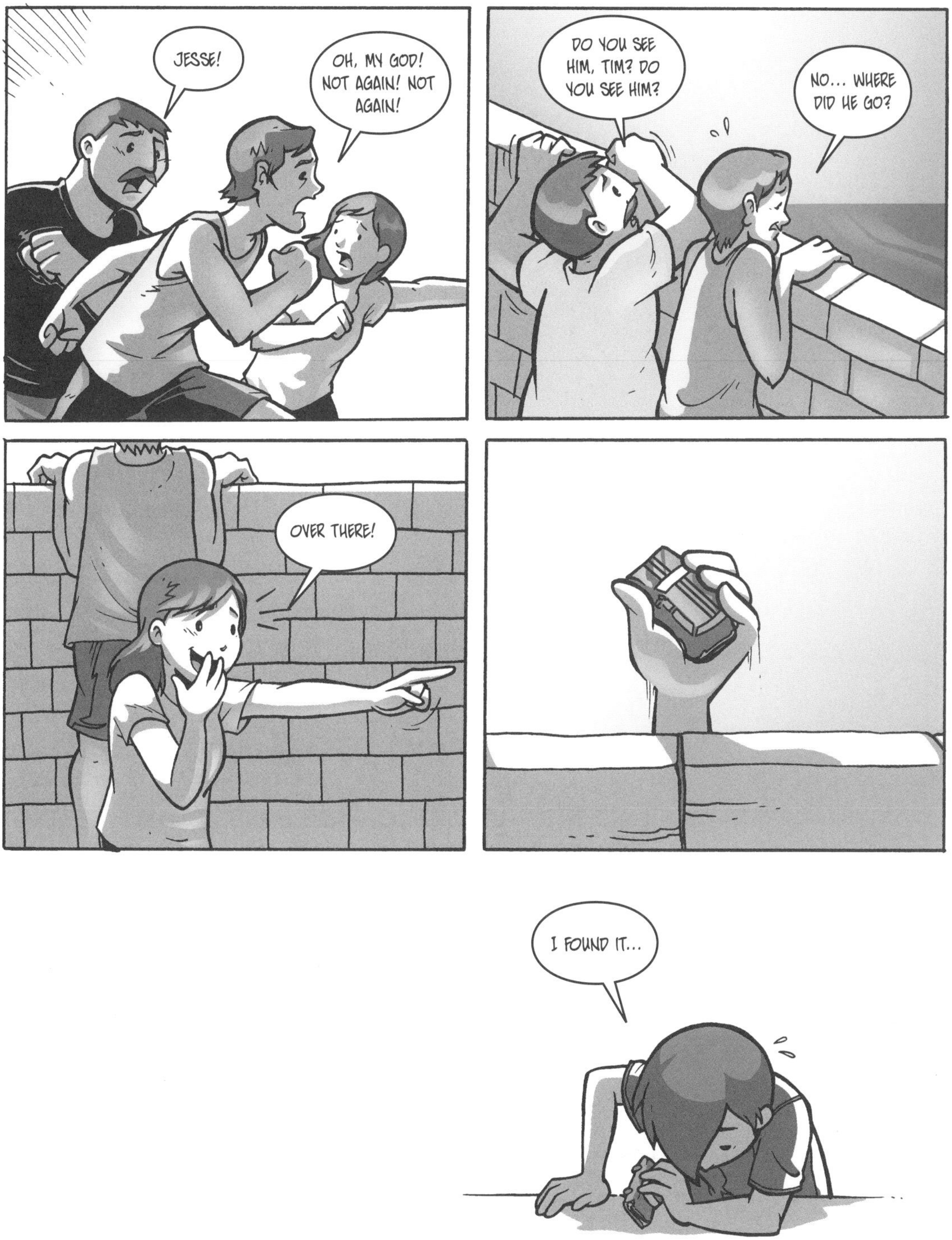
JESSE!
OH, MY GOD! NOT AGAIN! NOT AGAIN!
DO YOU SEE HIM, TIM? DO YOU SEE HIM?
NO... WHERE DID HE GO?
OVER THERE!
I FOUND IT...

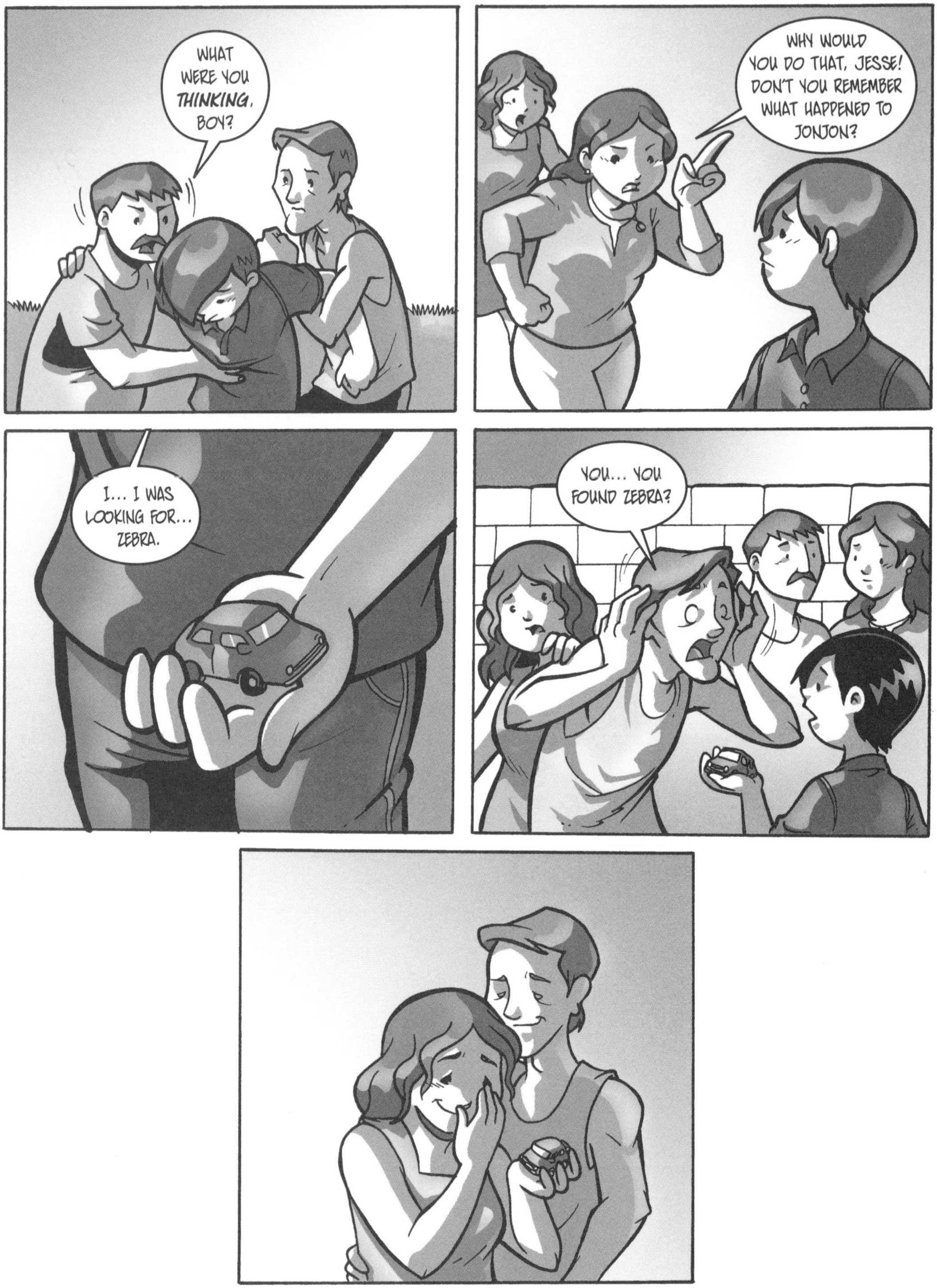
WHAT WERE YOU *THINKING*, BOY?
WHY WOULD YOU DO THAT, JESSE! DON'T YOU REMEMBER WHAT HAPPENED TO JONJON?
I... I WAS LOOKING FOR... ZEBRA.
YOU... YOU FOUND ZEBRA?

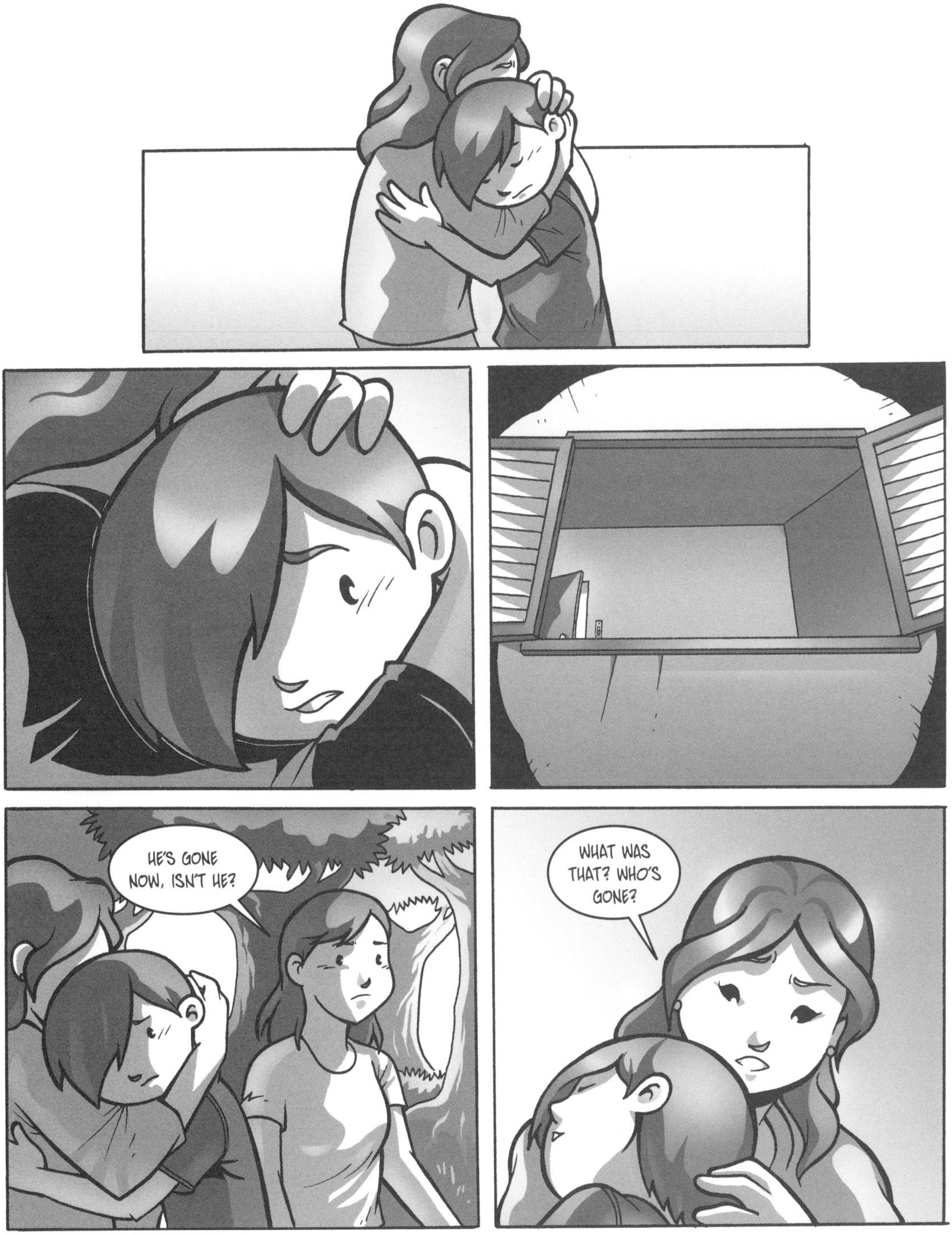
HE'S GONE NOW, ISN'T HE?
WHAT WAS THAT? WHO'S GONE?

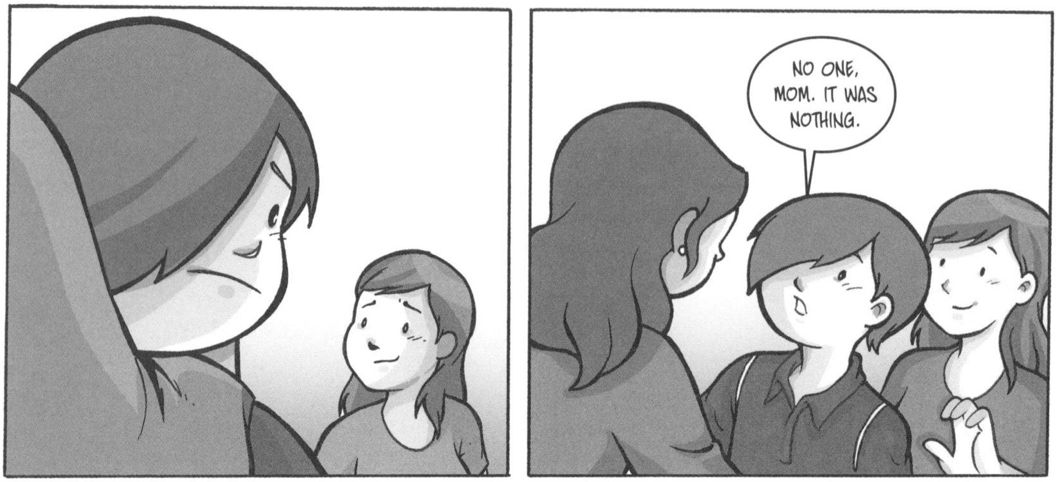
NO ONE, MOM. IT WAS NOTHING.

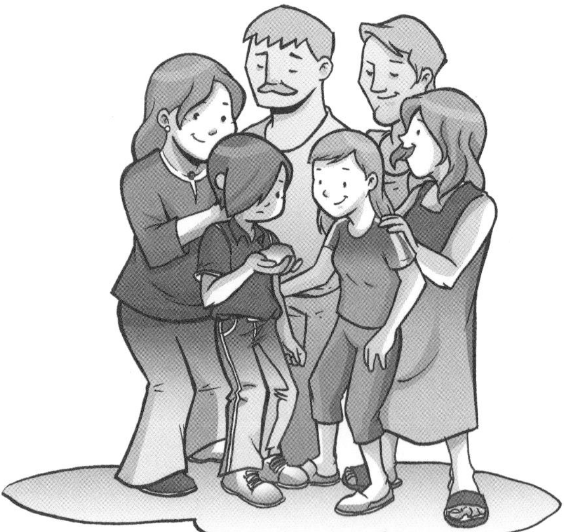

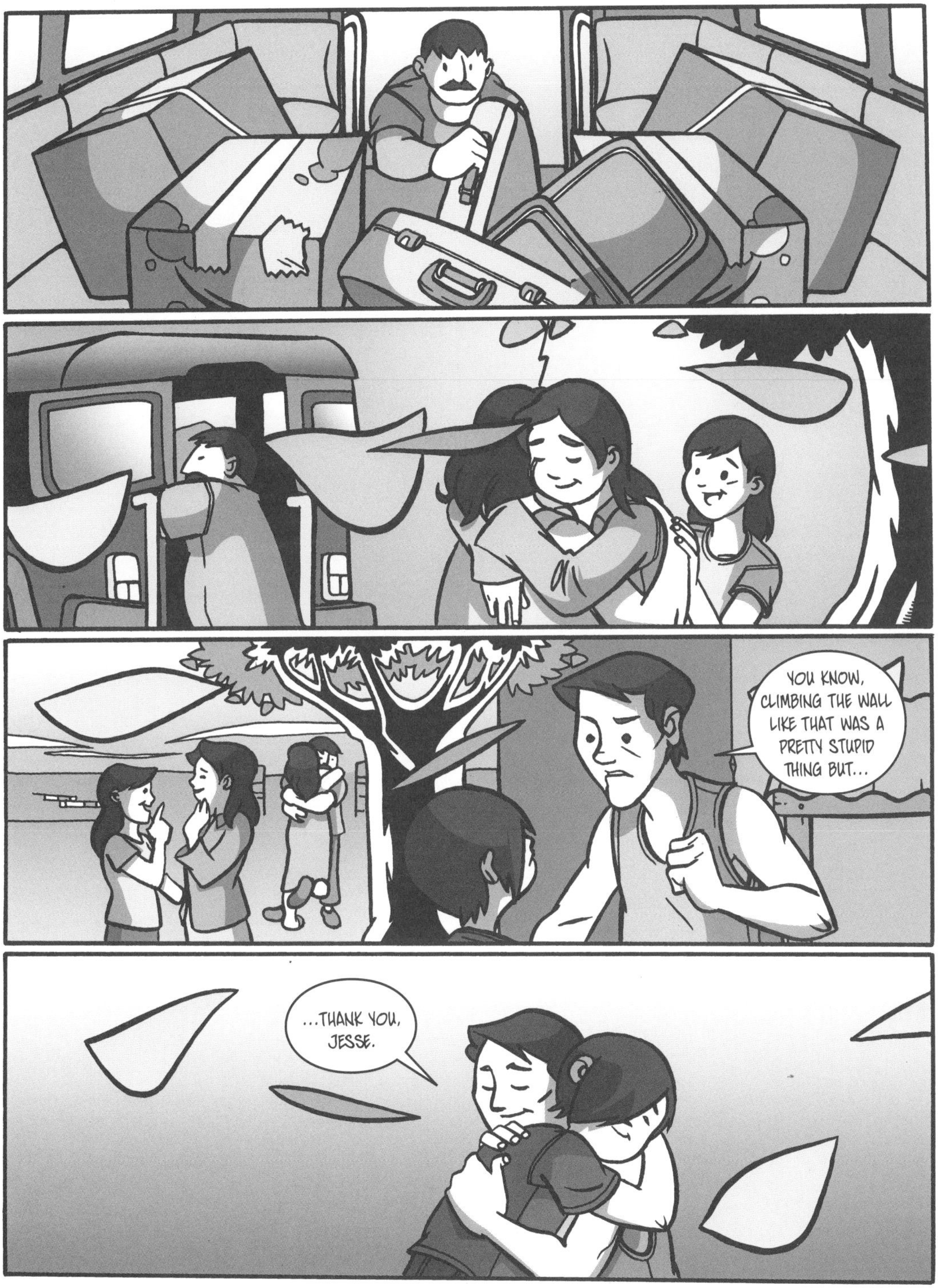
YOU KNOW, CLIMBING THE WALL LIKE THAT WAS A PRETTY STUPID THING BUT...
...THANK YOU, JESSE.

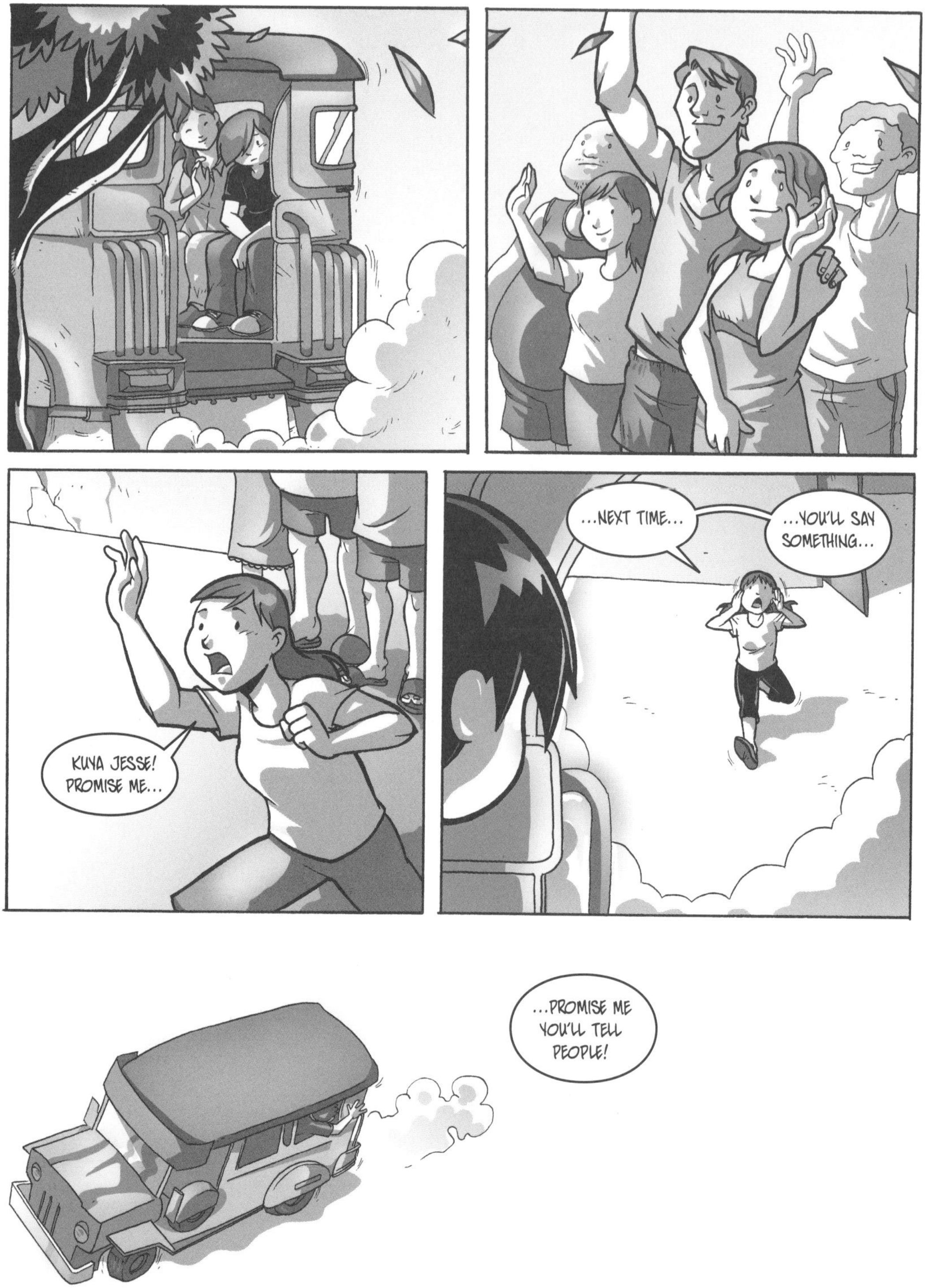
KUYA JESSE! PROMISE ME...
...NEXT TIME...
...YOU'LL SAY SOMETHING...
...PROMISE ME YOU'LL TELL PEOPLE!

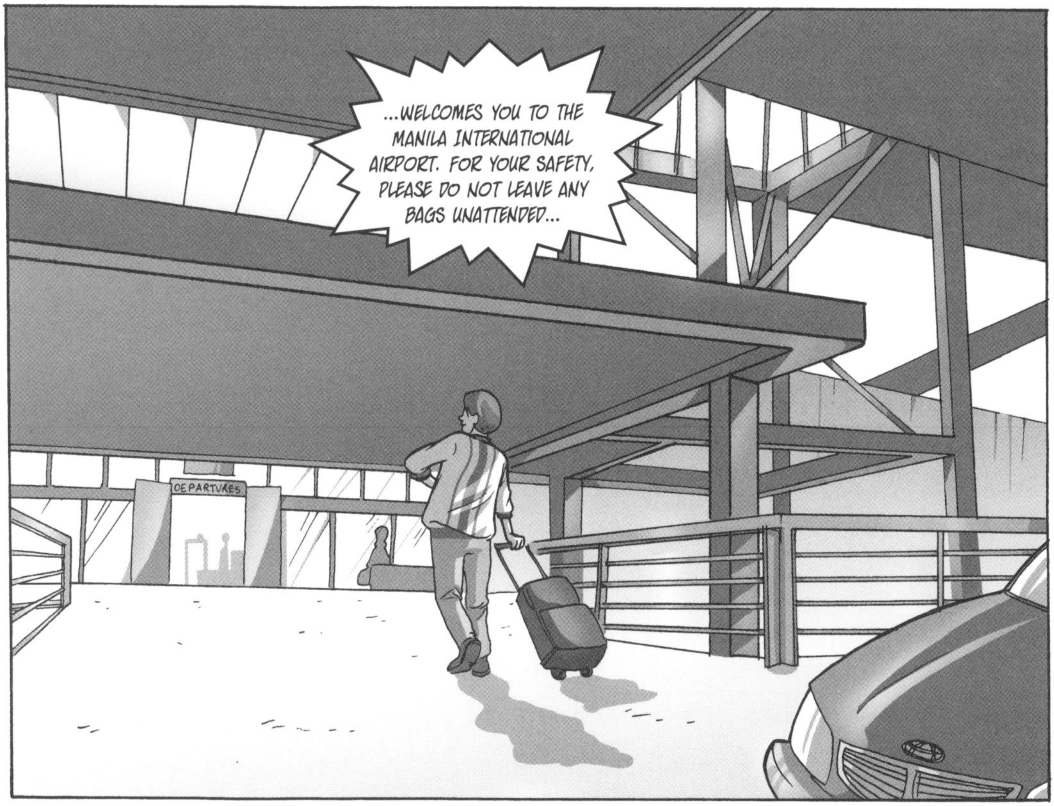
...WELCOMES YOU TO THE MANILA INTERNATIONAL AIRPORT. FOR YOUR SAFETY, PLEASE DO NOT LEAVE ANY BAGS UNATTENDED...
DEPARTURES

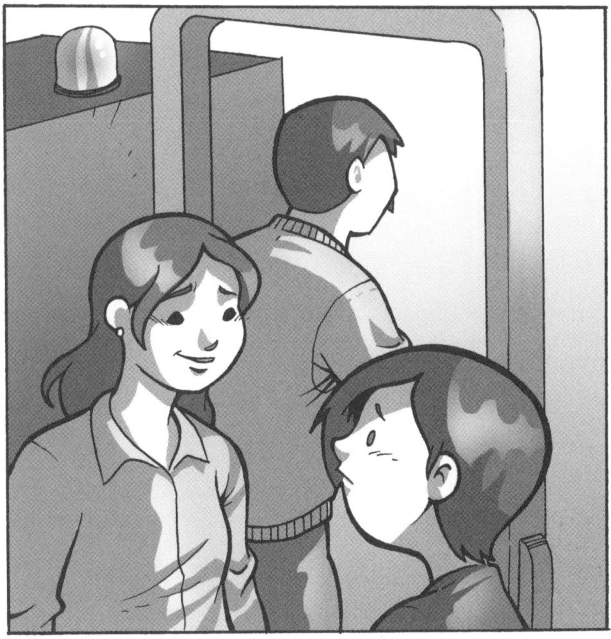

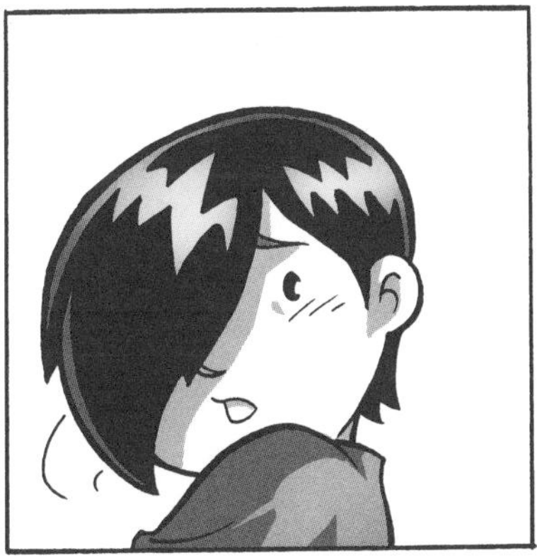

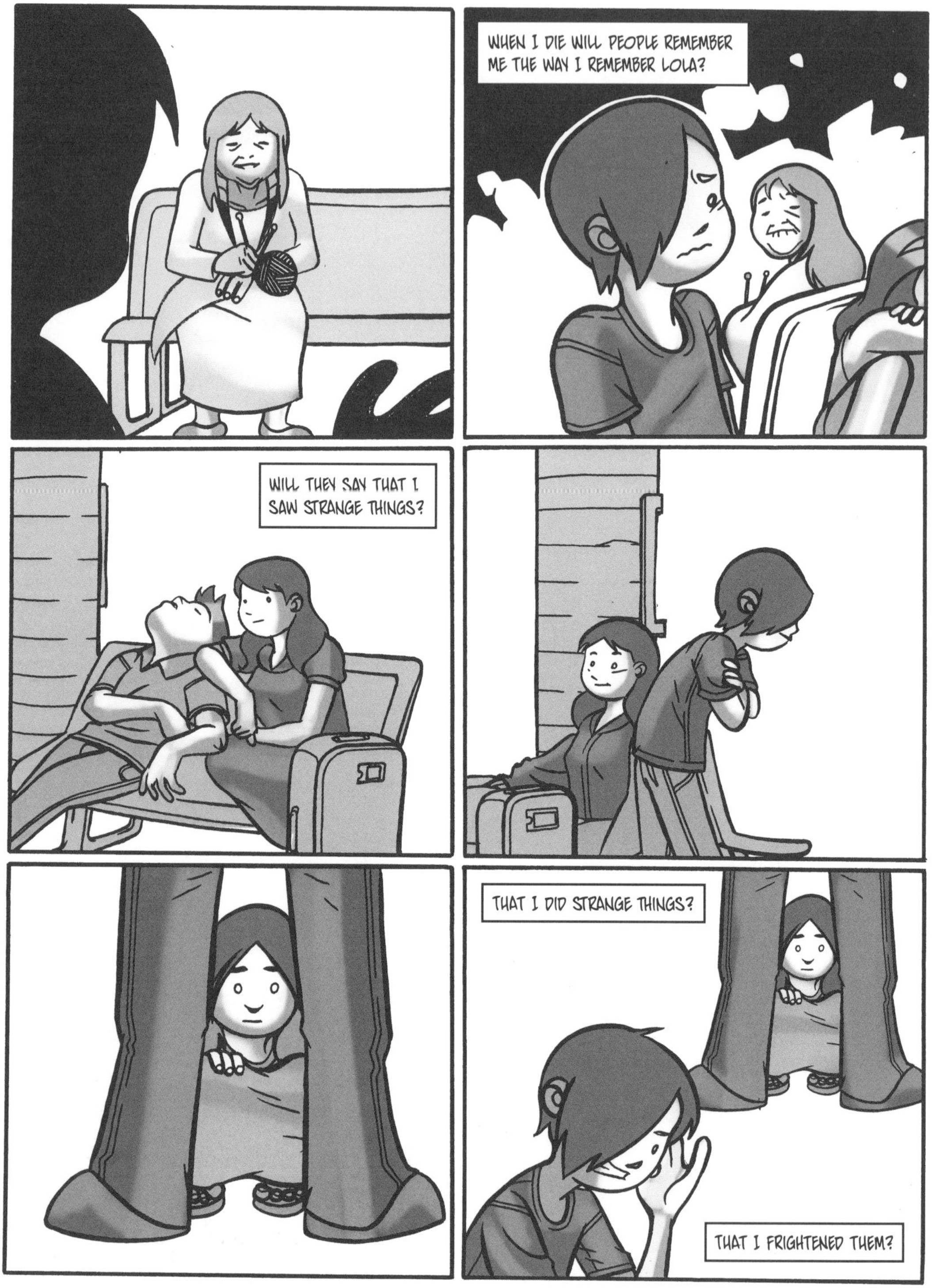
WHEN I DIE WILL PEOPLE REMEMBER ME THE WAY I REMEMBER LOLA?
WILL THEY SAY THAT I SAW STRANGE THINGS?
THAT I DID STRANGE THINGS?
THAT I FRIGHTENED THEM?

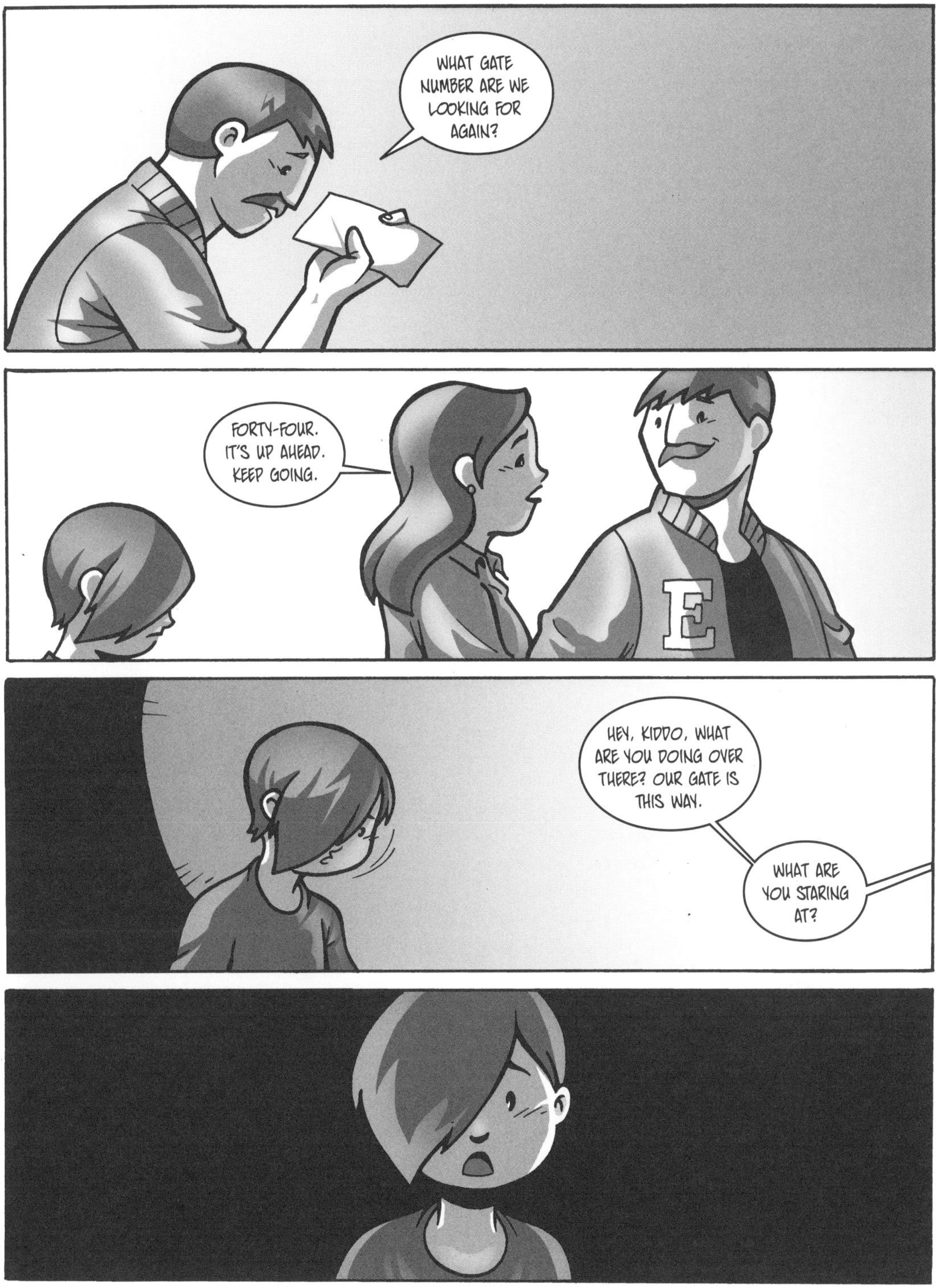
WHAT GATE NUMBER ARE WE LOOKING FOR AGAIN?
FORTY-FOUR. IT'S UP AHEAD. KEEP GOING.
HEY, KIDDO, WHAT ARE YOU DOING OVER THERE? OUR GATE IS THIS WAY.
WHAT ARE YOU STARING AT?

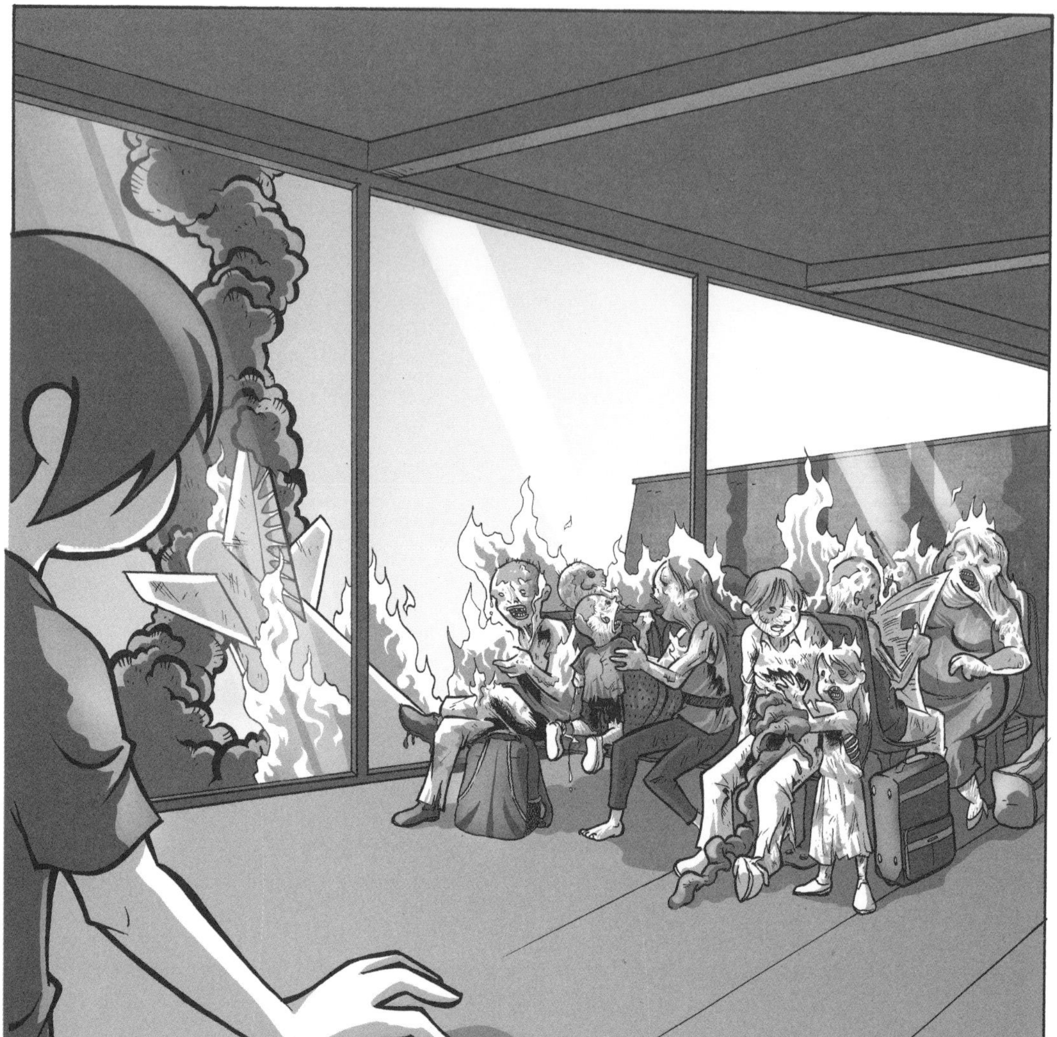

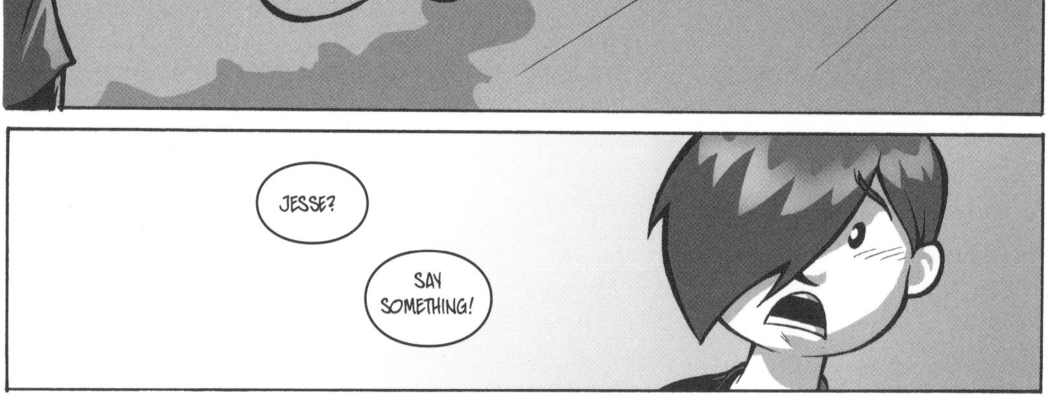
JESSE?
SAY SOMETHING!

THE END

LOLA

A GHOST STORY

ABOUT THE AUTHORS

J. TORRES IS THE SHUSTER AWARD WINNING AND EISNER AWARD NOMINATED WRITER OF *ALISON DARE*, *LOVE AS A FOREIGN LANGUAGE* AND *TEEN TITANS GO*. OTHER NOTABLE CREDITS INCLUDE THE ALA LISTED *DAYS LIKE THIS*, *DEGRASSI: EXTRA CREDIT*, AND *WONDER GIRL*. HIS CURRENT COMIC BOOK PROJECTS INCLUDE *BATMAN: THE BRAVE AND THE BOLD* AND *WALL-E*.

VISIT HIS WEBSITE AT WWW.JTORRESONLINE.BLOGSPOT.COM

ELBERT OR WRITES AND ILLUSTRATES COMIC BOOKS IN MANILA, PHILIPPINES. HIS WORK HAS SEEN PRINT IN TITLES SUCH AS NAUTILUS COMICS' TEEN-ORIENTED SERIES *CAST*, THE NATIONAL BOOK AWARD-WINNING *SIGLO* ANTHOLOGIES, AND HIS CREATOR-OWNED *BAKEMONO HIGH* SERIES FOR KIDS. IN ADDITION, HE ILLUSTRATES CHILDREN'S PICTURE BOOKS, DOES GRAPHIC DESIGN, HATES WEB-RELATED WORK, AND LOVES CHOCOLATE MOUSSE. HE IS ALSO TEACHING COMICS PRODUCTION CLASSES AT THE ATENEO DE MANILA UNIVERSITY, AND THINKS THAT WORKING WITH ONI PRESS IS JUST THE COOLEST THING EVER.

VISIT HIS WEBSITE AT WWW.MUNIMUNISTORIES.COM.

Other books from Oni Press...

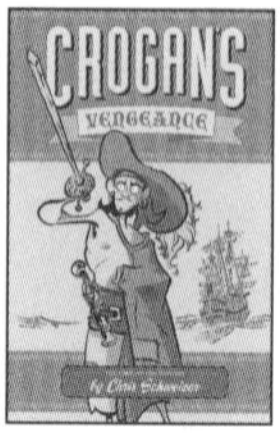
CROGANS
VENGEANCE

CROGAN'S VENGEANCE
By Chris Schweizer
192 pages • hardcover
B&W interiors • $14.95 US
ISBN 978-1-934964-06-4

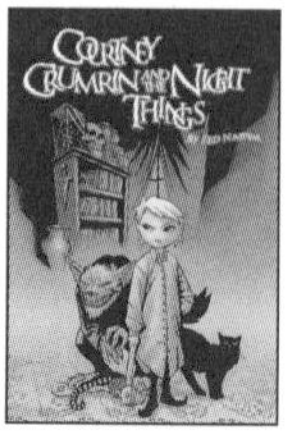
Courtney Crumrin and the Night Things

COURTNEY CRUMRIN, VOL. 1:
THE NIGHT THINGS
By Ted Naifeh
128 pages • digest
B&W interiors • $11.95 US
ISBN 978-1-929998-60-9

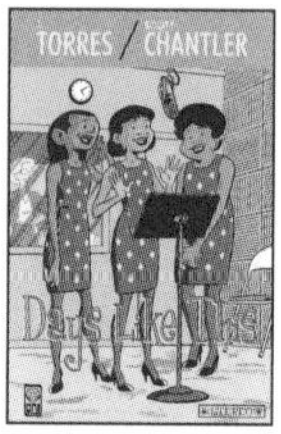
TORRES / CHANTLER
Days Like This

DAYS LIKE THIS
By J. Torres & Scott Chantler
88 pages • digest
B&W interiors • $8.95 US
ISBN 978-1-929998-48-7

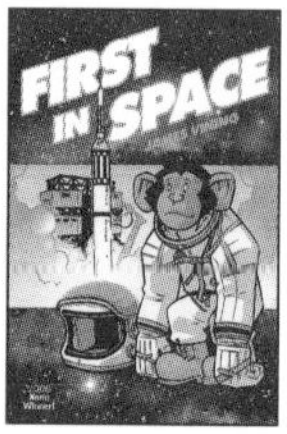
FIRST IN SPACE

FIRST IN SPACE
By James Vining
96 pages • 6x9 trade paperback
B&W interiors • $9.95 US
ISBN 978-1-932664-64-5

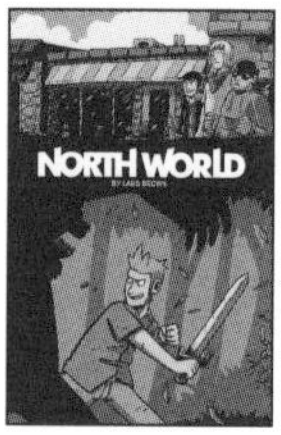
NORTH WORLD

NORTH WORLD VOL. 1:
THE EPIC OF CONRAD
By Lars Brown
152 pages • digest
B&W interiors • $11.95 US
ISBN 978-1-932664-91-1

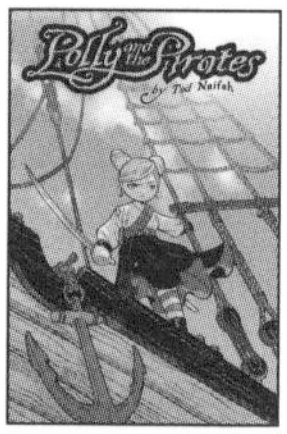
Polly and the Pirates

POLLY AND THE PIRATES,
VOL. 1
By Ted Naifeh
176 pages • digest
B&W interiors • $11.95 US
ISBN 978-1-932664-46-1

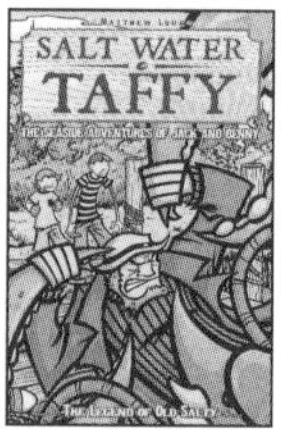
SALT WATER
TAFFY

SALT WATER TAFFY, VOL. 1:
THE LEGEND OF OLD SALTY
By Matthew Loux
96 pages • digest
B&W interiors • $5.95 US
ISBN 978-1-932664-94-2

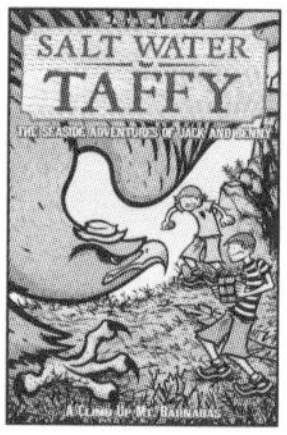
SALT WATER
TAFFY

SALT WATER TAFFY, VOL. 2:
A CLIMB UP MT. BARNABAS
By Matthew Loux
96 pages • digest
B&W interiors • $5.95 US
ISBN 978-1-934964-03-3

Available at finer comic book shops and booksellers everywhere!

To find a comic book store near you visit www.comicshops.us.

For more information on these and other fine Oni Press titles, visit our website at www.onipress.com.